¡Viva Vivas!

Essays in Honor of Eliseo Vivas
on the Occasion of his Seventy-Fifth Birthday,
July 13, 1976

¡Viva Vivas!

Henry Regnery, *Editor*

Indianapolis

Liberty Press is the publishing imprint of Liberty Fund, Inc., which was established to encourage study of the ideal of a society of free and responsible individuals.

Library of Congress Catalog Card No.: 76–9432
ISBN 0–913966–08–8

Eliseo Vivas

Philosopher, Teacher, Man of Letters

Contents

¡Viva Vivas!

For and About
Eliseo Vivas

Henry Regnery

Henry Regnery was born in Hinsdale, Illinois, in 1912. In 1948 he founded the Henry Regnery Company.

It is the purpose of the present collection of essays by his friends, colleagues and former students, to honor Eliseo Vivas, but we are well aware that in associating ourselves with him we also do honor to ourselves. The immediate occasion for this undertaking is the seventy-fifth birthday of our friend, but the impelling reason for it is to recognize a life of achievement.

As those who know Eliseo Vivas are well aware, he divides the members of his profession into various categories: there are those who write footnotes to philosophy, there are those who think seriously about philosophy, there are those who add creatively to philosophical knowledge, and there are those who teach philosophy. He has taught philosophy, effectively and vigorously, at many places: among others at the University of Wisconsin, the University of Chicago, Ohio

State University, and after his retirement as John Evans Professor at Northwestern University (where he spent eighteen years), two years as Distinguished Visiting Professor at Rockford College. He has also thought seriously about philosophy. In such books as *The Moral Life and the Ethical Life* and *D. H. Lawrence: The Failure and Triumph of Art,* and in many essays, he has made his contribution to understanding and knowledge.

Eliseo was brought to New York from Venezuela as a young man to study engineering. His father, who had been in politics and had been exiled by the dictator Gomez, was determined that his oldest son should enter a profession which would insulate him from the temptations of politics. Engineering seemed a good choice for such a purpose, but a choice that failed to take into account the inclinations of the young man involved. While a student at Brooklyn Polytechnic Institute, Eliseo attended an English course given by a young teacher at the beginning of his career, Joseph Wood Krutch, which came as a great revelation to him and changed the course of his life. Eliseo made up his mind to become a "man of letters." He was not quite sure, he says, just what a "man of letters" was, but this is what he told his family he wanted to be. He read widely, hungrily, he says, wrote essays and book reviews for such publications as the *Literary Review* (the first, on Pio Baroja in 1922), the *Nation,* the *New Leader,* and *New York Herald Tribune Books,* and in 1928 graduated from the University of Wisconsin. Following his graduation, he received a comfortable sinecure as Venezuelan Consul in Philadelphia, for which he conscientiously stamped the required documents, and which enabled him to do a semester of graduate work at the University of Pennsylvania and to study the rest of the year at the Albert C. Barnes Foundation, an opportunity for which he has often expressed his gratitude. However difficult Barnes may have been as a man, Eliseo says, he showed him how to see a picture. By this time Eliseo knew what he wanted: in the fall of 1929 he accepted an appointment as instructor in philosophy at the University of Wisconsin at exactly one-quarter of the salary he had received as consul, and was on his way. He became the assistant, but by no means a disciple of the leading man in the department, Max Otto, and, as he has told us elsewhere,[1] as a fiery young University of Wisconsin radical, spent more of his time indoctrinating than teaching his students. He was granted a Ph.D. by the University of Wisconsin in 1935, and became an assistant professor the same year.

Eliseo's first philosophical passion was Unamuno, which is probably reflected in the fact that from 1925 to 1927 he wrote five reviews of books by Unamuno, two of them of the *Don Quixote*. He soon discovered, however, that as much as he admired Unamuno's vigorous, seductive literary style and his brilliant insights, that the systematic thinking he was looking for was lacking,

---

[1] "Alonzo as 'Teacher,'" *Modern Age,* Fall 1975.

that for him, Unamuno led into a blind alley. Unamuno, I think Eliseo would say, had a philosophical mind, but not the mind of a systematic philosopher. His next stage, not surprisingly, was Nietzsche, whom he read and discussed with his friends, as many young men have done before and since, with the greatest enthusiasm. He soon discovered, however, that they were concentrating on the passages they liked and agreed with, and were skipping those they did not like. At this point he decided that Nietzsche was a thinker he had to accept as a whole or not at all. From Nietzsche (as one might have expected, considering his cultural background and sense for literary style), Eliseo went on to Santayana. He reviewed Santayana's *Platonism and the Spiritual Life* in 1927, the same year in which his last review of a book by Unamuno appeared. What attracted him to Santayana was not only the grand style in which he developed his ideas, but the fact that he wrote as a poet. When Santayana wrote about poetry, Eliseo says, he wrote about it from the inside. As Eliseo read more of Santayana, however, he came to feel that concern for elegance of expression was gradually replacing hard, logical thinking; again he had to look farther.

As a young man in search of a philosophical base, at the University of Wisconsin during the 1930s, it was almost forordained that Eliseo would turn to naturalism, to the philosophy, that is, which holds that "man is a part of nature, that there is nothing besides or outside nature, and that therefore man is fully explainable in terms of science,"[2] of which John Dewey was the leading spokesman. It was not, clearly, Dewey's literary style that attracted Eliseo to him, but he learned to read Dewey in spite of his style, and became a firm believer. Naturalism is the philosophy of liberalism, so that in adopting naturalism, Eliseo doubtless felt that he had found the philosophical counterpart to the political position to which he had fully committed himself. With the social and moral crisis that culminated in World War II and as his own search for answers went deeper, he began to discover inadequacies in naturalism. It had no place, for example, for the tragic or for the heroic dimensions of the human experience, inadequacies which the world of the 1940s made vividly apparent. As if this were not enough, the physicists had demonstrated that science can be concerned with other things than the search for truth or "explaining" man. Naturalism, Eliseo began to see, was not only philosophically inadequate but suffered, in his eyes, from the further fact that it was part and parcel (like the liberalism with which it was allied) of the secularist spirit of the time, and, in his opinion, "one of the essential marks of decency today is to be ashamed of being a man of the twentieth century."[3] The proper role of the student of philosophy, he had come to believe, was to be a critic of his time, not an apologist for it.

The discovery that the philosophy to which he had

---

[2] *The Moral Life and the Ethical Life* (Chicago: Gateway Edition, 1963), p. 15.

[3] *Ibid.*, p. xi.

committed himself had been washed out from under him came at the same time as a shattering personal crisis. To this was added the realization that in giving up his old loyalties he was not only cutting himself off from many old friends and associates, but was isolating himself from the intellectual position that dominated the academy, of which, for better or for worse, he was a part. Whittaker Chambers, he says, prepared the way for him and made the decision easier than it would otherwise have been; the thought must have sometimes occurred to him, as it did to Chambers, that he was leaving the winning side to join the losing, but for a man who took his convictions seriously, there was no other possible choice.

In 1945 he became an associate professor in the College of the University of Chicago. By this time, things had begun to fall back into place for Eliseo. He had surmounted his personal crisis, and after much thought, study, and reading, among others, of the works of men he had scorned during his naturalist period, he was beginning to feel that he again had solid ground under his feet. In April 1946 he published an article in *Ethics,* "Animadversions on Naturalistic Ethics," in which he set forth the reasons for his rejection of naturalism, and in so doing, publicly renounced what he often calls the "reigning orthodoxy" of academic philosophy. A basic element of his new position, which he would develop further as time went on, among other places in his theory of artistic creativity, was the conception of value he had come to accept. The philosophy of naturalism, as he says, "pretends to account for values in terms of interest (or desire or drive or some similar term)";[4] rejecting this position, Eliseo went back to what he called "the high road of Western orthodoxy in respect to values," to the idea, which is as old as Plato, that "values have a status in being independent of our apprehension of them,"[5] that values are of themselves a part of the structure of reality.

The article in *Ethics* led to *The Moral Life and the Ethical Life,* one of his most important books, and one that helped to establish Eliseo Vivas as one of the creative thinkers of our time. "What the book tries to do is to examine the theoretical ground on which we sometimes resolve moral conflicts morally."[6] It was originally published by the University of Chicago Press. The immediate stimulus to write it came from the director of the press, William T. Couch, and his assistant, Fred Wieck, who suggested that Eliseo develop the ideas he had outlined in *Ethics* into a book. This is an example of the constructive role that an imaginative publisher can play. In his Introduction to the Gateway Edition, Joseph Wood Krutch has this to say about *The Moral Life and the Ethical Life:*

---

[4] From *Statement of the Major Ideas that have Controlled my Work* (unpublished).

[5] *The Moral Life and the Ethical Life, op. cit.,* p. xxv.

[6] *Ibid.,* p. xxiii.

This is a serious, learned, and searching exploration of some of the most difficult questions which have ever concerned the human mind. It is also tough-minded—in the sense that it recognizes all the difficulties, begs no questions, offers no easy solutions and, unlike conventional protests against modern skepticism, makes no pleas for a leap in the dark to an unexamined faith.[7]

The publication of the essay in *Ethics* marks a turning point in Eliseo's life and career. During his "orthodox" period, he must have appeared to be just another left-liberal young instructor of philosophy at a big university, Marxist in politics and philosophically a follower of John Dewey, with a conventional academic career ahead of him. As his publications of the time make clear, however, he was also a serious student of philosophy, of philosophy not as an abstraction but as a body of knowledge necessarily related to his experience of the world around him. It was this fact that made it possible for him to put the "orthodoxy" of the time behind him, to strike out on his own, and to establish his own position. It is a significant fact, and one which can give us reason to believe that the life of reason is not dead in our society, that Eliseo's recognition and influence beyond a narrow academic discipline came *after* he had broken with the prevailing orthodoxy of the academy, when he had ceased to be a yes man to his age and had instead assumed the role of critic.

---

[7] *Ibid.*, p. 1.

The road Eliseo has travelled has not been an easy one, as I hope I have been able to show in this brief account of his struggle to find a philosophical position that would accord with his own demands on himself and his experience of reality. There have been many twists and turns, but his development has been consistent and in the same direction. He would be the last to assert, needless to say, that his long search had led to certainty; as he put it in *The Moral Life and the Ethical Life,* "The quest for certainty thus defines man's destiny and to dissuade him from it is to strip him of his armor against despair. But it is the quest and not the result of it that defines his destiny, for certainty is not given to man to possess."

How does our friend Eliseo—this man who has thought hard and seriously about the great questions and who has never hesitated to look into the depths of our time nor to recount what he has seen—how does he, after his long quest, see his role as teacher and as student of philosophy? The teacher's task, he has said, "must be to guide man to grow to his full stature as human. This he does not do by enlisting him in a party, but by making him the possessor of the sustaining intellectual structures of civilization." How far he has come since his days as a cocksure young instructor at the University of Wisconsin! But, it is fair to ask, would he have attained his present depth of understanding without having gone through this experience? As for his role as student of philosophy, in the privately distributed

Statement of the Major Ideas that have Controlled my Work, Eliseo has this to say:

> Insofar as I am able to judge correctly the direction and purpose of my work, it is addressed to combating through criticism and constructive work, the dominant tendencies of contemporary American philosophers, who are positivistic in the broadest sense of this term; for they espouse the primacy of science as means to truth, they deny ontological reference to religious convictions, they reduce value judgments to purely psychological terms, they have no adequate theory of the person, and they lack a serious notion of the role played by art in culture.
>
> I think of myself, in my own way, and with the limited talents and learning at my disposal, as trying to do in this country the job that was done in Germany by men of great stature like Cassirer and Dilthey—as attempting to devise a normative notion of culture and of man that will guide our national talent and resources along lines worthy of our tradition. But the work I would do, I would do in the American idiom, and in view of American experience, and for the American people—whose philosophers at the moment, as I see it, have failed them.

We may safely say, I think, that while Eliseo may not, after seventy-five years in this vale of tears, have found certainty, he has attained a degree of wisdom and understanding that is granted to few of us, and can look back on a life of accomplishment. It is because of this that those of us who have contributed to this book have come together in its pages to express our affection and respect.

January 5, 1976

Styled Thought: An Open Letter to Eliseo Vivas

William Earle

William Earle was born in Saginaw, Michigan, in 1919. He was both an undergraduate and graduate student at the University of Chicago, served in the army during World War II, then earned a doctorat de l'Université Aix-Marseilles. *He has taught philosophy at Northwestern University since 1948, and has held visiting lectureships at Yale, Harvard, and Stanford. His books include* Objectivity, The Autobiographical Consciousness, *and the recently-published* Public Sorrows and Private Pleasures.

Dear Eliseo,

No doubt It is almost in as bad taste to talk about the living as to gossip about the dead; and yet this double scruple would prohibit speech altogether, not so bad an idea, perhaps, yet inhibiting another of our liveliest desires, precisely to talk to and about one another. Well, there's no solution. My apologies, Eliseo. With the best will in the world, nothing I say can possibly be wholly true of you. I only hope it won't be false to you. The rest of this is addressed to those who have never had the privilege of knowing you personally or studying with you who must now, alas, appear in the third person singular.

· · ·

Perhaps the reader will excuse a bit of autobiography. I first met Professor Eliseo Vivas when I was a graduate student in philosophy at the University of Chicago, the Spring Quarter of 1946. It was a course on Santayana and what an extraordinary course it was! We students had already done our best under other professors to work through the arguments of Plato, Aristotle, Hume, Kant and the rest. There were no limits to our horizon, and we had some of the most distinguished teachers in the country; but, if memory serves, we or at least I, were dead. No doubt we had some secret aspiration to master all of human thought, place each system within some enormously complex matrix or, on the contrary, to defend some favorite system and annihilate the others with well-aimed, single-shot refutations. In any case, it was intellectually bold but personally bloodless and without confidence. Who could speak without a wavering voice when there was always something more in the Western tradition to be read? I remember my acute embarrassment one evening after I had held forth on both Plato and Hume when someone asked me which I believed. I believe I answered him that the question was irrelevant! In any event, there we all were adrift on an open sea of philosophical possibilities with no land in sight.

But now we found before us a philosopher of a wholly different stamp: a passionate scholar with an inimitable style in which the passion did not outrun the scholarship and the scholarship was itself passionate. The dignity of man was respected independently of either ideology or position, yet both were seen as reflecting back upon the theory of that dignity. As can easily be imagined we were both entranced and unsettled. I had many courses with Eliseo Vivas encompassing Dewey, esthetics, ethics, Santayana, but, unless I am mistaken, never explicitly in metaphysics, or epistemology; they were always there but *en passant*. And while others of our professors without actually saying so appeared to us as masters of all thought, Eliseo Vivas was the first to my recollection to respond to a question of fact with "I don't know . . . I'll try to find out," and proceeded to do so. If not a question of fact, he returned to it not so much with an answer as with a response. I believe also that Eliseo Vivas was the first to introduce to philosophy departments, rather hard-nosed for the most part, that then questionable subject, the philosophy of literature. It also opened our eyes. We saw that philosophy might be found elsewhere than in "thinkers" officially designated as such either by consensus or by the university librarian using the Dewey Decimal System. In fact it could be found in the most extraordinary sources; newspaper anecdotes, anthropological studies, psychoanalytic case-studies, D. H. Lawrence, Henry James, tales of the conquistadores, and above all, Dostoievsky. This atmosphere was a far cry from sifting arguments and yet it all bore directly on our real subject. It was not merely a question of imbuing an otherwise abstract argument with fresh illustrations, but the illustrations themselves reflected back upon the argument to modify it. The "literature" or poetry was itself a mode of thought not translatable into the abstract without severe loss of sense. What was a "paralogism" or "antinomy" for abstract thought was lived as that "flaw in the heart of being" which Professor Vivas loved to refer to long before Sartre came upon it. Further, the experienced diremption in life might be that source of meaning that the abstractions needed to retain their own sense. What was at stake then was not so much a logical dilemma but a dilemma of life, what might now be called "existential anguish" or *Grenzsituationen*. Still, that was all before the existential movement, and, if I may say so, in many ways far more existential than some existentialists, and far more lucid.

Now, what do these personal recollections have to do with the *philosophy* of Eliseo Vivas? Perhaps not much, and yet these notes will try to gather them together. But certainly not by way of an overview of the system of Eliseo Vivas; I do not believe he has one, wants one, and would do anything but *hoot* at any such thing. Which does not imply that his philosophy is unsystematic in any sense that would make it consist of occasional pieces on this or that, scattered observations, miscellaneous essays. Where then does the unity of point of view lie? I believe that it lies beyond system and in a deeply reflective *person*.

It is impossible to mistake an essay or book by Eliseo Vivas for the work of any other thinker. They are deeply personal both in subject matter and style. What

other philosophers would couch the most searching
analyses under titles such as "animadversions," "atrabilious thoughts," or "contra. . . ."? None, indeed. We
are so accustomed to that hideous neutralized jargon of
the profession—without the slightest evidence that the
writer has hatreds and loves, or is in fact *capable*
of indignation as well as affection—that Eliseo's language itself appears to go too far; and yet I do not
doubt that it is just *this* which we have to learn from
Eliseo Vivas. The assumed neutrality is either fake, in
bad faith, or on the other hand indeed announces a subject that no one *could* possibly get aroused about. If
there is an official chloroform given off by our acade-
mies, it is not to be found in the writings of Eliseo
Vivas. They sting; they also celebrate. In a word,
thought shapes a style. Santayana, also of Spanish heritage, wrote with style. Aside from doctrinal differences,
Santayana and Vivas at least share that in common with
Ortega and Unamuno: the thought bears upon the universal, but its manner of expression is personal and
poetic. In a word, one encounters a whole man in their
writings, not simply *Bewusstsein überhaupt* or a kindly
reader of all books. Even when he quarreled with non-
entities, their un-thought-through "thoughts" took on a
dreadful scope and implication they never dreamed of:
a beautiful sense of intellectual responsibility.

A few more remarks upon style before the question
of its source or original unity, a pretentious enough task
in itself. The thought itself I believe to be *dialectical,* by

which I mean a position is provisionally adopted, defended, only to be gradually *developed* by negation; the "positions" are but stopping places to orient thought, compass points for the actual journey. In Eliseo's thought, these "positions," whether attacked or defended, are well-known; something called "naturalism" was, and, I believe, remains, one of them. At the University of Chicago, we students never knew what "naturalism" was until we heard it partially defended then, but mostly examined and attacked in Eliseo's courses. The reader must understand that at that time, we students hardly lived in the modern world; our ears were turned back upon the ancient and medieval world, and heard of contemporary problems only by rumor. "Naturalism?" We searched our minds for classical examples: was Aristotle or Plato a "naturalist"? It didn't quite seem to fit Spinoza either. Still, that wasn't now the point; naturalism was something influential in the '20s and '30s, flying its own banners, and mostly it seemed *against* the supernatural, God, miracles, teleological causation, the soul except insofar as it could be observed in behavior, and then, by some free associations not altogether clear to us, ending with a liberal political policy, not remote from Roosevelt's New Deal. It had its own "metaphysics," more or less a reflection upon logic and the physical or social sciences; but what we had always understood by the name was either wordplay, guesswork, bad science, or crypto-religion.

Well, Eliseo then and perhaps still takes "naturalism"

seriously, seriously enough, that is, to fight it; he insisted that it must first be known if it is to be seriously opposed. His rejection of it came only after knowing it thoroughly and then smelling out those peculiar problems in human existence which *don't fit in,* and in that work, I think his study of Dostoievsky played a decisive part. At the very least, the "naturalists"—most of them collected at Columbia University and around New York but also scattered around the world in the persons of Freud, Carnap, Marx, Marcuse, and those philosophical biologists who thought the last word about evolution was said in random mutations surviving through a successful adaptation to the environment— all these were the *grands simplificateurs.* Theirs is the position Eliseo is determined to undermine. And yet not through a new simplification. Related in a fashion too complex for present discussion is his life-long quarrel with Aristotle's theory of imitation.

He has frequently admonished me for my fault of never taking any of these thinkers, with the exception of Aristotle, seriously. Indeed, he says, they *must* be so taken if only in order to win one's credentials to depart from them. One must be "post-Carnapian," "post-Freudian," etc., which meant "going through" naturalism first in order to overcome it. Again, dialectical thought and no short-cuts. Naturalism was a powerful and dominant *Weltanschauung* and not simply this or that position. And again the characteristic style: the whole man, moral, intellectual, political and passionate, must find philosophical expression. Thought which is passionate and passion which thinks. Life is at stake, after all. Depth of thought walks hand in hand with depth of feeling.

Passing in some quarters as a political "conservative," supposedly provided with automatic views on every contemporary problem, Eliseo has always remained free to mock its formulas and oversimplifications; passing as "religious" in others, he can also mock with uproarious laughter the creeds, hopes, and superstitions falling under the worst of that title. Passing among some who do not know him as "atrabilious," he is more capable of generosity and courtesy than almost any other man I know. At bottom, I can only find a deep piety and respect, so deep in fact that it *can,* when aroused, pass into anger too. Again it is a whole man one encounters with a capacity for mockery, piety, courtesy, anger, love, and outrage virtually unique on the professional scene. All of it passes into his thought, strict, informed and courageous unto belligerency. No one can imitate his style because it isn't artificial; it aims at the universal and expresses that aim through the unique person of one thinking man.

I noted above a certain absence of metaphysics, both in his courses at the University of Chicago where I was his student, and at Northwestern University where I was his colleague. Is this accidental or an oversight on his part? I believe neither, but that it is rather part and parcel of his own *Weltanschauung.* In a word it is part of his intellectual and personal *modesty*. It would be presumptuous to predict the future concerns of a thinker alive and most lively, and yet nothing he has written so far would lead one to suspect that he has any such work on his table. At best, in his writings one can find allusions to God, to what transcends nature and therefore positive science and "naturalism." But allusions they remain. One is reminded of the old rabbis who would never utter the name of God aloud, except when the shofars were blowing so loud that not even the rabbis would hear what they themselves named. A beautiful *tact* on the whole matter! An explicit theology, while aiming at "knowledge" of God or the Transcendent, articulating his nature and proving his existence, accomplishes the opposite: blasphemy. Some things are better left unsaid, and that out of piety, respect, and deep conviction of human honor and inadequacy. Silence may be more expressive than a *Summa*. Equally, I have always felt that Eliseo is extremely uncomfortable with abstractions. If they are used, he will give them an experiential sense or else become uninterested. In a word, *abstract* metaphysics is not his field of interest; and it has taken me a long time to realize that it is not mine either.

· · ·

There would be little point in summing up Eliseo's work to date; I do not believe it goes into summary. There is equally little point in "explaining" his distinguished books and articles; Eliseo already says, with a clarity hardly to be equalled, exactly what he means. But perhaps there is some point in looking at the origin of these works, that is, the spirit behind them, never exhausted in them, and in the last analysis unsayable, as a person is indescribable.

I myself would call him an *existentialist* neither proto nor post; but I know he hates the word, associating it mostly with the peculiar philosophical personality of Jean-Paul Sartre. Besides, Eliseo is older than Sartre, formed his philosophy in complete independence of the "existentialists," but rather through his own experience and reflection, revolting against the "naturalists." Nor does the term "existentialist" add anything whatsoever to his accomplishment except to introduce his unique work to younger readers under a more familiar rubric. The spirit behind the work remains alive, like any profound thinker's, and therefore not susceptible to categorization. It is, I believe, the spirit of a person eminently situated in his own times, the battles, excitements, and even rhetoric of our times, who, although I doubt he would use this language, might be said to have one eye on an ambiguous and distressing passing scene and another on the sacred about which he remains silent, but which animates both the affections and indignations which color his thought. Eliseo, for me, is an outrider into the official camps, emphasizing what those camps would most like to forget, causing intellectual embarrassment to those naturalists or positivists of whatever stamp, who imagine the universe of life more or less a closed methodological system. Eliseo touches with his acute diagnostic finger all the *sore spots*, the unresolved issues whose solution academic philosophy puts off into an indefinite future, but policy on which determines the sense of existence if it is to have any; who nourishes his spirit more on Dostoievsky, Kafka, Greek tragedians and Lawrence, than professor this or that's article in *Mind*. For Kant, reason is one thing, impulses and sensuality another; for Hegel, the two must be experienced as dialectically united into spirit, the whole man. For me, Eliseo Vivas is one of the very few seminal thinkers whose philosophy proceeds out of spirit. Without this, our poor philosophical scene would be hopelessly impoverished; and for this, we all owe an incalculable debt to him. No one can fall asleep again philosophically after a serious encounter with this thinking man.

· · ·

P.S.

No, Eliseo, this isn't really what I wanted to say, which was so much more, and to be said so differently. I already hear your mockery. Please forgive, and realize that I and so many others remain your fond but inept students.

—Bill.

The Theoretical Contributions of Eliseo Vivas

Murray Krieger

Murray Krieger is University Professor of English of the University of California, teaching at the Irvine and Los Angeles campuses. He studied under Eliseo Vivas at both the University of Chicago and Ohio State University. At Ohio State, he wrote his dissertation (later published as The New Apologists for Poetry) *under Professor Vivas, who held a joint appointment in the Departments of Philosophy and English. Together Professors Vivas and Krieger edited* The Problems of Aesthetics *in 1953. Other books by Professor Krieger include* The Tragic Vision, A Window to Criticism, The Play and Place of Criticism, The Classic Vision, *and his forthcoming* Theory of Criticism: A Tradition and its System.

There is some embarrassment attendant upon contributing to an occasion of this sort. The essays which are assembled—and this essay in particular—are justified by the honor they pay to a man who has had a long and distinguished career as scholar and teacher. And yet the appeal they are to hold for the potential reader (especially as a publisher might view it) is dependent upon the distinction of those whose essays are being assembled: due testimony of the rightfulness of the distinction being claimed for the honoree, that these would come together to acknowledge their debt to him. Hence the writers are in the awkward position of having to justify themselves in order to justify the presumed object of the occasion they are together creating. And there is a presumptuous ambiguity about who is being honored: the present writers or the absent personage whose work was to have inspired their dedication.

To avoid this embarrassing ambiguity and the unjust presumption behind it, it is important that the work of the honored scholar-teacher be seen as influential and as worthy of being influential without being treated as if in competition with those it has influenced: as if its splendid historical role must be proved by proving the excellence of its followers. For the work, at least in this case, is—self-evidently—its own best testimony. Yet it is difficult to speak of this work, if one sees oneself as having inherited it, without seeing it from one's own vantage point, seeing it—that is—as it has helped to shape his own vision and, hence, his own work. And this is to run the risk of creating an impertinent competition among the objects of praise and defense in the essay; in short, to create a potential conflict of interest that can only damage the occasion and distort the appropriate object of study. Yet one must try to let modesty do its work.

Few can claim a greater right than I can to bear testimony on the present occasion, in view of the extent to which my work has been shaped by the writings and the teaching of Eliseo Vivas, in and out of the classroom, before and after I went to school to him. And, feeling with him so completely the student with the teacher, I should be in a convenient position to keep first things first, and myself second. Since I have just written yet another preface to a book in which I acknowledge my indebtedness to him, I should be especially and gratefully aware of his influence and, thus, should welcome the opportunity to discuss his contributions to developments in theory these last several decades.[1] And I do welcome it.

Given this personal entrée into what follows, however, the reader should be alerted to the likelihood that, even in my case, what I claim to see as his contributions will be colored by my sense of what I have needed most indispensably to make use of in my own theoretical work. Though I shall try to look dispassionately at the state of theory and the extent to which it was Eliseo Vivas who worked to constitute it, I cannot help, as a former student forcefully shaped by his teacher, but have *my* Eliseo Vivas strongly influence my judgment about his shaping force upon theory itself. And the aspects of his theorizing which will most concern me may well not be those which history (or perhaps he himself) would properly think his most distinctive gifts to his philosophic beneficiaries, though they are what has most characterized his work for me. It is precisely these fears about the distortions produced by my subjective angle of vision and the special investment I have in it which have led me to those distrustful words about *Festschriften* with which I began.

As I see them, the contributions to theory of Eliseo

---

[1] I speak mainly of literary theory and aesthetics, although some of what I say may well apply to his work in ethics and value theory generally. Though I cannot claim the competence to make these connections myself, his contributions in these areas would certainly seem equally deserving of an assessment on this occasion.

Vivas must be traced through a lengthy and continually productive career, one controlled by a developing, finally unified philosophic vision, however varied the problems to be solved and the solutions found. But it is worth distinguishing the successive phases of his career, since it is in the development itself that I believe the unity, as a complex, dynamic entity, can be best discovered and described. The deepest and most obvious division found in his work is that between what we can crudely term his early naturalistic phase and his more mature, self-consciously metaphysical phase, which is militantly anti-naturalistic. Perhaps more important for the theorist, however, is the fact that these phases are reflected in the changing theoretical problems on which he concentrated, as well as, more obviously, in the differing sorts of solutions he proposed to them. So we must also begin by seeing separately the two major areas of his distinctive contributions: on the one hand, those emerging out of the essays of the late '30s and early '40s which throw a new light on the nature of aesthetic experience and, on the other hand, those found in the books and essays after the middle '40s, which reconstitute first our notions of creativity and values, and then our sense of the role played by art in shaping culture.

Yet his career gives us reason to resist polarizing these phases, though his earlier philosophic commitments seem opposed to the later and though the aesthetic issues on which he concentrates show a cor-

respondent shift. For, whatever the turnings in his development as philosopher and theorist, Vivas did not
reject the gains of his early theorizing (however he
may have rejected the philosophic substructure on
which they were based) even as he added his later
transformations in metaphysics and aesthetics. Yet I
do not mean to suggest that he merely piled newer
notions onto incompatible ones in an eclectic accumula-
tion. To the contrary, he remained always wary of
systematic requirements: he might make his system
complex, even apparently paradoxical, but never in-
ternally inconsistent, if he could help it. So the merging
of his early doctrine of aesthetic experience, seemingly
a by-product of Deweyan naturalism, into an anti-
naturalistic and metaphysical theory of objective value
and original creativity (with their anthropological yield
for society) is a praiseworthy example of philosophic
growth and not merely of ideological alternations.

Let me trace these phases more closely, relating them
to each other and assessing their roles in the unfolding
aesthetic of Eliseo Vivas. Very likely it was his early
attachment to the Deweyan tradition which disposed
him to do his most exciting work on our peculiar response to art. Given the centering of value on the ex-
perientially dominated interests of man, it was the more
consistent—with Vivas as with Dewey—that the heart
of our theorizing about art should be man's experiencing of it. But though in conformity with instrumentalist
value theory and the objective relativism which gener-

ated it, Vivas' aesthetic breaks with the concern for expression and emotion to the extent that these were the defining features of aesthetic experience for Deweyan and near-Deweyan theory. His early critique of expressionist and emotionalist theories, together with his development of his own theory of "rapt, intransitive attention" as a more adequate substitute for them, is his first, and remains a continuing, major contribution to aesthetics.[2]

As I have suggested, Vivas originally saw no need to break with Deweyan naturalism to develop this theory as (he thought) a more adequate extension of naturalism into the domain of aesthetic experience, which, for the instrumentalist, was the dominant moment in the "aesthetic transaction." The very notion of the "trans-action," so central to his argument, suggests the relational basis of his claims about the subject's response to the stimulating object, a comfortable notion for the instrumentalist. But he uses this relational basis, we shall see, to move from the experiencing subject to

[2] See especially "Four Notes on I. A. Richards' Aesthetic Theory," *Philosophical Review,* July 1935; "A Definition of the Aesthetic Experience," *Journal of Philosophy,* November 1937; "A Note on the Emotion in Mr. Dewey's Theory of Art," *Philosophical Review,* September 1938; "A Natural History of the Aesthetic Transaction," in *Naturalism and the Human Spirit,* ed. Yervant H. Krikorian (New York: Columbia University Press, 1944); and "The Objective Correlative of T. S. Eliot," *American Bookman,* Winter 1944. For a much later refinement of this argument, see "Animadversions on Imitation and Expression," *The Artistic Transaction and Essays on Theory of Literature* (Ohio State University, 1963).

an object that possesses certain normative properties. These features in the object lead in turn to the doctrine of the phenomenal objectivity of aesthetic value, and although he argues even later that this doctrine can be held by naturalists and non-naturalists alike, it is clear that the doctrine is held the more comfortably by the philosopher who would ground phenomenal objectivity in what the non-naturalistic Vivas would later term ontic objectivity. So the "new naturalism" he first worked for, a broadening of naturalism that would accommodate his (still naturalistic) theory of aesthetic experience, had to give way. As he joined to his concern with value a concern with a theory of mind commensurate with his notion of creativity, his naturalism had to give way to a metaphysical conception that began with ontic substructures as philosophical realities which came to be reflected onto the phenomenal level, thanks in large part to the artist and the experience of rapt, intransitive attention which his object has been organized to force upon us.

But let us observe more closely this aesthetic experience which his naturalism may have led him into, but which by its own implications ended by leading him out of naturalism. The advantage for Vivas of defining the experience as intransitive attention is that, in contrast to subjective notions like emotion and expression, it directs us to the object as the source of the power that compels our attention. His definition has the further advantage of inviting an experience which is unique to

its object rather than, as with emotion or even pleasure, being assimilated to a broad human response,
which is capable of being aroused by many sorts of
objects, aesthetic or not. For the attention, as rapt and
intransitive, is induced and controlled by the special
features of the object which prevent our escape from
it to the world of more general or stereotyped responses. Hence it is a response, *sui generis,* to this object that keeps our attention rapt, and as intransitive,
riveted on itself. Of course, the object should then be
seen by the critic as displaying features capable of
enforcing this attention upon it.

It is important to note in passing that Vivas makes
these claims about the object modestly and with quali-
fication. He continually professes his awareness that the
aesthetic experience, as defined by him, is a psychological phenomenon, a datum that will occur when it
occurs, regardless of any consensus we can reach about
the aesthetic quality of the stimulating object—indeed,
regardless of whether the object is even intended to
serve such an experience. If, then, it can be any object
and if no one can predict when the experience will
occur for any subject, how can we use the experience to
make the normative claims which I have suggested is
the main advantage of defining the experience this way?
Here Vivas would remind us of the relational basis of
his notion of the "transaction": that the object functions
as the object in what is conceived as an aesthetic experience only because it so functions and is so conceived

as it interacts with the subject of the experience. (We see again at this point the advantage for Vivas of his emerging out of the Deweyan tradition. But this notion does not commit him to naturalism, as he later came to discover. Even the ontologist must leave phenomena to the phenomenal world, relating subject and object in a mutual dependence that is implicit in the meaning of *phenomenon.*)

But this relational basis can support an objective claim of value if we seek an experience of an object that can be shared by many subjects rather than be found, idiosyncratically, in one subject. Granted that an experience which might satisfy Vivas' definition as aesthetic can result, for a single subject, from a confrontation with any object, we can still try to decide whether the ground for the aesthetic character of the experience is in the features of the object or in the projective powers of the subject. If we come to expect the experience to be aesthetic as we move from subject to subject before the same object, it must be because we are attributing the control of the experience—and the largest share of the responsibility for it—to the features of the object. We are claiming, in effect, that a knowing and submissive subject—accustomed to aesthetic transactions—*ought* to be led into an aesthetic experience by this object. Further, the lapses or deficiencies are in the subject if he fails so to respond. If we do not find such characteristics in the object, on the other hand, then we are likely to claim that it is the subject who is responsible for any claimed aesthetic experience, so that we would not expect it to be repeated with another subject. The experience would be seen as more idiosyncratic than appropriate as a response to this object with the features we are specifying for it. By this manner of proceeding, the experience, in the case of a particular object of the first sort, becomes normative after all—or at least the aesthetic response becomes normative since the object is seen as soliciting it. In short, we are making an affirmative claim of aesthetic value for the object. So the Vivas argument runs, as he uses a relational theory of aesthetic experience to get to an objective theory of value.

It is, of course, the characterization of aesthetic experience as intransitive attention that enables him to manage this movement. If the subject, in such an experience, is required to be contained by the object, searching out all the possible interrelations among its elements playing on its surface and in its depths but being held by it from searching beyond, then his experience—so long as one maintains that it is a response appropriate to this object—must point to the features of the object that enforce and sustain that containment. The object invites attention and, keeping it intransitive, holds that attention upon itself terminally, presenting its world as the subject's total world for the course of the experience, without leading to the commonplace world beyond that comes before and after—though it is this world to which its symbols seem, in a non-aesthetic context, to point. This leads Vivas to emphasize that its meanings, during the experience, are "immanent" and "reflexive" rather than, as with objects functioning in non-aesthetic experiences, "referential." Representation becomes presentation, as signs that normally point the subject to the world are forced by the pressures of his attention to become mutually sustaining with meanings that become self-sufficient. A work thus would be seen to be other than aesthetic (in the experience toward which it seeks to lead its subject) to the extent that its meanings are referentially directed, moving the subject's attention outside instead of constantly renewing the internal relations that trap him within.

As Vivas licenses him, the critic thus sees as the psychological "factors of advantage" (by which is meant factors of containment and control) for our intransitive attention those aesthetic features of the object as an entrapping structure. Antique criteria like unity come to be newly justified, and more recent new-critical criteria like irony or paradox or ambiguity— complexity in general—are theoretically earned in a philosophical context that has us looking for characteristics whose equivocal nature blocks our tendency to escape with a single referential meaning. It is the potential completeness of aesthetic system growing out of his concept of the aesthetic experience that led Vivas to be looked upon, *ex post facto* and not altogether accurately, as the aesthetician of the New Criticism. For these promising but hardly philosophically minded critics needed one, and the tendency of Vivas' work was corroborative of many of their findings. Certainly it is the case that, in the light of his work, the New Criticism, whatever its inconsistencies and divagations among its varied practitioners, was accorded a more understanding and useful role in the history of modern aesthetics.

Throughout his career, despite the disruption in his philosophical allegiance, Vivas has held to essentially the same notion of aesthetic experience. In the early and brief, but justly influential, "A Definition of the Aesthetic Experience," he acknowledged that a lengthier treatment was required. He provided this fuller statement in "A Natural History of the Aesthetic Transaction," written as early as 1939 though the Krikorian volume which contained it appeared only in 1944. The commitment to naturalism is the more evident as the presentation becomes the more detailed in the longer essay. Ironically, by the time the volume appeared Vivas had undergone serious doubts about the philosophical underpinnings that were the more apparent in that essay.[3] It was not until two decades later that he wrote the final and most complete version, this time in accord with the metaphysic he had adopted.[4] And it was a full statement indeed, one that incorporated his

---

[3] For this reason it was the less revealing "Definition," rather than the fuller essay, that he preferred to reprint in *The Problems of Aesthetics* (1953) and *Creation and Discovery* (1955).

[4] "The Artistic Transaction," *The Artistic Transaction and Essays on Theory of Literature* (Ohio State University, 1963, pp. 3–93).

total mature aesthetic. Yet it remains essentially compatible with his earliest statement.

As I have suggested earlier, the role of the object in
the aesthetic experience leads Vivas toward an objective theory of value insofar as that value is "anchored"
in the perceptible features of the object. Values, as
axiological or tertiary qualities, may well be intuitive
affairs which cannot be reduced to perceptible or sec-
ondary qualities of the object; yet, in the case of an
object whose features can be shown to lead the subject
toward the aesthetic experience by controlling his attention and rendering it intransitive, we can claim its
aesthetic values to be "anchored" in those features.[5]
This commitment to phenomenal objectivity, a claim
which he has always conceded is possible for the naturalist as well as the value realist to make, led him
nonetheless to an awareness of the incapacity of even
the "new naturalism" to account for the metaphysical
basis of such values. His growing attachment to ontic
objectivity had stimulated his attack on naturalistic
value theory in ethics before "The Objective Basis of
Criticism" extended it to aesthetics.[6] And, whatever the

---

[5] "The Objective Basis of Criticism," *Western Review,* July 1948.

[6] "Animadversions on Naturalistic Ethics," *Ethics,* April 1946. This
essay, which officially indicated his change of philosophical allegiance,
was an early version of what grew into the opening section of *The
Moral Life and the Ethical Life,* University of Chicago Press, 1950.
It is unfortunate that the strength and vigor of his attack kept some
readers from appreciating the force of his positive argument in the
balance of that book.

common elements in his naturalistic and anti-naturalistic phases, his new philosophical position would have to be reflected in the shift in the areas to be emphasized in his aesthetics.

His conviction about the inadequacy of naturalism led to (if it did not result from) his championing of a theory of mind and its creativity which suggested metaphysical consequences—and origins. If his theory of value was realistic, his theory of mind was idealistic; but both seemed to him equally to require a non-naturalistic metaphysic.[7] Nor is there any inconsistency, although there is a dynamic tension, between these two theories (of value and of mind) as he builds his aesthetic on the apparently paradoxical relations between them.

Far from being inconsistent, it is rather clear that his definition of aesthetic experience as intransitive attention would assume the radical creativity of the artist. This entails the claim, in accord with Coleridge's definition of "imagination," that the artist brings to his product a creative addition, the result of a spontaneity of mind that gives forth a synthesis beyond the materials that it has taken in. If the artist is author of the object whose features have a structure that holds us intransitively in its unity, then that integral complex of immanent and reflexive meanings which has trans-

---

[7] "Two Notes on the New Naturalism," *Sewanee Review,* July 1948. A portion of this essay appeared in *Creation and Discovery* with the appropriate title, "Naturalism and Creativity."

formed his would-be referential materials can have its source only in his creative act. Not that the artist's spontaneity is a literal one that creates *ex nihilo,* like the God of *Genesis;* but the changes he works upon the materials given him lend to his emergent object an apparent newness, for the rapt aesthetic observer, that makes it appear to be the product of a human genesis. In effect, it is, as Coleridge would have it, the lesser genesis, finite imitation of "the infinite I AM." And Vivas sees this doctrine of creativity, so dependent upon the aesthetic realm for its most dramatic demonstration, as one for which no naturalistic theory of mind can account. For the doctrine requires an idealistic claim, while the naturalist cannot finally move beyond the materialistic and behavioral. This inadequacy in accounting for creativity joins with an inadequacy in accounting for objective values to summon the philosopher to a less reductive position—or at least these inadequacies so summoned *this* philosopher.

But it should be seen from what I have just said that it is not altogether accurate to speak of Vivas' description of the creative process as representing an unqualifiedly idealistic theory of mind. For his insistence on the finitude of human creation as less than God's infinite creation, *ex nihilo,* arises from his concern with those materials given the artist from outside. To cite the artist's finitude is to remind us that he can create only mediately rather than immediately—in short, that he is dependent upon a medium. Vivas is drawing back from making the idealist's gnostic claim (of unmediated creativity) for the artist. The fact that his theory spins out of an aesthetic experience defined as intransitive attention requires that the artist work in a manipulable but sharable symbolic medium, one with properties that can be shaped into an objective structure which can perform its captivating function when confronted by the observer. It is this medium that he shares with his contemporaries and with all earlier artists. Thus the mind of the artist, for all its creative capacity, is dependent upon the sensory realities of his objective and traditional medium to express himself. And that expression is the result of the give-and-take between what the creative mind demands and what the limitations of the medium will allow, although that give-and-take may result in break-throughs by an artist who has forced a new plasticity upon the medium. Not that he has exceeded the limitations, but that they seem to have been reconceived so that they seem to be working for him. Thus, even where Vivas most approximates idealism, he brings in the real as ineluctably there, a formative element to be reckoned with in whatever is to be created.

In effect, Vivas is saying that what the artist is in one sense creating he is another sense discovering in the flexible potentialities of his medium. This paradoxical notion—that creation and discovery are equally just, and simultaneously present, descriptions of the relation between the artist's product and his reality—

persists throughout Vivas' complex system of aesthetics. It explains his impatience with the partiality of unqualified idealism or expressionism on the one hand and of traditional theories of imitation on the other. The artist must be seen as creating beyond his materials, the biographical materials of his experience and the traditional materials left him by the history of his art; but he must also be seen as discovering what his product is becoming only as he works it out in the objective form it must finally assume. It is not a prior mental creation which he then translates into the form we finally see; it is a creation only as it is discovered in the making, the making in those materials that fix it for us.

Yet we have seen that what is created is a great deal indeed, and—once created—it is an indispensable gift for us all. Perhaps the greatest contribution made by Vivas' work after the middle '40s was his analysis of the nature of the gift which the artistic creation makes to its culture. According to this analysis, through its symbolic structure the work of art gives its culture the perceptual norms that create an elementary order for the inchoate flow which is "the primary data of experience" which we all undergo. Vivas claims to find four "ideal" modes of experience, of which we have seen only his crucial examination of the aesthetic (as intransitive attention).[8] Unlike the other three—the re-

---

[8] The reader should have been reminded, in my earlier discussion, that what Vivas has been defining as the aesthetic experience must not be expected to occur in its pure form in our actual experiences,

ligious, the moral, and the cognitive—only the aesthetic has this peculiarly intimate relationship to "the primary data of experience." Indeed, it is likely that the other modes, rather than dealing with the primary data directly, deal with the symbolic forms provided largely by the aethetic mode. So it is the aesthetic mode that puts the world at our disposal for us to act upon it in the other modes, the various transitive modes.[9]

---

which in fact are various mixtures of the four modes he defines. The experiences we have, whatever their composite natures, contain elements which can be extracted for a definition of what an ideal aesthetic experience would be. And, as we have seen, we can move from there to the kind of object whose structure would appear to predispose its subject to such an experience. But Vivas does not confuse ideal with actual mixed experiences; nor does he claim any superiority for the ideal experience, though it is philosophically useful for him to deal with it.

[9] There have been several key essays since the early 1950s in which Vivas treats the relation of the aesthetic mode to the "primary data" and to the other modes. Chief among these is "The Object of the Poem," *Creation and Discovery: Essays in Criticism and Aesthetics* (New York: Noonday, 1955), in my opinion the single most important essay in aesthetics he has given us. At least two other essays in *Creation and Discovery* are especially useful:

"Literature and Knowledge" and "What is a Poem." The "Appendix—The Constitutive Symbol" in *D. H. Lawrence: The Failure and Triumph of Art* (Northwestern University Press, 1960) supplements these essays by applying a series of useful distinctions among kinds of symbols, and "The Artistic Transaction" (1963) adds a later refinement by determining the relation between all the modes of experience and "the basic symbolic activity." In the earlier of these writings the aesthetic usually appears to be prior to the other three and the basis for them, though there are moments when the aesthetic rather seems coordinate with the others. Vivas attempts to resolve this problem,

Vivas clarifies his argument for the role of art in culture by distinguishing, first, the moment *before* the poem when the "meanings and values" which are to become "the object of the poem" *"sub*sist" in the culture, secondly, the moment *of* the poem when those "meanings and values," as the "object," *"in*sist" in the poem, and, finally, those many moments *after* the poem has organized them for our symbolic perception when they become *"ex*istent" in the culture, thanks to the poem.[10] Meanings and values are only subsistent when they are potentially within a culture, unrecognized and unnamed, awaiting the creative act that will bring them to active entity-hood. The poet fulfills his role of organizing and presenting the primary data of experience, identifying them by giving them symbolic form, when he creates an insistent order for these meanings and values, the order which is his poem. Since they have had no proper existence outside the poem, prior to the poem, they can be referred to *through* the poem only by the "insistence" they achieve *in* the language of the poem. Having thus achieved a full identity, these meanings and values can enter the language and the discursive life of the culture by being ripped out of their

---

substantively as well as terminologically, in "The Artistic Transaction," where he introduces the notion of "the basic symbolic activity" (in some ways similar to, but not identical with, the aesthetic) as prior to all four of the modes, now viewed coordinately.

[10] See *Creation and Discovery*, pp. 137–41.

insistent context in the poem and being generalized to apply to other contexts, having been thinned for referential use. It is how the language of our meanings and values grows, though it becomes, as we use it, a debased and inaccurate language which refers to its object *through* but not *in* its words. Vivas sees culture as standing in continual need of the poet to enlarge as well as to refresh its language, although its need for his gifts forces it to use them badly. The poet indeed plays a major anthropological role as maker of culture by making his poem. "Thus to the extent that the poet succeeds in revealing meanings and values which are actually involved in an emergent sense in the social process, he becomes the creator of culture and the meanings and values thus revealed become constitutive of culture."

Here indeed is a statement of the poet's privilege and priority. Yet in reaching these heights Vivas still can be seen to have traced a path leading back to his original definition of aesthetic experience. What he has now done is to demonstrate how the enclosure of that experience is transformed, when we turn from the object to the world beyond and to the other modes of experience, so that what has served for its own sake now serves our total humanity. Meanings have to be "immanent and reflexive" when they are *in*sistent since they are organizing primary data which do not yet exist discursively in order to be pointed to. But meanings that are immanent and reflexive during the course of the aesthetic experience in its intransitivity can become transitive and referential once they enter the language of the culture by allowing us to point to objects through them. This change can occur only after the aesthetic mode of experience has given away to the service of the other modes.

Here, then, is a second view of the artist's creativity though the two views are clearly wedded in Vivas' theory: as the artist created a unique structure to contain and control our response as intransitive, so he creates what comes out of that structure to stay with us after that response—the symbolic identities which form the constellation of meanings and values that constitute our culture. The artist's aesthetic creation is matched with his anthropological. But the anthropological creativity of the artist is as much qualified by the notion of discovery as was his aesthetic. We observed Vivas modifying the incipient idealism of the notion that the poet was radically creative by treating him as dependent upon the objective medium, co-conspirator with him in the expressive act. The poet's role as creator of culture by way of its meanings and values is even more circumscribed by external reality.

To begin with, we have seen that the meanings and values which the poet forces into "insistence" within his object are hardly arbitrary ones; rather they are those which are historically potential within his culture, awaiting the conferring of identity. They are, in other words, awaiting his discovery of them, although we do not know they have been waiting there until he has discovered them for us. In this obvious sense his act of creation is indeed—or had better be—an act of discovery. He may seem free to create as he will and persuade us by the vigor of his invention to accept his creation as what we were ready to discover (with his help). But there is, outside him, a reality that is ready to clip his wings if he flies in the face of it.

More than this realistic limitation is imposed by Vivas. When, in their pre-poetic state, the meanings and values are termed "subsistent," it is clear that he means the word literally, in its technical philosophical sense. Not only are the meanings and values potentially within the culture, beginning to stir and helping to move the culture, though as yet without name or recognition; but they also, as subsistent objects, have "status in being" or "ontic status." Since they "are actually to some extent at least operative in the culture prior to their discovery by the poet," they *are* before we have phenomenal awareness that they are: just the essence of "subsistence." What the poet discovers, what he brings to our phenomenal awareness, appears to be a creation, except that it is a revelation of an ontological structure. "Insofar as the objects of poetry subsist prior to their revelation, they have the same status, for ontology, as is enjoyed by the operative invariant relations in nature— the 'forces' and 'powers' and the actualizing potencies which subsist as the structures of the physical world and which the scientist 'discovers' and formulates as his 'laws.' "[11]

Here is philosophical realism indeed, although Vivas never permits it to undo his commitment to what, at the phenomenal level, he defends as significant and radical creativity. In emphasizing the aspect of discovery which paradoxically accompanies what the artist uniquely brings to our awareness, he seems to have moved beyond Kant and Croce, and more strikingly, even beyond Cassirer, but only after having absorbed his lessons from them fully. Though challenging the philosophic temper of our times by calling himself an "axiological realist," Vivas would rather court paradox than do less than justice to the creative capacities of mind as it interacts with matter to produce its utter originals. The object may itself function only at the phenomenal level, but the meanings and values it brings to that level, making them visible, it has transformed from the ontological seat where they were found. Thus the conjunction in his theory of creation and discovery echoes on the one hand the unlikely conjunction of the phenomenal and the ontological and on the other the equally unlikely conjunction of idealism and realism. But, Vivas would

---

[11] *Creation and Discovery,* p. 139. "But," lest he lose all that his aesthetic has gained for us, Vivas hastens to add, "we must not forget the all-important difference between the objects expressed through the scientific hypothesis and the objects revealed through and in poetry."

claim, his need for more adequate descriptions of the aesthetic experience, of aesthetic value, and of the role of art in creating our cultural vision has led him to his theoretical claims; and, as a dedicated empiricist (as he defines this term), he must follow. As he follows, in the complexity of his struggle he may indeed have moved beyond Kant, Croce, and Cassirer in the precision of his claims for art's symbolic workings on us and on our culture.

It is Vivas' most remarkable trait as a philosopher that he tests his problems and himself so relentlessly.[12] If his observations of those problems warrant it, paradox does not frighten him, though inconsistency does, as he tries to resolve the paradox without reducing any part of it in a way that would cheat experience. So he worries those problems continually and never lets them stop worrying him. When naturalism would no longer serve, he had the metaphysical courage to turn to axiological realism if there was where his answers were to be found, though he also had the empirical courage to retain the experiential basis of his theory and the

---

[12] He has been equally relentless in testing his contemporaries, producing many polemical studies, "animadversions" that took courage but were hardly calculated to give comfort within a fraternal order. Much of his best work is found in these searching studies—I think of the essays on Jordan or Wheelwright or Leavis or Morris or Wimsatt just offhand—and, though sometimes harsh and unsparing, they have never seemed to me to be personal or petty. His eye and pen are dedicated to the problem at hand, and philosophy is not to him a game for sensitive egos.

creative claims for the poet consistent with it. He thus has worked to preserve the freedom of the poet, justifying the best of the experimental tradition in poetry, but binding that poet to his traditional medium and his culture's history by way of the fixed objective structure he has made. Though not himself one of the poets of his theory, Vivas has been his own example of the gifted mind that need not imitate or fall prey to the expressed idols of its culture, the mind that insists on its moral and aesthetic freedom to struggle with its materials in order to create beyond them. But he is exemplary of his philosophy also in denying himself pure creativity, the license to spin out any wishful theory; for he has also the conviction that this theory must be put into the service of solutions and underlying truths that— found or unfound—are surely there, there to be hunted.

The Ethical Life and the Political Life

David Levy

David Levy was born in London in 1947. Educated at Stowe, Christ Church Oxford, and the London School of Economics, he now teaches sociology at Middlesex Polytechnic. He is the author of Against the Stream *and of various articles that have appeared in the United States, France, and Germany as well as in the United Kingdom.*

It is now twenty-five years since the first publication of *The Moral Life and the Ethical Life*. In that re-markable book, Eliseo Vivas discussed many of the central issues of moral philosophy and nothing that has happened in the world in the last quarter-century has made their discussion any less essential. If, as Professor Vivas suggests, "experience is the plasma of relevant, meaningful thinking,"[1] then the last twenty-five years of human experience have reconfirmed both his iden-tification of the problematic center of the human moral and ethical experience and his insistence that one of the roles of the philosopher is to be a critic of his age.

Though few were so open in their admission, many

---

[1] Eliseo Vivas, *The Moral Life and the Ethical Life* (Chicago: University of Chicago Press, 1950), p. vii.

readers of the book must have sympathized with Professor Vivas' confession that he was "a man radically opposed to the present drift of historical events and therefore unsympathetic with those who employ their talent in the manufacture of an apologetic for the direction of contemporary history."[2] The "yes men to the age" whom he then attacked were the naturalist moral philosophers among whom he had once numbered himself. The first part of his book consists of a series of chapters which, as it were, clear the deck for his statement of his own position. Santayana, R. B. Perry and the Interest theory of morality, Charner Perry, D. C. Williams and the Postulational theory are among the targets of his blows but his deepest hostility is raised by his encounter with the Instrumentalist moral theory of John Dewey. It is not difficult to see the reason for Vivas' hostility. Not only was Dewey's philosophy uniquely influential in the America of the day, but it represented in a peculiarly pure form the mixture of brash secularist optimism with the primacy of action over contemplation which Vivas rightly regards as fatal to our understanding of the moral and ethical dimension of life.

"Dewey's central effort in the analysis of moral theory . . . has been addressed to elucidating the manner in which 'inquiry' or thought brings about an

---

[2] *Ibid.*, pp. ix-x.

'*existential* transformation and reconstruction of the material with which it deals.' "[3] Well, since the publication of *The Moral Life and the Ethical Life,* the influence of Dewey has certainly waned, but the conception of moral and ethical thinking as something concerned with changing the world rather than discovering and describing its properties has certainly not. The restless ideologies of East and West have continued to eat away the subject matter of the philosopher, the lover of wisdom and the explicator of the real. The moral realism of Eliseo Vivas, a scandal to the Deweyites and a stumbling block to the skeptics, is a pernicious heresy to those in the forefront of today's intellectual life who see no reality beyond the merciless process of history. Deweyite moral philosophy inevitably resolves itself into reformist political activity; the result is a vulgar progressivism blind to the inherent limitations of the human situation, a pseudo-metaphysical underpinning for what one might call the philosophy of inflation. The equally activist Marxism, which has now become the favorite ideology of progressives, also sees our task as "not to contemplate the world but to change it"; its own concept of the moral life is also one of devoted political activism, more ruthless and all-embracing than that of Dewey's liberal disciples but recognizably sprung from the same lineage.

---

[3] *Ibid.,* p. 115.

The essential characteristic of both Deweyite-liberal and Marxist conceptions of politics is that both regard political action, constitutional or revolutionary, as means for operationalizing a typically private, partial notion of the good. The implicit argument of both runs as follows: There is not enough "X" in our present situation ("X" may be Liberty, Equality, Public Ownership, etc.); "X" is a good, in fact, the overwhelming good, since human fulfillment (Progress, Historical Reason, etc.) is defined in its terms; political action is the most powerful means we have for pursuing this end; therefore, there is no room left for any ethics, any account of the good life, that does not subject all else to the political struggle.

It is, I think, this conception of politics that Professor Vivas has in mind when he speaks out against belief in the primacy of politics: "Against belief in the primacy of the political, the truly humanist teacher—and properly viewed, the teacher must share with the statesman, the priest, and the poet, the ultimate responsibility for the success or failure of his people and culture—must conceive the fundamental problem today, yesterday, and always to stave off the snarling beasts of barbarism that are always and everywhere on the alert to get out of their inward cages into which culture drives them. The teacher's job must be to guide man to grow to his full stature as human. This he does, not by enlisting him in a party but by making him the possessor of the sustaining intellectual and moral structures of civilization."[4] If the primacy of the political is conceived with the Deweyite/Marxist conception of the role of politics in mind, then what Vivas says is certainly directed against it. But if we operate with a different conception of politics, namely, the Aristotelian and Thomist conception, then the fundamental job of staving off the beast within and the means of doing so, through the transmission of "the sustaining intellectual and moral structures of civilization," are both included within the notion of man as an essentially political animal.

A moment ago I reconstructed what I take to be the implicit argument underlying reformist and revolutionary politics. Let me now balance it with a schematic account of the nature and place of the political according to Aristotle and St. Thomas Aquinas. Man is a social animal whose potential can only be realized with his fellows in society. His potentialities are given him in his nature, but whether he realizes them or not depends on his participation in the social and political life. Man is a rational as well as a social animal; he can understand the vital necessities that draw him to the construction of the commonwealth. In man, reason replaces the instinct of the lower animals as the motive for sociality. Human political reason supplements brute necessity. Politics is the science that discovers the conditions of man's human fulfillment. Professor Vivas'

---

[4] *Ibid.*, p. 132.

"sustaining intellectual and moral structures of civilization" can only be realized and transmitted within the city, and it is for this reason that St. Thomas, following Aristotle, holds that politics among the practical sciences occupies "the first and architectonic position in relation to all the others, as concentrating on the ultimate and perfect good in human things."[5]

In this perspective, the political life completes, and in a sense defines, the moral and ethical life of which Professor Vivas speaks, as the forms of political organization define the likelihood of man's achieving his full earthly potential. There is nothing subjective or partial about such a conception of politics; it is based simply on the observation that under certain conditions human beings flourish more than under others, and on the knowledge that human action can materially increase the chances of such a flowering even though the conditions themselves are given us by our nature and by its place within a natural order which we did not create and which we do not even necessarily will. The choice lies between cooperation with natural necessity, reason completing nature, or rejection of necessity, reason defying nature. The first is objective politics in the sense that the place and ends of politics are given us by our human station within the object world; the second is the politics of subjectivism in which the ends

---

[5] St. Thomas Aquinas, "Prologue to the Commentary on the Politics of Aristotle," paragraph 7.

of political activity are pure projections of more or less permanent human desires not necessarily related to the objective potentialities of man's earthly being. Success crowns the first, though for various reasons never permanently; frustration and failure follow the second.

If the objectivity of the political, which I take to be implicit in the Aristotelian/Thomist view, is accepted, then there ought, theoretically, to be no irresolvable conflict between the ethical and the political good. However, in *The Moral Life and the Ethical Life,* Professor Vivas talks of situations in which precisely such a conflict can occur: "To kill a king may be a *political* necessity which a Lenin can argue about with a Suarez. It can never be an *ethical* necessity, since the only necessity that the ethical man would recognize is that of living according to his primary insight. When the two necessities—the political and the ethical—clash, you may be facing a tragic conflict in the sense that whichever way you choose to resolve it involves irreparable loss."[6] The "primary insight" of which Vivas talks is the discovery of the absolute value of the person as person, and it is this discovery that thrusts one from the moral to the ethical plane.[7] To live the ethical life is to acknowledge the primacy of the person among all the values discovered in experience, but the acknowledgment of this primacy is not a simple subjective

---

[6] Vivas, *The Moral Life and the Ethical Life,* p. 345.
[7] *Ibid.,* p. 291.

choice (of the type "let 'X' be the supreme good"), which would make Professor Vivas a postulational moralist of the type he rejects in the first half of his book.

"I believe," we read in the Preface to Vivas' book, "that the moral man *discovers* the values he espouses, in the same way in which the scientist or the logician discovers the laws of his science. There is a difference, of course, between the laws of nature and laws of morality and of logic, but the difference does not concern us here. Values are real and antecedent to our discovery of them; this is what I mean when I say that they have 'ontic status.' They are a peculiar kind of fact, since they possess 'requiredness' to which we respond, and it is this aspect of value that is the source of the moral imperative."[8] Among the many values discovered, the ethical man espouses the primacy of the person. He differs from the postulational moralist in that he does not manufacture his morality as a logical system deducible from the postulation of that primacy. Professor Vivas argues against drawing an analogy between moral and logical systems. "Morality, if it is a deductive system at all, is a material system"[9]; morality deals with the right, the fitting, organization of existential relationships between human beings. If the primacy of the person is a postulate in any sense at all,

---

[8] *Ibid.*, p. viii.
[9] *Ibid.*, p. 94.

it is not an arbitrary subjective moral statement from which an ethical system may logically be deduced; it is, says Vivas, "a 'postulate' in a totally different sense: in the sense Kant meant when he spoke of the 'postulates of the practical reason.' The ethical man in the situation in which he discovered the necessity for 'postulating' the primacy of the person was not picking out arbitrarily one sentence or proposition among many to lay at the base of a deductive, purely symbolic system. He was completing the moral process by discovering the necessary conditions required to resolve the problem of evil."[10] Evil, as a problem of morality, is discovered in the experience of objective injustice and unrighteousness, the undeserved, "unfitting" end of the victims of concentration camps, for example.

The inmate of Maidenek, calling out for justice, does not merely demand the satisfaction of his subjective desire; that would place his cry on no more secure basis than his murderers' equally subjective decision that he should die. In calling out for justice, he means that there is no justice now but "there ought to be, in order to satisfy the demands of a situation which, as it exists at present, is awry, which inherently and intrinsically lacks something it ought to have to be a fit human situation."[11] The notion of the "unfitting" is a perfectly objective derivative from our knowledge of the ontic

---

[10] *Ibid.,* p. 316.
[11] *Ibid.,* p. 304.

status of the human being, his nature and status in the surrounding universe.

Eliseo Vivas' recognition of the ontic status of value is derived from the realist wing of the phenomenological movement, Nicolai Hartmann and Max Scheler; his personalism from his readings of Nikolai Berdyaev and Francisco Romero. However, the ethical theory of *The Moral Life and the Ethical Life* suggests to me a strong kinship with the moral philosophy of Jacques Maritain, which develops the natural law position of Thomism in the direction of personalism. This resemblance is even more marked when we note the way in which Vivas sees the discovery of a system of objective relationships entailing certain consequences for human action as pointing to the existence of a rational creating agent, and thus as a warrant for belief in God. Eliseo Vivas, like the Thomists, holds that the nature of existence is such as to suggest the existence of God; indeed, that if God did not exist there would be no intelligibility in being. As an axiological realist he is convinced "not merely that the order found by him is a projection which is only a descriptive correlate of his mental deficiency in his capacity for apprehending utter chaos but that it has ontic status and that that order entails some sort of agent, somehow analogous to the human agent, and therefore also an end."[12]

Problems arise, however, when we ask what is the

---

[12] *Ibid.,* p. 322 ff.

status of the primacy of the person in this metaphysical scheme, a primacy which for both Vivas and Maritain involves in extreme situations a necessary clash between the ethical and the political in which man only secures his destiny by rigid espousal of the ethical. Jacques Maritain and Eliseo Vivas each handle this difficult area in a way that reflects their own philosophical backgrounds. For Vivas, as we have seen, the primacy of the person is explained in Kantian terms as an imperative of the practical reason, and it is easy to sympathize with this approach in an age which has seen the misuse of political reason and force on a scale inconceivable in the past. Only espousal of the primacy of the person secures us against the horrors of totalitarian politics and the arguments that can be used to justify them. In a Kantian framework this is a good enough justification of the position adopted; indeed, it is the best possible justification for anyone who cannot accept a realist metaphysics. However, it is clear that Professor Vivas does accept just such a metaphysical structure as Kant felt unable to recognize, and this, as I shall argue, puts a rather different complexion on matters.

Of Maritain's commitment to philosophical realism there is no doubt, and with his Thomist background he sees no need to introduce any such Kantian notion as a postulate of the practical reason as justification for the primacy of the person. Instead, he builds his argument on the basis of two parallel texts from St. Thomas. The first states, "Each individual person is related to the

entire community as the part to the whole." The second
adds, "Man is not ordained to the body politic according to all he is and has." Maritain expands on these
texts as follows: "Man is a part of and inferior to the
political community by reason of the things in and of
him which, due as they are to the deficiencies of material individuality, depend in their very essence upon
political society and which in turn may be used as
means to promote the temporal good of the society. . . .
On the other hand, by reason of the things in and of
man, which are derived from the ordination of the personality as such to the absolute and which thus depend
in their essence on something higher than the political
community and so concern properly the supra-temporal
accomplishments of the person as person, man excels
the political community."[13] Maritain, accepting the
Aristotelian notion of man as composed of body and
soul, sees the roots of individuality in human materi-
ality and human personality as rooted in a spirituality
directly ordained to the absolute. However, it is not
merely our material individuality that cries out for the
support of society; human personality, too, develops its
potential only through society. The point here is the
absolute sense in which the highest and ultimate ends of
personality, the desire for beatitude, transcend the
social political realm. Thus, for Maritain, the primacy

---

[13] Jacques Maritain, *The Person and the Common Good* (South
Bend, Indiana: University of Notre Dame Press, 1966), pp. 73–74.

of the person is not merely "a postulate of the practical reason," but a philosopher's recognition of the metaphysical composition of the human being, a rendering to God what is God's that apparently respects the realm that is rightly Caesar's.

Remember here that both Eliseo Vivas and Jacques Maritain are philosophical realists. That is to say that both recognize the patterns of intelligibility apprehended by the mind in experience as being truly present in the object of apprehension. It is my contention that this axiological position has important implications for our understanding of the relationship of the ethical to the political, implications that severely limit the extent to which we are justified in talking of the primacy of the person as the foundation and completion of a true ethics. It is a fine thing to say that the right, the humanly fitting, pattern of our conduct must be organized around our recognition of the dignity of the other precisely insofar as he is another person, but we must also consider another type of question related not to personality as an isolated quality recognized in a certain type of being we encounter in experience, but to the status of personality in relation to the intelligible patterns of being that our realism compels us to accept. Such questions, I suggest, lead us to recognize that there is a limit to the primacy of the person as a defining imperative of the ethical life, that the limits of personalism are given us by the limits of personality. The primacy of the person can only be the sort of absolute into which both Professors Vivas and Maritain make it if we treat personality in isolation from all else that we know about human nature and the status of its being.

My argument here owes much to my reading of the work of Marcel De Corte and in particular to his recent book, *De la Prudence: La Plus Humaine des Vertus,*[14] but, while Professor De Corte is concerned to restate the Aristotelian and Thomist doctrine of prudence as a counterfoil to the fantastic schemes of illusion thrown out by modern ideologists, the aim here is to suggest a conception of political philosophy and the political life which will, as it were, round off the noble conception of the ethical life found in Professor Vivas' book. In setting human personality against its necessarily social and political background, we may approach a correct understanding of the relationship of ethics and politics. Needless to say, the concept of the political, with which we will be operating, has nothing to do with that of the Deweyites and Marxists. Between their salvationist politics, which look to political action to transform the very nature of man, and realist ethics grounded in a recognition of the ontological structure and status of human nature, there cannot be anything but a fundamental conflict. We avoid the radical conflict of ethical and political imperatives which Eliseo Vivas suggests is

---

[14] Marcel De Corte, *De La Prudence: La Plus Humaine des Vertus* (Jorge: Dominique Martin Morin, 1974).

a necessary characteristic of the human condition only when we operate with a correct understanding of the nature and purpose of politics. This understanding—while restricting the scope we can allow the primacy of the person as a determinant of correct ethical practice—also restricts the operation of political reason to areas where it cannot challenge the integrity of the personality.

The essential thing to remember here is that man is a social animal. He depends on his fellows not merely for material satisfaction made available by the division of labor in society, but for the development of his personality as such. If, as Professor Vivas argues, he discovers moral values as imperatives of conduct somehow fitting to him, then these discoveries are made within the bounds of society. Even his recognition that the society in which he lives precludes the attainment of his full potential is largely based on a belief that he is precluded from establishing and maintaining a fitting relationship with his fellows.

It is in the context of his argument against Dewey's conception of the primacy of politics that Eliseo Vivas tells us that "The teacher's job must be to guide man to grow to his full stature as human," and he is surely correct in maintaining that this is not accomplished through enlisting him in a cause or party. It is the transmission of "the sustaining intellectual and moral structures of civilization" that draws out the full potentiality of the human child and inducts him into civilized social life. But can we talk of sustaining structures of civilization without talking of the political as much as the moral and intellectual? Furthermore, in relation to the moral and ethical, the code of fitting conduct with regard to our fellows, does not the political have just the "first and architectonic position" of which St. Thomas spoke? As L. Lachance puts it, "Man's ultimate temporal achievement is not to be found on the steppes or in the forest. It is found by participation in all the excellent goods that a well organized society is able of offer him. To the extent that, in the order of practical realizations, the city appears a supremely efficacious potential, the only concrete reality capable of producing the human good with a certain degree of abundance and integrity."[15]

In a certain sense, Eliseo Vivas' discussion of the ethical life opens out onto theological issues, as he recognizes when he talks of the apprehension of an agent in the surrounding order and the spiritual nature of personality, but in quite a different sense it requires a discussion of Politics in the sense in which Aristotle and Aquinas understand it. "The discovery of the ethical entailed the discovery of a moral order proper to human beings: a system of objective relationships involving them in their activity as human beings and thus defining their destiny as consisting in the actualiza-

---

[15] Louis Lachance, *L'Humanisme Politique de Saint Thomas d'Aquin,* quoted in De Corte, *De La Prudence: La Plus Humaine des Vertus,* p. 52.

tion of ideal values in a certain hierarchical manner controlled by one absolute value."[16] Fair enough, but these values are ontically based, are discovered in human experience which, so far as the ethical is concerned at any rate, is by definition experience of the other as a human person, in other words, social experience. Thus, the system of objective relationships is not only a system of relationship of one value to another, but of human beings to one another. These human beings are not simply persons, each constituted as a person by his espousal of values; they are sons and daughters, fathers and mothers, princes and subjects, existentially related to each other prior to any espousal of values by the very fact of being born.

Political philosophy is concerned with understanding these relationships. With the help of such disciplines as history, anthropology, sociology, and psychology, it can lead us to an understanding of the degree to which any particular political structure is the product of passing circumstances or a necessary structure of human social existence.[17] Though we can never know exhaustively the potential of human nature, we can recognize that at certain periods and under certain conditions human beings have reached a higher level of civilization than at others. Professor Vivas' discussion of the absolute

[16] Vivas, *The Moral Life and the Ethical Life,* p. 321.
[17] For an excellent discussion of the nature of political philosophy, see Thomas Molnar, *L'Animal Politique* (Paris: La Table Ronde, 1974).

cultural relativism of Melville Herskovits is admirably to the point in this context.[18] Somehow we must make sense of what I take to be the basic conundrum of political philosophy: that man only achieves his full humanity through participation in the life of society; and his full potential is only realized in a condition that of its very nature imposes restrictions on his freedom of action.

There are, therefore, conditions in which men can only be guided to the realization of their full stature as human by acting on the recognition that there is a higher requirement than the primacy of the person. The very end of the achievement of full human stature, which is an achievement in and through society, cries out for the acceptance of the primacy not of the person but of the organization and order that makes that achievement possible. I will not talk of the primacy of society, for in an age that has experienced the hideous parodies of human society produced by totalitarian ideologies and movements, such a phrase would be fatally equivocal unless explained at great length; instead, remaining with the vocabulary of St. Thomas, let me speak of the primacy of the common good.

It is easy to make of the phrase "Common Good" just such an empty slogan as is flung around *ad nauseam* by politicians at election time. In fact, however, it has a very precise meaning. Given that man is a political

---

[18] Vivas, *The Moral Life and the Ethical Life,* p. 25.

animal who achieves his potential through society, the common good can be defined as everything that unifies and links human beings in society. That which disrupts, even though it springs from the depth of a personality or the deepest fantasies of the human mind, is against the common good. Jean-Paul Sartre may define man as "the desire to be God"; Rousseau may, at times, talk of the truly human as being the isolated savage. Human experience is enough to teach us that neither is true; that both are pathological definitions applicable only to those unable to accept their status as human beings. We are all inheritors, heirs to a determinate human nature which constitutes us what we are, heirs to a particular civilization or culture each of which is ultimately little more than a particular more or less satisfactory gloss on the human condition, heirs to particular parents to whom without our choice we stand in a certain relationship implying mutual consideration and duties. Our nature makes us social, our culture fixes the way we participate in the life of the city, our parents reveal to us by their own success or failure in communion with each other and ourselves our destiny as participants and partakers in the common good. The ethical life is lived around the realization of the unique value of the human person, but politics alone teaches us the conditions in which that person can realize the potential within him. Those conditions are entailed in the common good. Political science and philosophy are concerned with the discovery of those conditions; good political practice with their implementation and maintenance. It is the acknowledgement of the primacy of the common good over all private or sectional interests, and the will to achieve it over the conflicting claims of ideology and utopia, that marks out the politician worthy of his task, the man or woman who lives the political life in its ancient honored sense.

Essay Four

The Sacred and Golden Cord

William T. Couch

William Terry Couch was assistant director of the University of North Carolina Press from 1925 to 1932, director from 1932 to 1945. He was director and general editor of the University of Chicago Press from 1945 to 1950; editor in chief of Collier's Encyclopedia *from 1952 to 1959; of the* American Oxford Encyclopedia *from 1959 to 1963 (finished but never published); and editor of* These Are Our Lives. *He is the author of* The Human Potential, *published in 1974, and of many articles. He is now living in Chapel Hill, North Carolina.*

ONE

I had the privilege while I was the director and general
editor of the University of Chicago Press (October
1945—November 1950) of considering the manuscript
of Eliseo Vivas' *The Moral Life and the Ethical Life.*
On examining the manuscript, I judged it to be the kind
of intellectual work that was most needed and that I
wanted most to support. I was fortunate in having on
my staff an editor, Fred Wieck, whose ideas on matters
of this kind were in complete accord with mine. The
philosophy faculty had members who could be relied on
to recommend publication of the work if it proved tech-
nically competent and even if it attacked their own
writings. The more cogent the attack, the more certain
they would be to recommend the work with enthusiasm

for publication. This was an extraordinary situation and I was fortunate in being a part of it.

The Moral Life and the Ethical Life is first a general attack on contemporary discussion of ethics at the theoretical level. It then passes on to particular theories: the interest theory of Ralph Barton Perry; the postulational theory of Charner Perry; and the instrumentalist theory of John Dewey. Finally, Vivas goes beyond attack and states a theory of his own. Because his theory made better sense to me than any other with which I was acquainted, I was more than ordinarily interested in publishing his book. It might be said that in allowing my beliefs to influence my action, I was abandoning the objective role appropriate to one in charge of publishing under university auspices. I have never believed, however, in that type of objectivity illustrated so well by the old story of Buridan's ass. I have published books with which I have thoroughly disagreed and have considered it my duty to do so when they have been given the necessary academic approval. I have pushed them, too, even though I had to hold my nose at times while doing so. One can have opinions, and strong ones, without believing oneself omniscient. One's intellectual muscles must have exercise if they are not to ossify.

I shall begin with Vivas' general attack on contemporary ethical discussion. Vivas is writing for the specialist in ethics who should know the subject well enough to know against what and whom his attack is directed. In this discussion I shall attempt to provide what I (not a specialist in the field but a much interested spectator, and, as far as possible for an outsider, a participant or perhaps a victim—and as a person inescapably so) believe to be the information needed by a nonspecialist to understand Vivas' attack. Since ethics is not something set off by itself and surrounded by impenetrable walls but open to, and actually penetrated by, influences from what we may call "outside" for lack of a better way to describe the real situation, I shall discuss what I consider the more important of these nonethical influences.

In his Preface, Vivas says he would like to call himself a "personalist." Personalism in its main doctrine asserts the ultimate value of the person. Vivas agrees with the main doctrine. But personalism as developed has gone off on tangents with which he does not agree. So he cannot call himself a personalist. He would like to call himself an "empiricist," but the term "empiricist" would be even more misleading. It has been, he says, "preempted by men given to methodolatrous, *a priori* lucubrations about the possibility of extending the methods of the positive sciences to all fields of human interest. The result is a positivistic scientificism." For this reason he has to refuse this label. He would like to call himself an "existentialist," but the existentialist Sartre with his "atheism and total lack of Christian love" stands in his way. He then finally chooses the label "axiological realist," by which he means that value is not something conferred on objects by interest, or something that has the less than shadowy existence conferred by postulation, or something that one can fail to find in things, actions, and relations and be true to human experience where human beings generally find it. The failure of instrumentalism to find value in the ordinary and ethical objects of human experience, despite its professed acceptance of naive realism—which certainly finds values in these objects—disqualifies instrumentalism. "Values are real," says Vivas. "They are a peculiar kind of fact." This is the meaning of axiological realist," and this is why he chooses to call himself an axiological realist. "A person," he says, "is constituted by the values the self espouses and which he is able to espouse because the spirit which inheres in him is capable of objectivity, whereas the selves of the lower animals are not."

Vivas had, he says further in his Preface, "uncritically accepted" what he thought of as the "new naturalism." He had taken "seriously what the founders of contemporary naturalism" had said "about the need for progressive correction of empirical truth." "I had," he says, "expected that the social crisis which came to a head with the holocaust of World War II would lead to a rebirth of philosophy; and I hoped that the limited insights of the American philosophies (the idealisms no less than the naturalisms) which developed in the age of the 'Robber Barons,' with their shallow vitalistic optimism, would be enlarged in the light of the tragic experience of our own days. It is natural that until our day American philosophy should have neglected the tragic dimension of experience. . . ." But it could reasonably be hoped that the two World Wars of the century would awaken the academic technicians from their dogmatic slumber. This hope was not realized. So Vivas had to give up naturalism and search for a better philosophy.

The Introduction to *The Moral Life and the Ethical Life* urges attention to moral philosophy as both a practical and a theoretical science. Practical moral philosophy, in the sense in which Vivas uses the term, asserts the validity and importance of theoretical inquiries; that is, inquiries that try to discover a valid basis for the making of decisions that involve immediate practical interests. It tries to avoid both the shallow practicalism that confirms the layman in his myopic prejudices, and the academicism which drifts further and further away from the real problems of morals, that follows the trends of the times and falls into the "specialization which shapes our institutions as our society becomes more and more complex. The effect of specialization on philosophy is to turn it into an autotelic activity and . . . to 'bureaucratize' the philosopher. . . . The professional philosopher develops his own outlook, and by degrees his professional and private vision becomes effectually insulated so that he can use it to build his own world. . . . The isolation sharpens the critical faculty of the philosopher toward his own pure discipline, but it blunts his interest in other disciplines and in broader social needs." It would hardly be true that the moral philosopher then engages *only* in the making of false distinctions, but he certainly does some of this and he also tends to work on smaller and smaller problems. His "skills and procedures become a special kind of pure virtuosity, extremely complex and demanding the highest talent, developing its own intrinsic and absorbing interest."

"The shrinking of the specialists' horizon in turn leads to the recruiting of talent possessed of the proper myopia necessary to carry on the pure specialized activity without being consumed by a sense of futility or triviality." Thus vitality and relevance, "as measured by a broad humanistic standard have been lost." Academicism in philosophy, Vivas says, "consists of at least three cooperating factors: autonomy defined as freedom from social responsibility, substitution of exclusive concern with method for the subject matter proper to the discipline, and the consequent loss of wisdom and its replacement by logomachy. In short, it consists of a prodigious increase in technical competence to a point where the subject matter of philosophy—human experience—is abandoned."

TWO

As I have said above, the specialist will know, but the nonspecialist will not, who and what furnish the occasion for Vivas' attack. It should be general knowledge by now (but our education, especially that called higher, is so bad that it is not) that the developments in physical science that began with Copernicus, gained momentum with Galileo and Newton, and were broadened by Darwin to include the biological sciences, showed that there are problems in human existence that previously had been practically unknown except in sheer speculation. The possible existence of some of these problems had been implicit, and to some extent explicit, in the thought of the early Greek atomists. This thought was superbly summarized in the Latin poem, *The Nature of Things,* by Lucretius. It was reflected in different form in the amazingly prophetic speculations by Galileo and Newton that predicted the direction in which modern physical science would develop. Darwin's writings had further revolutionary implications. These developments raised such questions as: If the universe consists only of invisible particles in motion, how did life come into being; and, particularly, how can what appear to be purely mental activities in human beings be explained? How did human beings get their various notions of morals and religion, and what is the status of these notions in reality? If these questions are given serious consideration, and intellectual honesty requires that this be done, the something called "nature" that the physicist studies, as ordinarily conceived, cannot possibly provide reasonable answers to them.

There has been, as far back as human records go, discussion of aspects of these questions, in their different ways, among the ancient Hebrews and Greeks. But modern science, both physical and biological, made questions practically important that previously had been only of speculative interest. First and foremost today is the problem of science. Once the great hope of man on earth, it has been transformed, in most important ways, into a curse rather than a blessing.

Is it in the nature of things that this should happen? Is it in the nature of man that he should abuse his blessings and turn them into disasters? It is possible to haggle indefinitely over whether that which is can provide a basis both for determining what ought to be and for bringing what ought to be into existence to some extent. Much of our talk about "that which is" has been an ignorant assertion of knowledge we do not have. In any case, some of what ought to be seems certainly to have been brought into existence. It is largely indistinguishable from that which we have put to worse than barbaric uses in this century. There are no good reasons (except what is widely thought to be, and, I fear, *is,* the nature of man) for believing that man may never be able to take a great step forward without opening the way to two or more steps backward, and very probably taking the backward steps. There is much evidence that this is the nature of man. Many of us believe that this is his nature. Even so in our support of law, education, and social work, and especially in the support many of us give to the Christian religion, we act upon the notion that man can change his nature with help from beyond himself. In all this activity, we express our faith that there is something inside or outside the universe, or both inside and outside, that is utterly unlike the nature of the physical scientist and that this is the source of both the nature of the physical scientist and that which goes beyond and is utterly unlike his nature. In other words, whether we know it or not, we are supernaturalists, and our supernaturalism includes naturalism—but a naturalism quite different from the currently popular variety. Of all bodies of doctrine, the Christian is by far the most radical on this crucially important point.

The development of modern science has seemed to require the naturalistic assumption that there is no supernatural intervention in nature; in short, that in all respects nature is the cause of itself, whether cause be taken as mere sequence or conjunction on the one hand, or necessary connection on the other. The crucial point here is that while modern science has seemed to require this as an assumption—and as an assumption it seems to us to be necessary to the work of the scientist—it has not been, and cannot be, proved to be true. And to hypostatize and take as true an assumption that cannot be proven, is to erect an insuperable barrier to the cultivation of knowledge, a barrier that can, in its own way, be just as effective as any ancient superstition. In all strictness, such a barrier is the modern equivalent of ancient superstition. To forget that this is an assumption, one that cannot be proved true, is simply to be false to the great principle that in human experience has been found necessary to the genuine pursuit of truth. This principle does not block the way to *believing* that an assumption is true or false, but it keeps assumptions, postulates, beliefs, and the notion of truth from being hopelessly confused. There can be no reasonable objection to the *belief* that an assumption that has been held necessary to scientific work is true, and to arguments to prove it is true. But until proof is provided, the belief remains a belief. The same is true of all assumptions.

It was not for nothing that many of the Founding Fathers in the period of the American Revolution were deists. They did not deny the existence of a supernatural power. They tended to disbelieve in rule by divine intervention and believed in rule by law. This was not an arbitrary shift in belief. It was a change that seemed to be required by basic principles in modern science and entirely compatible with belief in God as creator and ruler of the universe by His own laws. To ask whether God could break His own laws was entirely reasonable. So also was the assumption of omnipotence, an assumption required if Manichaeanism or an equivalent was to be avoided. The assumption of omnipotence required the answer that God could break His own laws. This assumption leads, of course, to other well-known difficulties for which no solution has ever been found, except perhaps that man, the creature, can never wholly understand his Creator.

Whatever the ultimate somethings assumed by physical science—particles or mere conveniences for purposes of calculation—the problems involved in understanding the world of everyday experience in terms of them are as difficult as any in theology. The assumption that such words as "emergence" can explain the problems with which they deal, such as that of life, is so childish as to be hardly worthy of notice. Such assumptions must be noticed, however, because they are often made, and employed to support claims to knowledge. If they were correctly understood, however, words like "emergence" would be recognized as labels for profound gaps in human knowledge.

I have used the words "life" and "mental" above. I do not mean to beg any questions by using them. But rocks and soil seem to me easily distinguishable from each other, and life or mental or mind even more easily distinguishable from them and from each other as exemplified in plants and animals on the one side and human beings on the other. I do not pretend to know in any final and complete way what any of the things are that the words "nature," "physical," "matter," "particles," "life," "mind," designate, but if all are derived from anything like what is suggested by the expression "particles," then the questions of the origins and natures of life, mind, and religion and moral ideas, as well as ideas in general—not to mention other questions—become almost unimaginably difficult. In ordinary discourse, we do not consider and attempt to answer these questions. We assume that we know and understand the answers. The ease with which we use the words creates the familiarity with them that creates the illusion of intelligibility. This principle that familiarity creates the illusion of intelligibility holds for the scientist as well as for the rest of us.

The early developments in modern science inevitably led to the attempt by thoughtful persons to understand these developments and particularly their bearings on the question of how there can be human beings and how they can know anything. If the universe consists of invisible particles in motion and nothing else, it becomes difficult, if not impossible, to believe that one particle, or one collection of particles—no matter how the particles are arranged or what their motions—can know another particle or collection of particles.

The theory of particles as stated by Galileo, as speculated on by Newton, and as generally accepted with some modification soon after their time, is that the particles as they exist in nature have *only* such qualities as extension, figure, motion, and number, that they are utterly devoid of such qualities as color or values of any kind, and that they have in them nothing capable of receiving and becoming conscious of the impressions that persons receive by means of their five senses. Even so, persons are composed of these particles, have at least five senses, receive impressions, and, despite all disclaimers, receive impressions in what even David Hume called the "mind." The invisible particles have both this power of giving and receiving impressions, a ghostly operation that somehow becomes unghostly and that is often said to be the exclusive basis for what in turn is called "human knowledge." This ghostly operation that somehow becomes unghostly becomes then the basis for what is called "naturalism," a body of doctrine that denies its basis. Eliseo Vivas does not accept this doctrine. Neither do I. The "human knowledge" that is generated in this way is just as much suspect as is the process by which it is said to be generated.

There is nothing in actual existence either as an object of the senses or of the mind that corresponds with the expression "human knowledge." What is called "human knowledge" is not in any one human mind, or any group of human minds, or in all human minds. It is not in any human habits and customs, and is in no sense human if the expression is taken to mean something that is the common possession of human beings, or, as I have already suggested, of even two persons. If it is said to be in print, it has to be answered that printed matter consists generally of ink on paper. While print can be used by human beings, it is itself in no sense human. We may say with some degree of truth that different parts of what is called "human knowledge" are in the minds and habits, even the muscles, of persons in different groups at different levels of what we are pleased to call "civilization." The problem of talking intelligibly is greatly increased by the fact that several groups of specialists powerful in the Western world today, the followers of Bertrand Russell and John Dewey among them, hold that there is nothing in existence that answers to what traditionally has been called the "mind."

From the time of Socrates, Plato, and Aristotle until that of Galileo and Newton, the discussion of morals—a division of the subject values—despite wide differences, was fairly simple. Aristotle held that values inhere in things, actions, and relations. Values in his view had no existence except in this inherence. Plato agreed as to the inherence of values in things, actions, and relations, and so did Socrates. But Plato held that values had prior and eternal existence along with other universals in a realm of their own. How far Socrates agreed with him on this is debatable but unimportant for our purposes. Our purpose is to suggest the almost incredible difficulties that the particle theory created for the development of any theory of morals, or theory of value wide enough to include morals, that would, because of its clarity and logical power gain general acceptance among scientists and philosophers and the general public.

The views of Socrates, Plato, and Aristotle that values inhere in things, actions, and relations is the objective theory. Then there is the theory that values *do not* inhere in things, actions, and relations, and that values are determined by opinion as shown by the opinions of different peoples about their different customs and habits. Each people is of the opinion that its customs and habits are the best. This is the subjective theory of value. In modern societies, both theories are held by different groups among the sophisticated. The general public is hardly aware of the existence of the two theories and, perhaps because of bad education, incapable of discussing the problems they represent.

Most of us do not know it, but the Aristotelian theory that values inhere in things, actions, and relations is the theory on which all of us act in our daily lives. We would be regarded as demented and almost certainly put away where others would be responsible for us if we tried to act otherwise. This theory, as it is generally applied, without knowing that this is what is being done, is called "naive realism" or "common sense." It is in the main in accord with what the expression "common sense" suggests, and no other theory is. But if one gives serious attention to one's own society, or to history —and history includes more than the past of the Western world—and to anthropology, one discovers that the common sense of one person or group, or of one people, often is not in important respects the common sense of another, that is, the notions of the values that are generally held to inhere in actions, things, and relations may be so different, so opposed, as to produce friction and conflict. Add this ground for conflict to that over things limited in quantity that many want and we have more than enough grounds for the wars of the past and the present.

The notion that thinking something is so can create

the conviction that it is so is highly sophisticated. And since human error can and does at times have terribly serious consequences, that which is not true, error, can create that which is true in the sense that it exists. It is conceivable that the transition to the *ought* from that which *is* that David Hume found so puzzling is no more puzzling than that from what is not true, error, to that which is true; e.g., the devastation of World War II, and the fact, beyond any reasonable denial, that somebody, or a collection of somebodies, made a terrible error in starting this war. Both objectivists and subjectivists can make the error of thinking something is so that is not so, but the subjectivist makes a virtue out of his theory. "Wars are fought," Patrick H. Nowell-Smith tells us in his *Ethics,* "over moral issues, and the only difference between the subjectivist and the objectivist is that to the former this fact is not surprising."

It is hardly open to doubt that war has always been a terrible burden on those involved in it except for the few who may gain greatly by it. But just how the subjectivist's denial of the existence of moral values can have any effect in the way of stopping or curbing wars is not at all clear. If he denies that he denies moral values, and says what he denies is that values are the same for all persons, he says something that in important respects is true and that also in important respects is not distinguishable from objectivism. It is fairly obvious that if I have fallen overboard from a ship crossing a sea, and the ship has left me, a raft that would be in the way in my living room, could be a lifesaver for me. Innumerable instances of this kind can be imagined and many occur. Let us ask the subjectivist whether he considers the life of a human being a value. He has to say *no* if he holds to his doctrine. He is, in this respect, worse than the makers of war usually are. For they certainly take a comparative view of the value of lives, sacrifice some to win for others, fight to preserve some and to destroy others that stand in their way, and generally to secure values for themselves and those on their side. The subjectivist, if true to his theory, looks on with indifference. Fortunately, the actual practice of subjectivism, as distinguished from wordy commitment to the theory, is possible only for human beings lacking both minds and hearts. Subjectivists generally are better than their words. The recognition of the negative value of war is still the recognition of value; and the subjectivist makes, at least in theory, the mistake of denying this negative value. The problems of war and peace call for the most serious possible thought about human values. War is an expression of the failure to discover and establish in their comparative importance the values that are necessary if life on earth for human beings generally is to be fit to live.

I repeat, the notion that thinking something is so can create the conviction that it is so is a highly sophisticated notion; and when one states this notion in a form that affirms it apparently without question—such as the form in which Shakespeare has Hamlet put it: "There is nothing good or bad but thinking makes it so"; or in the form in which Pirandello puts it in the title of his play *It Is So (If You Think So)* and which he confirms with the words Signora Ponza utters at the end of the play: "I am she whom you believe [think] me to be" —he is not writing without having reflected, no matter how mixed up the reflecting may have been. These utterances are highly ambiguous and, in the above cases, I believe were deliberately made so in order to provoke better thought about the problems they pose. They would be impossible for the primitive steeped in his ethnocentrism, and for the simple reason that they pose precisely a problem that he has not yet recognized as a problem. Such utterances, *with understanding,* are equally impossible for the modern person who is in certain respects mentally still in the primitive stage, and there are many of these, even in the highest of our intellectual circles. The modern primitive often repeats words, sayings, that have become familiar, but repetition is not evidence of understanding.

Now I do not know in any final and complete way that there is any truth about morals, but I think there is and I have beliefs on this subject which are, as John Dewey has said, programs for action. Perhaps my thinking deludes me into beliefs that are not true. But so far as I can see, neither I nor any other person on earth can escape this possibility. In this respect, the objectivist and the subjectivist are in exactly the same condition. Neither theory was handed down from heaven with a guarantee of its truth.

I pass on now first to consideration of problems that are common to all efforts to discover truth about anything, and then to problems involved in the effort to discover truth about morals.

THREE

"Pure mathematics," Bertrand Russell tells us in his essay "Mathematics and the Metaphysician,"[1]

> consists entirely of assertions to the effect that, if such and such a proposition is true of *anything* [Russell's italics], then such and such another proposition is true of that thing. *It is essential not to discuss whether the first proposition is really true, and not to mention what the anything is, of which it is supposed to be true* [my italics]. In pure mathematics we take any hypothesis that seems amusing, and deduce its consequences. *If* our hypothesis is about *anything* [Russell's italics] and not about some one or more particulars, then our deductions constitute mathematics. Thus mathematics may be defined as the subject in which we never know what we are talking about, nor what we are saying is true.

Now if Russell never went beyond this statement and never claimed truth for his mathematics, this basis for mathematics would still be extremely objectionable for

---

[1] In the volume *Mysticism and Logic* (New York: Doubleday, n.d.), pp. 71–72. Russell published "Mathematics and the Metaphysician" in 1901. He changed many of his ideas in the course of his life but in his 1917 Preface to *Mysticism and Logic,* he says, "Some points in 'Mathematics and the Metaphysician' require modification in view of later work. These are indicated in footnotes." No changes are indicated for the passage quoted above.

precisely the reason stated in the quotation above that *its foundations are put* (at least in intention) *beyond serious examination.* Russell has been clear and emphatic in his satiric way in his condemnation of Christion theologians for attempting to get unquestioning, completely trustful acceptance of their basic premises. He proposes acceptance of his mathematics on exactly this same basis. And he holds that in order to pass on his system, one has to get inside it, become thoroughly familiar with it, and that anyone who does not do this is not qualified to have an opinion on it. Many theologians have taken exactly the same position with reference to their theology. Neither Russell nor some of the theologians take account of the role of familiarity in creating the conviction of intelligibility and truth—a role illustrated in the customs and habits and beliefs of every people on earth from the earliest times to the present. The respect in which Russell offends here is not the only one in which he condemns in others what he himself does. He goes beyond the disclaimer of truth in his mathematics in the statement quoted above and makes explicit claims of truth; and he waves banners, clashes cymbals, and blows trumpets when he does so. I quote from his "Study of Mathematics" also in *Mysticism and Logic:*

> Mathematics, rightly viewed, possesses not only truth, but supreme beauty. . . . (p. 57)

> The solution of the difficulties which formerly surrounded

the mathematical infinite is probably the greatest achievement of which our own age has to boast. (p. 60)

The discovery that all mathematics follows inevitably from a
small collection of *fundamental laws* [my italics] is one
which immeasurably enhances the intellectual beauty of the
whole; to those who have been oppressed by the fragmen-
tary and incomplete nature of most existing chains of deduction this discovery comes with all the overwhelming
force of a revelation; like a palace emerging from the
autumn mist as the traveller ascends an Italian hillside,
the stately storeys of the mathematical edifice appear in
their due order and proportion, with a new perfection in
every part. (p. 64)

Note that Russell's premises with which we began
and that are not to be examined as to their truth have
now become true and even a "small collection of fundamental laws." There are no notes rejecting these large
claims.

The principles on which Russell proceeds open up
the way to the infinite multiplication of pure theories.
He himself says this many times and this in his case is
a merit. Russell was devoted to the use of Occam's razor
to eliminate the multiplication beyond necessity of the
theories and parts of theories of others. But what is a
fault in others is in his case a merit. He failed to apply
Occam's razor to his own theories, and not only in
the case of mathematics.

Now one does not have to know much about logic
to know that conclusions that are true, or that at least
appear to be true, may be derived from premises that

are false. Russell's claims to truth in his logic may therefore be valid—but there is no way of proving that they are. The same is true of the theologian's premises and conclusions. But again, Russell condemns that in others which he himself does. And many theologians rest their cases on belief, faith rather than on premises for which they claim truth indirectly. If we state in a formal way the principle involved in drawing true or apparently true conclusions from false premises, Russell's procedure is correctly stated in the formula: if p, then q; q therefore p. Russell parodies this mode of procedure despite the fact that he himself follows it, and incidentally shows something that those who use his formulas seem to me to fail to understand: that easily understood words, in their conventional use, show absurdities that formulas do not. Here is Russell's unrecognized parody of that which he himself does: If pigs have wings, then some winged animals are good to eat; now some winged animals are good to eat; therefore pigs have wings. In his article in P. A. Schilpp's volume, *The Philosophy of John Dewey* (p. 149), Russell uses this formula and this parody to condemn the logic in Dewey's *Logic: The Theory of Inquiry.*

When Russell claims truth in his mathematics without distinguishing between his consequents and their antecedents and making it clear he is *not* claiming truth for his antecedents, he does exactly that for which he condemns Dewey's logic. His consequents might be true despite the purely postulational nature of his antecedents, but if they are, they are true only by accident.

Russell's conduct in acknowledging some of the possible defects within his mathematical logic has been admirable. But his forbidding anyone to look seriously at the foundation of his structure is not. The child must not look at the king parading in what have been heralded as the king's wonderful new clothes and in his simplicity utter the plain truth: Why, the king has no clothes on, he is naked. All of us are children when we deal with the specialists of our time; and all specialists are children when they deal with specialists in other fields. It is a matter of some importance whether we can trust each other.

I have, in the foregoing, pointed out problems in Russell's writings that seem to me to invalidate much of his thought. But I have not meant to suggest that his writings are not worth study, or that there is nothing in them that will not stand the test of time. I simply do not know about this. The writer that I have read and re-read and studied most closely over a period of around fifty years—and to whom I would have given far more attention if I had had the time—is David Hume. When I started reading Hume, he provoked me so that I went to him again and again. I disagreed with him from the start almost completely, but, for a long time, I could not say why in a way that continued to satisfy me. I made marginal notes from time to time as I read and re-read, and I began understanding what he was saying and why I disagreed with him. I cannot imagine any process more genuinely educational than this one. When I began reading Russell some decades ago, I had

had preparation of this kind, but Russell too, while easy on the surface as was Hume, also required close attention. I am grateful to him, as I am to Hume, despite the fact that I disagree profoundly with him. He has the great merit, as has Hume, of asking and trying to answer questions of basic importance, though he does at times, as Hume did not, slip into utter triviality. I will give an instance of the triviality.

In his account of his mental development in *The Philosophy of Bertrand Russell* in the P. A. Schilpp series, Russell tells us:

> For three years I thought about religion, with a determination not to let my thoughts be influenced by my desires. I discarded first free will, then immortality; I believed in God until I was just eighteen, when I found in Mill's *Autobiography* the sentence; 'My father taught me that the question "Who made me"? cannot be answered, since it immediately suggests the further question of "Who made God"?' In that moment I decided that the first cause argument is fallacious.

Russell seems never to have abandoned the belief that the question any bright child might ask, "Who made God?" when told God made him, disposed of all grounds for serious religious belief. It seems hardly credible that a great logician could fail to see that one has to believe, whether consciously or not, either that nature is a cause of itself, or that something beyond nature is a cause of itself. One may, of course, never imagine this problem in its final simplicity and ask about it the most serious question that can be asked.

I believe a good case could be made for the view that no discussion in which human beings have ever engaged has had so much effect on the quality of life possible, and in large measure actually achieved by some human beings on earth, as the discussion and achievement of certain ideas on this subject has. This discussion has had to do with ultimate truth and no other is so important. For the beliefs that human beings form on this question seem inevitably to be reflected in the quality they manage to establish in their daily lives. John Dewey was, I believe, not entirely right in his view that beliefs are only programs of action. There appear to be important exceptions, but the very concern with truth, even if the truth one is concerned with seems to be completely negative as in the case of the utter skeptic, often appears to have a purifying, health creating, effect on life; and we are still too ignorant to be certain that appearances do not have any degree of reality.

Russell was, I believe, far too much inclined to the view that the cultivation of the ability to think correctly began in modern times and culminated in his mathematical logic. There is, so far as I can see, little room to doubt that this was a great achievement, but Russell's estimate of it could be far too great. And he not only gives no credit to aid he received from ancient times, he disparages the great source without which he could not have done anything. Consider the following statement from him:[2]

---

[2] Bertrand Russell, *Our Knowledge of the External World* (New York: Mentor, 1960), p. 33.

> Logic, in the Middle Ages, and down to the present day in teaching, meant no more than a scholastic collection of technical terms and rules of syllogistic inference. Aristotle had spoken, and it was the part of humbler men merely to repeat the lesson after him. The trivial nonsense embodied in this tradition is still set in examinations, and defended by eminent authorities as an excellent 'propaedeutic,' i.e., a training in those habits of solemn humbug which are so great a help in later life.

If any one principle that Russell has clarified and stated for the first time ever achieves anywhere near the status in human thought and life that the law of contradiction in logic first stated by Aristotle in Book Gamma of his *Metaphysics* has achieved, Russell will have earned a secure place among the immortals. His mathematical logic would have been impossible without this tool, even though he "proves" it with his admittedly uncertain premises. The training during the Middle Ages in the use of this tool is no less important than the tool itself. This training was probably cultivated more intensively in the Middle Ages than in any other period in human history. It was the great instrument in both the defense of and the attacks on the ancient gods. It was the great instrument in the arguments over Christian doctrine, in the shaping of both heresies and orthodoxies. It made perfectly clear to the mind willing to consider and not trapped in some superstition, that no statement of either fact or theory could be both true and not true either as a whole or in any part at the same time and in the same respect. It was the indispensable tool of the great skeptics as well as the great believers. Its use that is probably the most important of both early and later modern times was made by Copernicus when he made his arguments that, in view of later developments, ought to establish beyond doubt for the informed modern mind the absolute indispensability of the law of contradiction in distinguishing appearance from reality. The great achievement of Copernicus is not understood unless it is understood that he began the proof once and for all time that knowledge gained by means of the human senses may be untrustworthy, and that the rational faculty of the human being using the law of contradiction as Aristotle stated it can show beyond any reasonable doubt that the senses alone at times can be grossly deceptive.

We still speak in the English language, and other peoples doubtless speak in their own languages of the rising and setting of the sun. And on any clear day, when our vision is not obstructed, if we look in the right direction at the right times, we see the sun rise or the sun set. Norwood Hanson in his *Patterns of Discovery*[3] says that for Galileo the horizon drops, but Galileo says otherwise and I quote what he says in my book, *The Human Potential*.[4] But if we dwell on these questions, we miss the real point which is that the sun could not

---

[3] Norwood Hanson, *Patterns of Discovery* (Cambridge: Cambridge University Press, 1958), p. 182.

[4] William T. Couch, *The Human Potential* (Durham, North Carolina: Duke University Press, 1974), p. 270.

both rise and not rise at the same time and in the same way.

Copernicus told us that in this case our visual sense deceives us, that the appearance of rising or setting by the sun is created by the rotation of the earth on its axis. His chief reason was a purely rational one: that the heavens are vast, the distance the sun would have to travel made it extremely improbable that the sun moved around the earth and with it all the heavens as appearance said and still says it and they did—that this appearance could easily be created by the rotation of the earth on its axis. Copernicus did not prove this. Later evidence was, until the advent of relativity theory, accepted as proof. I do not believe the principle of relativity that one can choose one's point of rest at will has disturbed the argument of Copernicus on this particular motion, for it is hardly possible, even if current notions as to the highest possible speed should change, that the sun could move around the earth, carrying the whole content of the heavens with it as it appears to the visual sense to do. Whatever the final truth may be, of one thing we can be certain: the motions cannot be what they are and at the same time and in the same respect be something else. This undoubtedly was what emboldened Copernicus to make his argument against the almost-all-powerful orthodoxy of his time.

Now, as I have shown, there is no room for reasonable doubt that there are times when the evidence of the senses is untrustworthy. But here is Bertrand Russell, the great logician of our time, asserting the finality of the senses in all cases[5]:

> What does not go beyond our own personal sensible acquaintance must be for us most certain; the evidence of the senses is proverbially the least open to question.

Again[6]:

> I think it may be laid down quite generally that, in so far as physics or common sense is verifiable, it must be capable of interpretation in terms of actual sense data alone.

Again[7]:

> The first thing that appears when we begin to analyze our common knowledge is that some of it is derivative, while some of it is primitive: that is to say there is some that we only believe because of something else from which it has been inferred in some sense, thought not necessarily in a strict logical sense, while other parts are believed on their own account, without the support of any outside evidence. It is obvious that the senses give knowledge of the latter kind; the immediate facts perceived by sight or touch or hearing do not need to be proved by argument, but are compeletely self-evident.

No one who has understood the law of contradiction has ever claimed that it, by itself, provides or guarantees truth. When it is understood, it is seen that Russell's errors in these statements are so obvious it is difficult to understand how he could make them. It is hardly credi-

---

[5] Bertrand Russell, *Our Knowledge of the External World*, p. 57.
[6] *Ibid.*, p. 68.
[7] *Ibid.*, p. 58.

ble that he never learned the lesson taught by Copernicus, but if he did, so far as these statements are concerned, he forgot or ignored it.

When the law of contradiction is understood, it is seen that it performs a sort of judicial office of a sharply limited but absolutely necessary nature if there is to be any quest for more rather than less truth. Its great function is to show, in the case of claims to truth, how the universe of possibilities can be so divided as to make it clear beyond any reasonable doubt that one claim is necessarily true and the other false, but it never says which is which. It only makes clear to those with minds to see, that more evidence may be needed to decide this question. If, as in the Copernican case, less weight is given to reason than to the visual sense, as was done before Copernicus and as in the quotations from Russell above, the answer given necessarily is that the sun goes around the earth and carries with it all the other heavenly bodies. What reason does is to try to imagine the whole situation and to conduct what amounts to an imaginative experiment in order to see whether any facts might be involved that are not available to the visual or any other senses. It is sheer nonsense to assume, as is often done, that in advocating the necessity of the use of reason, there is any intention to ignore any relevant facts. On the contrary, the proper use of reason calls for the discovery of such facts—facts that the human senses unaided cannot discover.

The law of contradiction does not authorize the notion that sufficient evidence can ever be discovered to decide any of the great questions finally and completely, nor does it say this cannot be done. The role of the law is superbly illustrated in the arguments between Copernicus and his adversaries over the motions of the heavenly bodies. It is inconceivable that Copernicus could have made his arguments as well as he did without the training in the use of the law of contradiction, derived from Aristotle and kept alive and active in the Middle Ages. Certainly there were absurdities in Medieval times—but absurdities did not end with the Middle Ages. We, too, most certainly have ours, and far more dangerous ones than in any previous period in human history.

Despite these grave lapses in Russell's thought that I have shown above, he undoubtedly had one of the best minds of our time. I cannot help wondering *why* this failure on Russell's part to use knowledge of which he certainly must have been aware. The answer to this question I believe is that he, too, was steeped, and lost, in the specialization that has become the rage of our time; that he, like the rest of us, needed, but did not have at hand, the aids that, if used, could have kept him from blunders such as those we have recorded. Russell was at least vaguely aware of the blight that extreme specialization has brought, but never concerned himself seriously with the effort to find and propose a corrective. The only possible aid that I have been able to imagine is a properly made encyclopedia. None of our encyclopedias, including the new (1974) Britannica, tells us in its article on Copernicus of the problem of deceptive appearance created by the visual sense in the case of relations of the sun and earth, and how Copernicus showed the role of reason, and particularly of the law of contradiction in logic in distinguishing reality from appearance. I have stated elsewhere (*The University Bookman,* Winter 1975) in a way on which I cannot improve what seems to me the indispensable part the law of contradiction plays in the cultivation of knowledge and I will repeat this statement here.

> Is there any discipline that is, more than any other, necessary to the cultivation of knowledge and particularly the distinguishing of it from error? *Yes,* says D'Alembert in his famous "Preliminary Discourse"[8] to the great French encyclopedia that he and Diderot inaugurated: Logic is "rightly considered the key to all our knowledge." I would agree if the meaning "determining factor in" were given to the words "key to"; for observation unchecked by reason, says the sun moves, whereas checked by reason, it suggests that the earth moves. If it is assumed that the suggestion made by reason is true, then if the same weight is given to observation and reason, as D'Alembert appears to do ("Preliminary Discourse," pp. 6, 7 vs. p. 30), both are true. But both cannot be true at the same time and in the same way. The understanding of this is what forced further obser-

---

[8] Tr. R. N. Schwab and W. E. Rex (Indianapolis: Bobbs-Merrill Library of Liberal Arts, 1963), p. 30. I still believe that the word "determining" in the phrase "determining factor in" in the quotation above is right, but an apparent contradiction could have been avoided by using the word "judicial."

vation and reasoning. This is the role that the law of
contradiction plays in the human thought that has been
necessary to the cultivation of knowledge.

Why do I harp on this subject? For a reason that is
compelling. When we discuss ethical theory, the question will arise whether values are objective or subjective. The argument is often made that if values are not
and cannot be objects of ordinary sense experience,
they are not and cannot be objective, but must be subjective or perhaps even non-natural, whatever that
would be. Now it seems to me clear beyond any reasonable doubt that the reasoning process involved in
the use of the law of contradiction and the law itself,
both are not and cannot be objects of sense experience.
They are never and cannot ever be visible as is the yel-
low patch that has played such a large part in the discussion of ethics during this century—under influences
that, it happens, were powerful on Bertrand Russell.
Does their inaccessibility to sense experience prove their
nonexistence? If so, then we have to ask of the wise
men of our time how it happens that nonexistence can
be a predicate when existence cannot be one? The very
ideas involved here are absurd. If they were true, there
would be no way of distinguishing between objective
and subjective and both expressions would be sheer
nonsense.

The reader will remember that I have quoted Vivas
to the effect that morality and ethics involve a peculiar
kind of fact. I believe I have shown in the discussion

above the possibility that there is such a class of facts. There is, so far as I can see, no reason whatever to consider this class of facts non-natural as G. E. Moore does in his *Principia Ethica*—no reason, I should say, other than the spurious doctrine or prejudice which holds that all knowledge is derived from the sensation of sense experience, and none from the rational element in sense experience. Moore as a "realist" of the type of Russell had to hold this doctrine, and this drove him to assume nonsensuous intuition of ethical values. The view that is held here is that disciplined intuition, intellectual intuition is necessary to knowledge. This is one of the many important views that Vivas holds in his book, *The Moral Life and the Ethical Life,* and this is one of the reasons for my conviction that the book was important and deserved publication and strong support. There is nothing new in the notion of intellectual intuition and that intuition to be trustworthy has to be disciplined. It is perhaps a little too rigidly illustrated in the story of Plato and Antisthenes in which the latter says, "I see a horse but not horseness," and Plato comments that this was because though he had eyes, Antisthenes had no intelligence. I would say it takes a mind or intelligence even to contemplate the problem of what it is with which one sees and what one may see, even though the answer that one gives is wrong. The mind can create problems for itself, and the discussion of morals and ethical theory in our time is by far not the only evidence that can be produced for this fact. If the bog that I believe Bertrand Russell has created for human thought—even some of the best of the thought of our time—is real, it will be a long time before the human mind escapes from it without at the same time creating other and possibly even worse bogs.

I believe that the strictures in which Vivas engages in his Preface and Introduction are directed more toward such bog-making as that which I have described than toward the theories of Ralph Barton Perry, Charner Perry, and John Dewey that he describes in his book. Russell was, in my view, aided greatly by G. E. Moore, one of the great leaders in our time in the making of intellectual bogs, and Russell and Moore's many followers will in all probability continue for a long time floundering in the bogs they made.

FOUR

The subject of "morals" is one of the great subjects of all times. When one reads contemporary discussions of morals, one may wonder, as H. A. Prichard[9] of Oxford did, whether moral philosophy has been a mistake, a waste of time; and one may, as Prichard did, begin developing a sense of extreme dissatisfaction with the whole subject. The subject is vast, enters into all human life, but at first, and especially to those who have never given it serious attention, it may seem small,

---

[9] Harold Arthur Prichard, "Does Moral Philosophy Rest on a Mistake?" in *Moral Obligation* (Oxford: Clarendon Press, 1949).

easy, so easy as to raise the question why it needs study. The state of the savage generally, as Herodotus[10] knew and as anthropologists have shown over and over in our time, is that of unquestioning acceptance as right of the customs under which he lives, and almost any discussion of morals that goes beyond the superficials is to him abstruse and obscure. This condition has been expanded in civilized societies into one in which most people, while accepting the customs and habits of their society, also on being given the chance to express themselves may seize the chance and tell how all the problems of the time can be solved. This knowing how to fix things up has become a part of the established customs and habits of civilized societies and a major difference between them and the primitive, but hardly an advance over the latter. Many of us, even many in positions of influence in the intellectual world, are little if any beyond the savage state despite all our educational machinery.

I have quoted previously from P. H. Nowell-Smith's *Ethics*. Let us now look at the passage from which the previous quotation was taken:[11]

> Wars are not fought over logical or empirical issues, just because men do in the end agree about what they see to be the case or "see" to be logically valid. But wars are fought over moral issues, and the only difference between the

---

10 Herodotus, *History,* Bk. III, par. 38.
11 Patrick H. Nowell-Smith, *Ethics* (London: Penguin Books, 1969), p. 46.

subjectivist and the objectivist is that to the former this is not surprising.

But Nowell-Smith's whole book is devoted to the thesis that thinking about morals is so mixed up with "the logic of words, sentences, and arguments" that we have to straighten out this logic before we can think correctly about morals. Nowell-Smith informs us, for instance, that logically there are three classes of adjectives: "aptness," "descriptive," and "gerundive" adjectives; that the word "sublime" used to describe a scene belongs to the class of "aptness words."[12] He also tells us that if a person looking at the same view that someone has called "sublime" calls it "extensive," he would be stating a "question of empirical fact." The sublimity of the view, says Nowell-Smith, is not a part of its contents and no description of the view would logically entail the truth or falsity of "the view was sublime."

Now suppose you are eating an apple and you say to someone standing by that the apple is good and he then asks you to show him the goodness, I think you would have to admit that you couldn't; but then you might also wonder whether the question made any sense. For even though the taste of goodness certainly was in you, the cause of this taste was also certainly in something beyond you and your identification of the apple as the cause, if not accepted, would raise large, general questions about empiricism that empiricists

---

[12] *Ibid.*, p. 70ff.

generally could not answer. Further, as to logical entailment, the very words that Nowell-Smith uses to designate his classifications of adjectives show the absurdities in his argument. For among the ordinary meanings of the word "apt" are the meanings "fitting," "suitable," "correctly descriptive." So Nowell-Smith does not have three classifications of adjectives.

Nowell-Smith touches on a subject of very great importance when he says:[13]

> There are a few fundamental rules of conduct that have never changed and probably never will; indeed it is difficult to imagine what life in society would be like if we abandoned them. The more we study moral codes the more we find that they do not differ on major points of principle and that the divergencies that exist are due partly to different opinions about empirical facts, for example about the effects of certain types of conduct, and partly to differences in social and economic organization that make it appropriate to apply the fundamental rules now in one way, now in another. Thus all codes agree that we have a duty to requite good with good; but obedience to this rule will involve behaving in ways that will differ according to the view that a society takes of what it is to do good to someone.

In the course of this statement, the great importance of the suggestion that there are principles of universal validity, whether they are known or not—and even perhaps that human thought and conduct to some extent testify to this universal validity—this suggestion is

---

[13] *Ibid.,* p. 18.

here and there whittled down either to the trivial or the opposite of validity and universality. Let us look briefly at the whittling down and virtual denial. The whittling down is done, perhaps inadvertently, by questions that are suggested, such as, Do all codes from the earliest times "agree that *we have to* [my italics] requite good with good"? What sense is intended for the words "we have to"? Necessity? If so, of what kind, moral or physical? What known society has such a code and enforces it? Was Shakespeare maundering when he wrote as he did in many plays of the returning of evil for good as in *King Lear, Macbeth,* and perhaps most bitterly in *Timon?* Milton showed real understanding of this problem when he had his Satan deliberately resolve: "evil be thou my good." Most of us undoubtedly and unquestionably conduct ourselves in accord with the customs and habits of our society, and if there is evil in these customs and habits, most of us also engage in it innocently, though some may do so deliberately as Satan did. When we realize this, we may consider our customs and habits seriously—and we may even go on to the consideration of the customs and habits of other societies, for instance, Mr. Fortune's Dobuans. Even Ruth Benedict, with all her tolerance and commitment, at least in words, to the doctrine of cultural relativism that holds all cultures to be of equal validity, has no good words for the Dobuans. Among them lawlessness and treachery are endemic and "every man's hand is against every other man."

We have not finished with the questions that the quotation from Nowell-Smith above suggests to us. If the meaning of "good" can vary so far as to go from one notion of good to its opposite, can it be that any meaning is left in the word? And what about requiting evil with evil? Here, in order to make sense, as with good, the notion of evil in certain codes is fairly definite, e.g., an eye for an eye and a tooth for a tooth. What about requiting evil with good? Jesus says, "Turn the other cheek." Socrates says, "It is better to suffer than to do evil." Shakespeare's Isabella and Mariana forgive Angelo. And what about torturing with the at least declared purpose of saving souls? Or the Aztec practice of making war to get captives to sacrifice to the Aztec god Huitzilopochtli for the benefit of the Aztecs? The quotation from Nowell-Smith simply falls to pieces when it is examined.

On the page preceding the statement just examined, Nowell-Smith says "the view that no progress has been made in solving the fundamental problems of ethics is an illusion based on the fact that some of these problems were solved very early in the history of mankind."[14] What are these problems, or some of them, who did the solving, and what are the solutions? Nowell-Smith does not tell us. He says "From Plato, Aristotle, and Epicurus, from Hobbes, Spinoza, and Butler you can learn how, *in their opinion* [my italics],

---

[14] *Ibid.,* p. 17.

you ought to live." So the solutions that are offered are mere opinions. Tom, Dick and Harry have opinions, doubtless different ones, some conflicting as do some of those of the persons in Nowell-Smith's list. We do not look to Tom, Dick, and Harry for guidance on moral questions. Our reason is that we want something better than mere opinion. And if we look, say, to Hobbes and to Plato to whom Nowell-Smith in the quotation above suggests that we look, we find opinions about as far apart and as completely opposed as is possible. Why Nowell-Smith omits Socrates and Jesus is beyond me. Further:[15]

> Suppose someone were to ask me to give him a moral code to live by. I should reply—as Aristotle in effect did—"I can't give you a code; go and watch the best and wisest men you can find and imitate them."

But how could anyone, without first knowing signs by which wisdom and goodness can be recognized, identify the "best and wisest"? This is like assuming that a persons knows what by his own admission and clear statement he has said he does not know. There probably is some knowledge of this kind, as Socrates showed with the slave boy in the *Meno*. But the eliciting of this knowledge—the bringing of it to the consciousness—requires genius, and this genius is exceedingly rare. Aristotle gives in his *Ethics* important clues that would

---

[15] *Ibid.,* p. 17.

help in the recognition of the best and the wisest, but for those of us who are unskilled in reading and thinking about such subjects as ethics—and this means most of us, including most in the intellectual world—even Aristotle, with his simplicity and directness, is not easy to read. Nowell-Smith gives no clues—though the unskilled reader may easily find passages that he thinks provides clues, but that, when read as Nowell-Smith intends them (if I understand him), most certainly do not.

Many candidates could be found who *in their opinion* and even in the opinion of others are the best and wisest. Some of the worst have been of this opinion. Is ethics always to be merely a matter of one opinion against another? Socrates, Plato, Aristotle—all three and many others have held that there is nothing else to begin with in the study of ethics but opinion. But they also held that the expression and discussion of opinion could be so conducted as to rise above opinion to truth about the kind of conduct most conducive to human welfare. Those who are able to satisfy others that they somehow have done this, whether in discussion with others or in silent meditation (discussion with themselves or an ideal self), have been accepted as authorities. But when authorities disagree, as they do today, where shall the questing person go? How can he tell a genuine from a bogus authority? This is not an easy question to answer—if it can be answered at all in a way that is wholly trustworthy. We have good reasons by this time in human history to be somewhat dubious of all human authority.

When Nowell-Smith says,[16] "It is logically absurd to ask a question without knowing how the answers to it are to be judged to be good or bad answers," I have to say it is logically absurd to assume, if we are ordinary persons and not great teachers such as Socrates—or far lesser teachers who merely know the answers that the textbooks give—that when we ask questions we are qualified to judge whether the answers are good or bad. If we were so qualified, we would normally not ask others. We would work out the answers for ourselves.

If the discussion of opinion on ethical problems cannot be conducted fruitfully—and Nowell-Smith seems implicitly to say that it cannot—what alternatives are possible? The example of the Dobuans seems to me to say about as clearly as is possible that there are better and worse among codes and practices; but here we are back again with opinion and the problem of distinguishing between opinion that is reliable and opinion that is not reliable. The question cannot be escaped: can opinions be developed that are trustworthy, and, if so, how? So far in human history, we have been unable to answer this question in a way that has gained acceptance that transcends national and racial boundaries, and especially the allegiance of the intellectual leadership of people generally.

---

[16] *Ibid.*, p. 175.

Aristotle's notion of fixed species is, of course, not tenable if evolutionary doctrine is true. I see no good reasons for believing it is not true, though it raises perhaps as many questions as it answers. Evolutionary doctrine leaves open the possibility that the majority of us, perhaps all, are in certain respects still at or below the level of the most primitive savages. If there is anything certain about us, it is that we have not made progress in a most important respect: we have not yet learned how to use reason to settle questions between groups and nations, questions that lead to violence and to war. The two world wars of this century speak with horrible eloquence this appalling truth about us. The fundamental problems in ethics are protean in nature: grasp them at this point, perhaps even appear to solve them at this point, then they appear at another point and perhaps elude all grasp at the most important points. If Nowell-Smith has discovered this fundamental fact about ethics, he gives no evidence of his discovery in his *Ethics*. He comes close to this when he agrees with Aristotle that a "scientific morality" is impossible. If he had gone carefully into this question, he could not easily have escaped discovering the fundamental problems in ethics, involving as they do the volatility in the nature of man, the volatility that makes ethics protean in nature. Vivas makes this clearly in highly luminous passages in his book. The subjection of Proteus to control was in the myth an almost impossible task; but he was subjected. The lesson for human beings today, and particularly for Americans, I believe is: either we discover and subject ourselves to the real interests of the general public, or we will have to reconcile ourselves to being, in the course of time, subjected by others.

The real interests of the general public cannot be discovered without far more serious attention to ethics than Nowell-Smith gives in his book. Eliseo Vivas, I think, points to the way that has to be followed in his book *The Moral Life and the Ethical Life.*

The notion that linguistic analysis can illuminate the problems of ethics is an illusion and a terribly dangerous one. This is not to say that language is unimportant and that care with it is unnecessary. On the contrary, we insist on care, and especially of concern with the question whether language is being used in ways that help or hinder the discovery, as well as is possible, the nature of the subject being discussed. We have given examples that seem to us to show that Nowell-Smith's focus on language has been of no help to him in the cases that we have examined, that it has, on the contrary, helped to hide from him the real nature of his subject.

Nowell-Smith is, of course, only one of many in his addiction to linguistic analysis. I have dealt with him only because his *Ethics* has achieved the status of a Pelican-Penguin volume and this means large printings and sale to the general public in large quantities. How much real reading and study of the subject there has been is another question that cannot be answered by knowledge of large printings and large, general sales. I will now discuss briefly one other addict to linguistic analysis.

"The function of the philosopher," says A. J. Ayer in his enormously influential *Language, Truth, and Logic,*[17] "is not to devise speculative theories which require to be validated in experience, but to elicit the consequences of our linguistic usages."

What is there to keep this from being a license to more and more binges in the metaphysics of which Ayer so thoroughly disapproves in this same book?

"If these things are only to be known through names," said Socrates in his discussion with Cratylus,[18] "how can we suppose that the givers of names had knowledge, or were legislators before there were names at all, and therefore before they could have known them?" "I believe, Socrates," said Cratylus, "the true account of the matter to be, that a power more than human gave things their first names, and that the names which were given are necessarily their true names."

It is possible, without complete absurdity, to agree on this with Cratylus. But it is not possible to make sense and agree and at the same time deny the existence of the supernatural power that Cratylus assumes. It is

---

[17] A. J. Ayer, *Language, Truth, and Logic* (New York: Dover Editions, n.d.) with a new introduction by Ayer, dated 1946.

[18] *The Dialogues of Plato,* Tr. Benjamin Jowett (New York: Random House, 1937), pp. 227–28.

certainly possible also to make sense and hold, as Socrates did, that the origin of language was not supernatural, without denying supernatural powers, and
that, as Socrates said later in the dialogue, "the knowledge of things is not to be derived from names."

One is reminded of the hilarity that swept the Western World when a certain scientist of some prominence
asked the question, when the name Uranus was given to
the newly discovered plant now known by this name:
"What guarantee have we that the planet regarded
by astronomers as Uranus is really Uranus?"[19]

I have entitled this discussion "The Sacred and
Golden Cord" because I do not believe human beings
are necessarily puppets of fate but have in their reasoning faculties the power to make life better or worse. I
believe that there are undeveloped potentials in the
mind that hold possibilities for man, possibilities long
more or less vaguely imagined, but still almost as far
from development as in the time when Plato wrote in
the *Laws* (I, 645), the words that gave me the title of
this discussion. I have tried in the above to show some
of the aberrations in which a few of the best minds of
our time have engaged. I confess that this spectacle
has filled me at times with a deep pessimism and the
feeling that there is no hope for man on earth, that the
very notion that man can go far toward the excellence

[19] C. K. Ogden and I. A. Richards, *The Meaning of Meaning* (New
York: Harcourt, Brace, 1956), p 109, n.1.

that is his best hope has been made by the horrors of our time into a torturing dream that makes one at times want only to escape into oblivion.

It is not necessary, not in the nature of things, that the United States of America illustrate again the rise and fall of great hopes, the strict discipline and labor and rise of the fathers, the extreme moral relaxation and dissolution and fall of the sons. It is not necessary that the wisdom of the primitive with its stability-creating discipline be forever at war with the near-creative powers of the human mind. If we learn to recognize aberrations, abuses, of our reasoning faculties, we may in time learn how to escape from them. We should know by now that the faculty which enables man to be a very special kind of animal can be abused, can be the great instrument in the fostering of destructive superstitions and prejudices and conduct in daily life, as well as a cleansing, freeing, and almost creative power. The superstitions and prejudices that govern the man of "enlightenment" and science are far more destructive than those of any primitive people have ever been. But the brotherhood of man, so horribly caricatured in our time, and the fatherhood of God, need not be no more than a torturing dream.

There are tasks of pressing urgency. The ancient Hercules, if reborn today, and if as well-qualified to clean up the discussion of ethics as his prototype was to clean the Augean stables, if he attempted to clean up the discussion of ethics would have an almost impossible task on his hands. The propensity of some of us toward the cultivation under other names of one or another variety of wild metaphysics is unbelievably powerful, and checking this propensity, not to speak of stopping it, may be beyond even extra-human powers. This is the great need in human thought today. David Hume was clear on the real problem when, as if rebuking those who imagine it is possible to get rid of all metaphysics, he said: "We . . . must cultivate true metaphysics with some care, in order to destroy the false and adulterate."[20] That Hume himself gave great impetus to the false does not minimize the importance of this caution from him. Brand Blanshard has made heroic efforts toward the recovery of the true use of metaphysics during a lifetime of work in the field. In scope, clarity, and cogency, Blanshard is matched by very few in our time. Of all the writers on ethics in this generation, only Vivas is worthy to rank with him. I regret that I have used much more space than that allotted to me and cannot give more attention to Vivas' book, *The Moral Life and the Ethical Life*. But anything I said would, with only a very few minor disagreements, underline the excellence of the work. It is the superb expression of a great spirit on a great subject. To read and study this expression would be more rewarding than spending any time on anything I could say about it.

---

[20] David Hume, *An Enquiry Concerning Human Understanding* (Oxford: Clarendon Press, 1902), Sect. I, par. 7.

Essay Five

The Aesthetic Theory
of Eliseo Vivas

Peter J. Stanlis

Peter J. Stanlis was educated at Middlebury College, the Bread Loaf School of English, and the University of Michigan, where he took his Ph.D. in 1951. He has taught English at several colleges and universities, since 1968 at Rockford College in Illinois. He was chairman of the English department at Rockford from 1968 to 1974, and in 1973 was appointed Distinguished Professor of English and Humanities, the first such title granted in the college's 130-year history. In 1959 he founded The Burke Newsletter, *later called* Studies in Burke and His Time. *He edited this journal for twelve years. His books include* Edmund Burke and the Natural Law, The Relevance of Edmund Burke, Edmund Burke, the Enlightenment and the Modern World, *and* Robert Frost: The Individual and Society.

The aesthetic theory of Eliseo Vivas, as revealed in his seventeen essays in criticism and aesthetics in *Creation and Discovery* (1955), is at once very simple and very complex. It is profoundly simple in part because in its most developed but unsystematic form it is the distilled essence of that part of his total philosophy which deals with the nature and function of art, that is, of "poetry" in its generic meaning in Western civilization. Yet his aesthetic theory is not abstracted and isolated, but remains organically connected with the ethical, intellectual and social elements in his total philosophy. Vivas' aesthetic theory is also simple because it is presented with clarity and force, in his full maturity, untrammeled by any of the out-of-focus gropings of youth. These essays show his intellectual brilliance, candidness, courage, and native simplicity.

Like a skilled archer who hits the bulls-eye again, and again, and again, Vivas does not waste time and energy shooting in the dark at random targets. Cross country archery is not his aesthetic game. His aesthetic theory appears simple because he goes straight to his mark. In the process of advancing his aesthetic principles, he often points out and refutes the errors of less skilled archers, who do not merely miss the bulls-eye, but frequently have no clear notion of where the target is located. How does Vivas avoid the common errors of aestheticians, whose theories are so frequently plagued with obscurities and dubious refined complexities? In this essay it will become increasingly clear that Vivas' aesthetic theory is valid and clear because it rests upon the assumption that human nature and values are not limited to a merely physical or material reality, but have a metaphysical or spiritual basis in reality. Vivas never loses sight of this great and simple truth. When he has explicated and clarified a principle of art, and placed it in its proper place in the galaxy of our aesthetic universe, a reader comes to see that what once was obscured by cloudly mechanistic speculation stands revealed, clear and sharp as in a cloudless sky, like self-evident intuitional truth.

But beyond this great clarification in theory is the complexity inherent in his subject. Vivas not only identifies and isolates the basic elements and principles of aesthetic theory. He also defines and analyzes their nature, function and interrelationships; and this complex, organically-related context of aesthetic theory is connected with practical criticism, and with his whole philosophy of life. This essay will limit itself to a description and analysis of two cardinal subjects in Vivas' aesthetic theory: his conception of the nature of art, and of its function in society. It will include Vivas' strictures on aesthetic theories he has rejected, because his own principles are often most clearly revealed in his criticism of inadequate theories. Vivas has summarized in question form the two essential subjects of his aesthetic theory: "What is it that the artist does to his subject matter when he creates a work of literature, and how does the created work function in human experience?"[1] In order to avoid the usual confusions of aesthetic theorists and literary critics, the two parts of this question will be kept clearly separated: (1) What is the nature of literary art as an individual creative process and aesthetic product? (2) What is the private and social function of literary art as a finished aesthetic product in society? In the essay that follows, Vivas' answers to these two vital questions provide the basis of both his aesthetic theory and critical practice.

ONE
The Nature of Art

Like Emmanuel Kant and Ernst Cassirer, Vivas assumes that values have no status in Being independently

---

[1] Eliseo Vivas, "Literature and Knowledge," in *Creation and Discovery* (Chicago: Henry Regnery Co., 1955), pp. 180 81. All quotations in this essay are from this book.

of men. But Vivas goes beyond Kant's premise that the cognitive power of the mind provides the measure and norm of external or objective reality and values. Kant's premise is inadequate for him in aesthetics, because art cannot be wholly explained by human reason. Taking his cue from Cassirer, Vivas rejects the German philosopher on this point: "Kant did not reckon with the problems which evolution forces on us, and he did not recognize that the mind functions in other modes than the narrowly cognitive one."[2] To Vivas, human reason is more than mere discursive logic operating upon empirical data. Such a process may be adequate for science in its ordinary experimental method. But it is wholly inadequate for art, which involves a super-rational process of creation and intuitive discovery: "In its original Kantian formulation," that is, "in its unqualified idealistic sense,"[3] Vivas rejects Kant's premise that the relationship of the human mind to external physical reality is one of simple direct perception. He provides three reasons for going beyond Kant's rational idealism: (1) Kant failed to account for evolutionary changes in the human mind. (2) Kant did not understand, as modern science and linguistic studies have proved, that "all perception involves a modicum of interpretation."[4] And (3) Kant ignored the subconscious mind, which Freud and others have since underscored as a very vital

---

[2] *Ibid.,* p. 112.
[3] *Ibid.,* p. 134.
[4] *Ibid.,* p. 123.

part of the creative process in art. In brief, the difference between Kant and Vivas is Darwin, modern science and linguistics, and Freud.

To Vivas, "the mind is constitutive of the world"[5] because "the artist perceives creatively."[6] The logical implications in this vital principle of philosophy and art form the whole basis of his aesthetic theory. He argues convincingly that in the very process of aesthetic creation the literary artist provides meaning and values in life through art as a self-sufficient product: "In the act of creation the mind adds something to what was there before the act took place."[7] Therefore, "a genuine work of literature contains novelty. . . ."[8] Unlike the scientist, philosopher, or historian, the true artist is like God in His original creation of the world: he brings into existence something unique, mysterious, and enduring. But unlike God, the artist does not create something out of nothing, but works with the materials provided for him in the natural and social world. But in the final analysis the creative process of the artist is a God-like power, a divine mystery that transcends the perceptive power of human reason to explain it adequately. As Vivas observes, ". . . there is . . . a profound truth in the Platonic myth of poetic inspiration."[9] With the ancient Greeks, and with all men who understand the utterly unique nature and power of art as creation and dis-

---

[5] *Ibid.*, p. 122.   [8] *Ibid.*, p. 163.
[6] *Ibid.*, p. 162.   [9] *Ibid.*, p. 193.
[7] *Ibid.*, Preface, xi.

covery, Vivas believes that art is finally a divine mystery, a gift of the gods to mankind.

Part of the unique and mysterious nature of literary art consists of its difference, in kind, from the historical world of men's practical affairs, and also from the structure of the physical universe and external nature as abstracted in the world of mathematics and physical science. The world of literary art is utterly different from the worlds of social history and of science. Vivas believes that these three distinct areas of "reality" are each "real" in a sense different from the others. Therefore, the norms of each world apply only to itself, not to the other dimensions or types of reality. Just as it would be fallacious to take as historical fact the fictions of historical novels, so too the factual, empirical and rational norms of practical life and of scientific reality do not apply to the imaginatively created fictional reality of literary art.

The absolute distinction between the world of literary art and practical life is obscured to many people because the illusion of probability in the fictional world of art, created by the skill of the artist, breaks down the psychic distance between fiction and common-sense empirical fact. This process is extended through the reader's "willing suspension of disbelief" in the fictions of art as reality, and in his recognition of many points of reference similar to the familiar world of practical affairs and nature, in the setting, actions, characters and language of fictional literature. Thus, many people who asume that the world of practical affairs and external nature is the only true reality, therefore also assume that practical life and physical nature provide the norms for judging the validity and value of literary art. This common error, that art is "an imitation of life," is by no means limited to simple, unsophisticated people. Indeed, it is the most common error of many famous aestheticians and practical critics of poetry, from Plato to the present. Vivas is perfectly aware of the many subtle ways this error disguises itself in the modern world. But in his own aesthetic theory he constantly insists that literary art creates a fictional world of its own, and that it must be judged by its own nature —that is, through fictional and aesthetic criteria, and not by the norms of practical life or scientific truth.

Implicit in Vivas' criticism and rejection of many modern theories of aesthetics is another vital philosophical assumption in his own aesthetic theory: that "reality" includes a metaphysical realm of the human mind and spirit. This is a dimension of reality beyond the reach of any mechanistic conception of reason based upon materialism. Art, like religion, transcends the empirical-rational realm of scientific materialism, not by denying or ignoring physical reality, but by including it in a complex dualism of matter and spirit. To Vivas, art mediates between the physical and the metaphysical: it expresses mind and spirit in terms of matter, and matter in terms of spirit and mind. Vivas would heartily agree with Robert Frost's definition of poetry in "Education By Poetry," as "the only way we have of saying one thing and meaning another." Vivas' assumption that "reality" includes a metaphysical dimension, and that art mediates between the physical and the metaphysical realms of reality, explains the unique power of literature to simultaneously express several themes on several levels of meaning. Literary art leaps from sight to insight, from sense to essence, from the physical to the metaphysical realms of being. Poetry has this unique power only because, unlike the empirical-rational logic in the methods of experimental science and discursive expository scholarship, the method of the poet in using language is not literal and logical, but wholly metaphorical, analogical and symbolic. The ambiguities of figurative and symbolic language in poetry are both consciously and unconsciously functional in conveying meaning on several levels. As Vivas notes, "For a consistent mechanist the very demand for meaning is nonsensical."[10] If materialism provided the only reality, the multiple meanings of poetry would be impossible.

Critics of Vivas' aesthetic theory object that he claims too much for art, that he attributes to it a unique nature and value which, in our age of modern science, is quite unwarranted. With great wit Vivas turns the table on his critics. It is not that he claims too much for art, but that they have a seriously deficient total

---

[10] *Ibid.,* p. 18.

philosophy and aesthetic theory, and therefore do not understand the unique and vital nature and function of art, and claim too little for it. In brief, many modern aesthetic theories are based upon a wholly materialist philosophy of life, in which human nature and reason are conceived in Hobbesian terms, as wholly mechanistic. As Vivas puts it, ". . . the majority of our contemporaries" are "loyal inmates of a secularistic culture,"[11] and are therefore content to explain the creative processes of the literary artist in mechanistic terms that apply to science but not to art.

Edgar Allen Poe was guilty of precisely this aberration when he explained in "The Philosophy of Composition" how he came to write "The Raven." Poe claimed that he pursued a totally rational and conscious method, and laid out a blueprint for his poems before composing any part of it, and pursued it in a logical manner such as in solving a problem in geometry. Vivas' criticism of Poe reveals the grounds for his own total rejection of any merely conscious and rational explanation of the creative process in literary art:[12]

> The genuine work of art comes from the unknown depths of the soul, where its growth is even more mysterious than the development of a fetus. The artist, moved by forces over which he exercises only limited conscious control, does not know clearly what he wants to say till the labor of the file is finished and he can discover his intention in his com-

[11] *Ibid.*, p. 216.
[12] *Ibid.*, p. 160.

position. . . . The analysis of these phenomena in scientific terms is something which, so far as I can discover, is still a long way off.

No genuine poet can know beforehand which "presuppositions" may enter into his work, because to put it in Freudian terms, "consciousness proposes and the Id disposes."[13] Vivas notes that Freud himself provided "the insight that the analysis of aesthetic values is not within the reach of his analytical method."[14] Neither in the creative process nor in the critical response to art does analytical reason satisfy Vivas as providing ultimate explanations.

Vivas extends his criticism of Poe to the behaviorists of the twentieth century. He agrees with Freud that the unconscious mind is paramount in the creative process, and that "those submerged processes of the psyche which we dimly envision"[15] in art are not subject to behavioral description and rational analysis. But the behaviorist ignores the subconscious mind: "Since for the behaviorist there is no consciousness, nothing can take place below its level."[16] As a complete materialist and empiricist, the behaviorist cannot reach to the unconscious mind; indeed, he even wants "to get rid of the category of mind altogether."[17] The behaviorist's attempt to explain the creative processes of art in scien-

---

13 *Ibid.*, p. 12.   16 *Ibid.*, p. 234.
14 *Ibid.*, p. 46.   17 *Ibid.*, p. 227.
15 *Ibid.*, p. 225.

tific, mechanistic terms is severely criticized by Vivas:
". . . The creative act remains a mystery for the behaviorist in spite of his scientific courage and precisely
because . . . he reduces the creative activity to a complex process of shuffling the already experienced. But
for all its appearance of contemporaneity, this does not
advance the theory of mind beyond the point where
Hobbes left it."[18] In practical literary criticism the behavioral aesthetics reduces poetry to mere linguistic
response. In attacking the inadequacy of the behavioral
explanation of art, Vivas implicitly asserts his belief
that "reality" includes a metaphysical realm of the human mind and spirit which transcends the material:
"The creative activity makes nonsense of the universal
applicability 'of the scientific method."[19] To Vivas, the
creative process of art, and art itself, transcends
empirical observation and logical analysis, and all
the materialist assumptions and methods of modern
science.

Vivas' criticism of Poe and modern behaviorism also
applies, with many subtle variations, to all modern
aesthetic theories based upon philosophical materialism
and scientific rationalism. The most obvious such theory is Marxist aesthetics, and on the level of critical
practice Vivas is sharply critical of how Marxists conceive of and use art. By making art instrumental to

---

[18] *Ibid.,* p. 233.
[19] *Ibid.,* p. 240.

dialectic materialism and ideology, the Marxists make the value of art depend wholly upon non-aesthetic criteria: art is good only as a means of making Marxism triumph in the world. On the level of practical strategy and tactics in fomenting class warfare, the Marxists reduce art to the ideological polemics and party propaganda for their social, political, and economic programs. The chief value of literary art is to make the proletariat aware of themselves as a separate class, to enlist their support in making Marxist revolution, and to sustain the Marxist state once they have triumphed. Art may also be useful in providing harmless pleasure and amusement to the masses, thus diverting them from criticism of the Marxist state. All of these conceptions of the nature and function of art are based ultimately upon a totally materialistic philosophy of man and reality, which Vivas rejects as woefully inadequate.

To the Marxist the ultimate "reality" for man is a hypothetical materialist Utopia beyond history and beyond art. Vivas' criticism of this important aspect of Marxist theory, as it applies to their aesthetics, is not as explicit or concrete as we would wish. It is implicit in his criticism that the materialist "real" is made antithetical to the aesthetic "unreal" in art, and that thus the fictions of art are dismissed as a mere lag in the historical progress of man toward a Marxist materialist Utopia. Apart from his use of literature in polemical propaganda, the Marxist believes art has a place in historical society only so long as society is imperfect and evil. But as society progresses toward the "reality" of a perfect Utopian world of future material happiness, men will want to live in the "real" world, and there will be no need to create the unreal fictional world of art. Thus the gap between art and society is resolved by Marxists wholly in favor of the latter. As society and therefore men become more perfect in fulfilling their material nature, art must be reduced and finally abolished. To atheists, fictional gods and real god-like men do not need the arts.

Yet there is a profound irony implicit in this Marxist view of art in relation to society, namely, their recognition that art, like religion, is rooted in the spiritual life of man. For if it is the object of the Marxists to use art and religion for political ends, and ultimately to get rid of them as illusions, the Marxists also see in the arts and religion major enemies preventing the realization of their future materialist Utopian state. Thus they acknowledge the enormous power and importance of art and religion in ways that other less total and vigorous materialists do not. Vivas notes this grand irony:[20]

> It is ironic, but it is sadly true, that the only body of men in our day who have had a consistently serious sense of the importance of literature are the very men who in their hearts least of all care for it—the Marxists. Their materialism makes them as blind as the hedonists and the

---

[20] *Ibid.,* p 419.

Freudians to the manner in which art actually functions in society; but at least they do not offer us the vulgarities of the hedonists or of the therapists.

Like Plato, the Marxists recognize and fear the great power of the artist, and thus they acknowledge the importance of art even while wishing to eliminate it from their hypothetically perfect society of the future.

Vivas identifies yet another example of aesthetic theory based upon scientific materialism in John Dewey's *Art as Experience*. His theory, that art is pleasure in "experience" and in "emotion" produced by art in an audience, clearly manifests itself as what Vivas calls "hedonistic secularism." Dewey thought "that literature has as its end pleasure produced through the play on the emotions."[21] Thus, he displaced the common didactic fallacy of art for the sake of morality with his own fallacy of art for the sake of pleasure in a heightened experience of the senses. Art was for him merely a form of higher amusement. Therefore, Dewey denied that literature is concerned with philosophical "truth," because in merely giving us "pure experience," without reference to its objective aesthetic nature in form and technique, he made subjective response the sole criteria for aesthetic value. Vivas objects strongly to Dewey's subjectivism: ". . . All subjectivism" assumes "that each individual's reaction is absolutely valid, and we must take it at its face value."[22] In brief,

---

[21] *Ibid.*, p. 418.   [22] *Ibid.*, p. 306.

subjectivism ends in aesthetic solipsism, in which no social agreement about literature would be possible.

In practical criticism Vivas also takes strong issue with Dewey's view that "the aesthetic object arouses emotion in the spectator," and that "the content or meaning of art, objectively speaking, is emotion."[23] In experiencing an art object, since various people feel various emotions, or little, or none, to Vivas this is evidence that "emotion is an accidental consequence of aesthetic apprehension,"[24] and is not the core content of art. Dewey naively assumed that there was some necessary correlation between emotion expressed in art and emotion experienced in the reader. Therefore, he believed, the emotion as experienced in life through art is transformed or transubstantiated into the emotion expressed in the art object. But despite this circular reasoning the two are by no means the same. For just as poetry may express an emotion without arousing that emotion in a reader, so too a reader may feel an emotion not actually expressed in a poem. Vivas notes that this leads to "one of the most frequent forms of the subjectivistic fallacy," which "consists in confusing the value of an experience with the value of an object in an experience. . . . Aesthetic value is not the quality of an experience but an object in an experience. . . ."[25] This criticism of Dewey is extended by Vivas with

---

[23] *Ibid.,* p. 143.
[24] *Ibid.,* p. 144.
[25] *Ibid.,* p. 301.

brilliant insight to T. S. Eliot's principle of the "objective correlative." Vivas asks the crucial question: ". . . Exactly how can feelings, something subjective, attach to images, something quite objective?"[26] Eliot's failure to explain this problem is at the core of all theories of art as self-expression. They invariably end up "by offering us as an explanation the fact to be explained."[27] Like Dewey, Eliot did not distinguish between the idea that "poetry arouses emotion in the reader," and the idea that "the poem expresses emotion in and through the poem itself."[28] But like I. A. Richards, Vivas believes that "no artist, however skillful, can possibly control the subjective responses of his readers."[29] Dewey's aesthetic theory is fallacious at its core, and presents a seriously inadequate understanding of the nature and function of art.

In his "Four Notes on I. A. Richards' Aesthetic Theory," and elsewhere, Vivas took sharp issue with Richards' claim that he had placed aesthetics and practical criticism on a scientific basis. Like the behaviorists, in practical literary criticism the later Richards tended to reduce criticism to linguistic analysis. But the psychological elements in Richards' early aesthetic theory, which contradicted his later behavioral positivism, provided him with insights of a kind that resulted in an aesthetic theory that "constitutes the most systematic

26 *Ibid.*, p. 273.   28 *Ibid.*, p. 274.
27 *Ibid.*, p. 273.   29 *Ibid.*, p. 275.

defense of poetry that we can find in the English language."[30] But although Richards exposed many errors long established in aesthetics and criticism, on a more subtle level he fell into similar errors himself. He assumed that his psychology was based on science, and in the end he turned "aesthetics into psychophysiology." He rejected the crude mechanistic assumption of behaviorists and other theorists who believed that literature provides us with knowledge of the practical world in the same manner as history or science, and he argued instead that art "organizes our attitudes."[31] Vivas dubs this claim of Richards the "therapeutic" theory of art.

The belief that art "organizes our attitudes" makes art a substitute for religion. Like Matthew Arnold, Richards held this conviction because he believed that modern science has made traditional religion obsolete, and that art could take the place of religion. As this belief applies to art, Vivas disagrees with Richards, and notes that he never understood "that art has a function of its own,"[32] and it is not merely a therapeutic substitute for religion. Also, if art can thus replace religion, could not psychiatry in its turn replace art? Vivas notes the tendency in Richards to substitute psychological terms for traditional literary terms, to make "all the objective features of the work of art become physico-

---

[30] *Ibid.*, p. 166.
[31] *Ibid.*, pp. 166 and 418.
[32] *Ibid.*, p. 167.

physiological stimuli. Rhythm becomes 'expectancy,'
. . . etc."[33] In the end, Richards merely reduced "objective phenomena to subjective terms."[34] He was aware
that practical criticism required a technical analysis of
literature, but as Vivas notes, "psychology does not
provide either the categories, or the criterion, or the
method, involved in that evaluation."[35] Richards ac-
counted for art "in terms of impulses, instincts and
sensory effects," but "somehow or other the work of
art has vanished, has become mythical."[36] To Richards
the objective categories of art and of practical criticism
were "merely fallacious 'projections' of the mind. . . ."[37]
Vivas draws out the disastrous implications of such a
position to practical criticism:[38]

> Now one of the most irreducible confusions in Richards'
> doctrine results from the fact that through his extreme in-
> tolerance of any other approach to aesthetics than the
> psychological there is no legitimate place in his system
> for technical analysis of an objective kind. But without
> objective technical analysis it is difficult to imagine what
> answer can be given to the question why good art should
> be preferred to bad.

Vivas' devastating criticism of Richards' theory rests on
his principle that whenever the aesthetic function of art
is made instrumental to some other supposedly higher
end, the distinction between good art and bad art be-

---

[33] *Ibid.*, p. 329.   [36] *Ibid.*, p. 330.
[34] *Ibid.*, p. 330.   [37] *Ibid.*, p. 330.
[35] *Ibid.*, p. 332.   [38] *Ibid.*, p. 326.

comes irrelevant. To Vivas, the act of aesthetic expression in art is always an end in itself, and not merely instrumental to organizing our emotions, propagandizing materialism, or any other end.

Vivas attacks the Marxist, hedonist, and Freudian literary theorists and critics because none of them do justice to the nature and function of art, nor explain why it is "one of the two most ineradicable, most indispensable modes of experience."[39] Like most modern critics "they work in a philosophical vacuum . . . ," because "philosophically, ours is a bankrupt generation."[40] These theorists are "for the most part philosophically pauperized and are, hence, devoid of a coherent sense of the place of man in society, the place of society in history and the relation of history to the universe. It is no wonder, therefore, that they should have only the most trivial notions of the use of literature."[41] All of them have "the same secular image of man,"[42] devoid of any metaphysical sense of reality. Therefore, they lack "a tenable notion of the destiny of man,"[43] and literature becomes for them mere entertainment, or an escape from the "reality" of practical life.

Vivas finds the chief source of the inadequate aesthetic theory of most modern critics in their anti-metaphysical materialist philosophy, and in their

[39] *Ibid.*, p. 418.   [42] *Ibid.*, p. 420.
[40] *Ibid.*, pp. 419 and 420.   [43] *Ibid.*, p. 419.
[41] *Ibid.*, p. 418.

Faustian pride in the supposedly unlimited power of human reason and knowledge through science. They have unlimited faith in the possibilities of applying the principles and methods of the physical sciences to the study of man and human values in aesthetics. This positivist faith blinds them to all evidence of the metaphysical dimensions of reality, beyond materialism. They refuse to admit any place for spirit and mind in their philosophy, because if such an admission were to be made, sociology and psychology could not be exact sciences, and therefore the admissions must never be made. The consequences of their materialist philosophy, beyond aesthetics, are well summarized by Vivas:[44]

> Science . . . has encouraged a swarm of false philosophies which claim its authority and whose business is to destroy the once solid metaphysics in the light of which we defined our destiny. In this Brave New World of science and of pleasure, humanity is not destroyed by forced labor in the frozen tundras of Siberia; it is destroyed by something worse: the social engineer painlessly performs a lobotomy on it and destroys its soul. . . . Such a society, taking God to be a silly and burdensome superstition, will substitute the image of Man for His image and under the illusion of humanism will worship naked power. This is the society that we have already begun to rear on both sides of the Iron Curtain.

Vivas observes that in the past all men, even the greatest sinners, "never seriously proposed a purely secular

---

[44] *Ibid.,* pp. 423 and 415–16.

conception of human destiny," but among modern theorists dominated by science the great aim is to establish "a totally secularized future."[45] This is what underlies "the threat-filled dialectic of the commissars,"[46] and less obviously the social scientists who "under the pretense of being pure knowers bore like termites at the foundations of our culture."[47] The result of the total denial of the City of God by scientific materialists is "the swarming secularized city of today . . . ,"[48] with its separation of the intellectual from the emotional life of man, leading to "the disintegration of the modern personality."[49] Modern man's worship of a "quasi-divine" independent abstract reason and science creates the contemporary "dehumanized man." Since such a man has no sense of metaphysical reality, he cannot imagine art as concerned "with the values men live by and the ends they serve."[50] Modern scientific materialists, hedonists, and positivists all fail to explain the vital role of the spirit and mind of man in the creative process of art. Their failure to do justice to the nature and function of art is part of a much larger failure in their total philosophy, which has disastrous consequences in man's culture and civilization.

Vivas is well aware that historically the dominant theory of aesthetic in Western civilization prior to the modern era, to the end of the eighteenth century, was

---

[45] *Ibid.*, p. 422.   [48] *Ibid.*, p. 428.
[46] *Ibid.*, p. 423.   [49] *Ibid.*, p. 426.
[47] *Ibid.*, p. 425.   [50] *Ibid.*, p. 420.

Aristotle's doctrine that art is "an imitation of life." He notes that ". . . outside of the 'Chicago school of criticism' the imitation theory has very few defenders today,"[51] having been almost universally rejected in favor of scientific and psychological theories. The Classical theory that art pursued the dual function of giving "pleasure" and "instruction," held by Horace, Ben Jonson, Dryden, Pope, Samuel Johnson and many others, was modified by the Romantics in favor of pleasure alone. This was the opening wedge for modern psychology and hedonism to enter. Yet some modern theories of art as psychological "self-expression" and of social "communication," are really only disguised versions of the Classical imitation theory which they reject. Like the theory of art as imitation, they assume that "the world of experience, the spacio-temporal world of culture and history . . . ,"[52] is the ultimate reality which art renders, and that the skill and value of an art object is determined by intellectual, aesthetic, moral and social norms drawn from that world. If this is so, then literature is merely a means of providing "knowledge" of life in nature and in civilization through an aesthetic medium. Unlike the modern Marxists and other scientific materialists, many writers who have held fast to the imitation theory believed in a metaphysical reality beyond the physical world and practical life. Yet by

---

[51] *Ibid.*, p. 161.
[52] *Ibid.*, p. 191.

equating "Being with existence" they too failed to do justice to both the creative process and the unique nature of art.

Vivas provides an excellent summary of his grounds for objecting to the theory of art as an imitation of life:[53]

> The theory of imitation is wrong on at least two counts: (1) the work of art gives evidence of novelty, originality or freshness, which aspect constitutes the addition the artist makes to the forms and the matter he takes from experience. Creativity, therefore, is no mere making, but a special kind of making that deserves its special name, unless we are to obfuscate important distinctions; (2) the object of the work of art can only be exhibited with adequacy *in* and *through* the work itself, and any paraphrase or rendition of it outside the work itself involves loss to the object and, in this respect, the destruction of the work itself.

These two reasons for rejecting the theory of imitation are woven through much that Vivas wrote about aesthetic theory. In ignoring the novelty of a work of literature, the imitation theory does not do full justice to the creative activity of the artist,"[54] because in constituting the world of aesthetic fiction in his art, the poet creates it in the very act of discovering it. Therefore, "art does not imitate nature; instead it breaks up its meanings and forms . . . under the impact of expe-

[53] *Ibid.,* p. 387.
[54] *Ibid.,* p. 131.

rience, and then fuses the whole into something utterly new."[55] The result is a vital difference in kind between objects in life and their identifiable equivalent objects in art. This difference is a strong argument against the imitation theory: "Not even the most realistic imitationist would claim that the object imitated by the work of art is the same as the object of imitation."[56] Therefore, if the literary art object has its own reality, and the subjects and themes of art derive their treatment from techniques and forms that belong to art and not to life, "the theory of imitation must be rejected by anyone who grasps firmly the difference between existential objects and the objects of poetry."[57]

Indeed, it is closer to the truth to say, with Oscar Wilde, that life imitates art than that art imitates life, because in literary art we discover "what the artist through his work tells us is there."[58] In brief, we judge the world through art as a norm, and not art through the the world as a norm. This is so because the creative artist has his own autonomy and his created object its own self-sufficiency. True art is never "referential" to the world, or "associative": it is its own end, and controls our total and undivided attention to itself. It will not do for critics to paraphrase a poem, to "substitute our own irresponsibly constructed objects for the care-

---

[55] *Ibid.*, p. 240.
[56] *Ibid.*, p. 389.
[57] *Ibid.*, p. 211.
[58] *Ibid.*, p. 189

fully structured and organically related self-sufficiency of the object the artist presents us with."[59]

Those who take the temporal-spacial historical world as their norm for literary art fail utterly to do justice to the unique way that language functions in literature to say or mean what it does. The fallacy of art as an imitation of life is perhaps most evident because "what a poem says or means is neither its paraphrase or translation nor what the paraphrase points to. . . . The best and most exhaustive paraphrase does not point to all the poem says. Somehow what the poem says cannot be conveyed by any other means than the poem itself."[60] The conventions of language in poetry, which are figurative and symbolic, determine how and what a poem means, rather than the conventions of discursive logic and nonfigurative language used in ordinary life in society. Therefore, images and objects referred to in poetry "pre-exist and are independent of the language through which we refer to them."[61] The very language of criticism precludes the possibility that any analysis will render the equivalent of the poem.

To Vivas, any critical concept which takes the world outside of the art object as the norm by which to judge the art object is fatal to any valid aesthetic experience in art. The doctrine of art as an imitation of life begs the whole question of the authenticity of a unique expe-

---

[59] *Ibid.*, p. 360.
[60] *Ibid.*, p. 121.
[61] *Ibid.*, p. 122.

rience in and through art. To Vivas, the aesthetic experience is valid and "pure" only "to the extent that in
the intensity of apprehension of the object before us it
appears as self-sufficient, that it excludes all conscious
external reference."[62] It is a basic principle of both
aesthetics and practical criticism that the art object has
a life and a reality of its own, with a method of language
of its own, that it is a self-sufficient aesthetic world
bounded within its own limits, and independent of the
practical ordinary world of external nature and historical society. The norms of literary art provide an anchored sense of form in our chaotic everyday world of
sensory flux: "Without the aid of poetry, our ambient
world remains an inchoate, unstructured chaos."[63]
Vivas' statement is identical with Robert Frost's claim
that poetry provides in the external world "a momentary stay against confusion."

To reach into the heart of Vivas' aesthetic theory it
is necessary to combine and refine his statements that
"the mind is constitutive of the world," and that "a
genuine work of literature contains novelty." Indeed, in
the same mysterious way that process finally becomes
product in art, these two arguments become identical.
Vivas lays far greater emphasis upon the process of
creation than most aestheticians. How does the creative
mind constitute a new, unique, self-contained world of

[62] *Ibid.*, Preface, xxi.
[63] *Ibid.*, p. 11.

poetry through the creation of images and symbols, casting them into new forms or structures? He insists that there is a mystery at the heart of aesthetic creation. No scientific and rational analysis can adequately explain the creative process. The poet does through symbolic language what Genesis reports that God did in creating the material world. Poetry is a form of prophetic revelation: it is as close as man can come to seeing "Being" as God sees it. God sees Being directly, but "what we know we know by means of symbols."[64] Vivas defines a poem as "a linguistic artifact, whose function is to organize the primary data of experience that can be exhibited in and through words."[65] Through metaphors, images, and symbols, constituting structured form, a poem at once overcomes the chaos of direct sensory experience of life, and creates values by which to understand life: "By means of the image we are able temporarily to frustrate the tendency to respond behaviorally to the stimulus. The image, when it arises, embodies values which seek our espousal."[66] Thus, process becomes product even for the reader: "What the poem says or means . . . is, genetically speaking, the full-bodied, value-freighted, ordered, self-sufficient world it presents to us for the first time."[67] Vivas also indicates how the poem finally becomes a revelation of metaphysical reality: ". . . The object of

---

[64] *Ibid.*, p. 136.   [66] *Ibid.*, p. 125.
[65] *Ibid.*, p. 111.   [67] *Ibid.*, p. 133.

aesthetic apprehension is a self-consistent structure, involving an ordered complex of values of a sensuous, formal and immanently meaningful nature. . . . They are, in the isolation of the aesthetic experience, final values, inherently interesting for their own sake and not as means. And beyond them we perceive an authenthentic vision of the structure of reality."[68] The mind is constitutive of both the material world and the metaphysical world through art.

The two most basic features of a poem as product are its self-sufficiency and its organic unity. Only if a reader approaches a poem in a purely aesthetic attitude, with a "captive mind" that is "utterly engrossed," even in a state of "ecstasy," only then can the organically unified poem function in its true autonomy: "In order for the poem to function as a self-sufficient whole, we must approach it in an aesthetic attitude. We do so when we read it with rapt, intransitive attention on its full presentational immediacy."[69] But as Vivas points out on several occasions, the literary art object "remains in complete monopolistic possession" of a reader's consciousness only if the relationship between its ingredients controls and compels his concentration: "A poem functions as a self-sufficient whole when it has . . . unity, when its discriminable elements are tied by organic interrelationships in such a manner that our

---

[68] *Ibid.,* p. 268.
[69] *Ibid.,* p. 116.

attention is not led off from them. . . ."[70] A valid and profound aesthetic experience of literature results only when both the poem as product and the mature reader as critic have perfect rapport: "An aesthetic experience is an experience of rapt attention which involves the intransitive apprehension of an object's immanent meanings and values in their full presentational immediacy."[71] To a reader who has a perfect rapport with a great poem, the poem is not about reality; it is reality. A poem, as a poem "and not as something else, means what it is and is all that it means."[72] The aesthetic experience in reading a poem is "structurally different from the moral, the religious and the cognitive."[73] Its technique and form presents a recognizable content through a principle of analogical identity between itself as fiction and the everyday world we know: as Marianne Moore said, a poem presents real toads in imaginary gardens. A poem has in metaphors and symbols a language of the imagination beyond the senses and logic of discursive reasoning, a language which designs the total structure of the poem, including sensory appeals, but simultaneously transcending objects of sense through cognitive insights which unfold as the poem is written or read. A true poem writes itself in metaphors and symbols. As Vivas notes, a poem while being composed gets "the whip hand" over the poet. No external

---

[70] *Ibid.*, p. 116.   [72] *Ibid.*, p. 360.
[71] *Ibid.*, p. 146.   [73] *Ibid.*, p. 360.

logic is imposed upon it, so that as a finished product a poem always remains autonomous and true to itself.

Yet there are two important senses in which an individual poem cannot be totally autonomous. First, a poem is part of the whole tradition of poetry, and an individual poem is like a star or planet in a whole galaxy or universe of poems. From previous experience both the poet and the reader have knowledge of the conventions and language of poetry. This knowledge forms their essential assumptions prior to writing or reading a new poem. Second, the unique self-sufficiency of a poem is not absolute because the art object "is dependent on the presuppositions that make it possible, and not all of these are purely aesthetic."[74] During the time that a reader considers a poem solely as a poem, as a fictional art object it enjoys "a sort of congressional immunity from moral and cognitive jurisdiction."[75] But apart from its aesthetic immunity from being judged by the non-aesthetic norms of the world, in its themes or content as a work which says something about the world, that is as "knowledge," a poem is open to non-aesthetic criticism. As Vivas says, the "moral and cognitive . . . presuppositions that make it possible"[76] also make the ideas or content of a poem subject to criticism in moral and cognitive terms. But these are philosophical and cultural considerations which in no way invalidate the aesthetic self-sufficiency of a poem.

---

[74] *Ibid.*, p. 179. [76] *Ibid.*, p. 180.
[75] *Ibid.*, p. 179.

TWO

The Function of Art

The personal function of art to the creative artist is the fame and satisfaction he experiences in creating an aesthetic object of intrinsic value, and in its enduring social importance as an emblematic revelation and a prophesy in history. As Vivas puts it: ". . . The artist creates novel objects and discovers the hidden reality of our practical, common-sense world."[77] During the process of creation, the artist's whole concern is the perfection of his form through technique; after the art object has been created and accepted into its aesthetic tradition, it assumes a cultural value and function beyond its aesthetic nature. An artist's primary accountability as an artist takes precedence over his role as a citizen of his country or a man of his civilization. He must be true to his own integrity as an artist, and produce first-rate art, before he can contribute to his culture: "The artist . . . cannot be at the service of the state or of a parochial morality or anything else. He must serve his art; that is the only way in which he can serve developing history."[78] Two novelists, Henry James and Dostoevski, provided Vivas with his ideal examples of how this primary personal function of art is best fulfilled.

---

[77] *Ibid.*, p. 191.
[78] *Ibid.*, Preface, xv.

Perhaps no man was more completely the literary artist than Henry James. Yet the concept of "aesthetic man" is an artificial abstraction, no more valid or real than "political man" or "economic man." Man as artist does not lose his civil character or common humanity in the practice of his profession. To compartmentalize the functions of life assumes a moral and intellectual, not an aesthetic conception of life. It is a way of defining our necessary duties and understanding distinctions within the whole context of life. But to avoid schizophrenia, in life as in art we attempt to see things integrated and whole. Thus, when we note that James as artist utilized totally aesthetic principles by which he selected his materials for fiction, and that his techniques and discriminations in shaping his materials were totally aesthetic, this does not mean that his aesthetic and creative sensibility precluded ethical and intellectual objectives. His total nature as a man was involved in his total artistic efforts.

The famous "ethical neutrality" of James as a novelist did not mean that he had abandoned his ethical principles in the process of creating his fiction. Rather, it meant that when he composed his fiction his only concern in his passion for technique and the creation of fictional order was concentrated totally in his response to what Vivas calls "the inner thrust of the dramatic incident which has been selected for treatment."[79]

---

[79] *Ibid.*, pp. 25–26.

James' absolute primacy in aesthetic technique did not derive from ethical indifference: art for art's sake applied to the technique, language and structure of his novels, but the content of his fiction was profoundly moral. Indeed, Vivas notes that in James the core of his concern as a novelist, and therefore the ultimate source of "his creative effort," was "his interest in the clarification of the ethical structure of his world."[80] James' moral vision of life is clearly evident in his fiction. Vivas notes the "sharp and shocking" contrast between Will James' utilitarian and Darwinian moral theory, in which calculated might makes right, and Henry James' fictional morality, in favor of "loyalty to the pledged word, kindness as against cruelty, honor as against expedience. . . ." These, says Vivas, "are basic to his vision of the world."[81] In their "conception of consciousness" and of "pure experience" based upon the empirical-rational flow of consciousness, Henry and Will James meet as one. The superiority of Henry James to his brother consisted in his ability, as a novelist, to organize his consciousness and experience in his fiction beyond anything that Will James could do through discursive reasoning in philosophy. As a novelist Henry James transcended ordinary and even refined rational philosophical life through his "acuity of perception organized by an intellect into self-contained

---

[80] *Ibid.*, p. 24.
[81] *Ibid.*, p. 29.

form."[82] This superiority was possible only because he was first true to himself as a novelist, so that he could fill the "crowded consciousness" of his characters' lives with meaning, through "subtle shades of character and mood, temperament and attitudes."[83] In thus being true to himself and the demands of his art, James fulfilled the primary function of the artist.

Likewise, Dostoevski's novels "contain . . . a dramatic organization of life which includes characters, most of whom are deeply interested in ideas."[84] Yet Dostoevski, as "a committed Christian and a political conservative," never allowed his religious or political convictions to intrude as propaganda into his art. In *The Possessed,* when he presented his character Shatov, a professed but pharisaical Christian who speaks non-Christian ideas, Vivas notes that "it was in the teeth of the latter's assertions that Dostoevski held his truth."[85] Dostoevski's fiction does not present a set of personal doctrines or views, nor any "systematic structures of abstract thought involving major affirmations and denials." No reader of his fiction can assume that any character speaks for the author. Each reader is compelled to understand the convictions held by each character at the dramatic level, in the interrelationships revealed to exist between him and other characters. Through his words and actions each character reveals

---

[82] *Ibid.*, p. 23.   [84] *Ibid.*, p. 75.
[83] *Ibid.*, p. 23.   [85] *Ibid.*, p. 75.

his personal understanding of life. Dostoevski is a true literary artist because he insists upon organizing and informing experience on the primary level, as pure drama.

Although his fiction exhibits "two levels or aspects of human reality: the psychological and the metaphysical,"[86] he is never a psychologist or a theologian, but always a novelist. One of Dostoevski's greatest achievements was his assertion of the "metaphysical dimension" of modern man "in empirical terms."[87] This is what is most troublesome to his modern materialist and rationalist readers. His fiction is a powerful attack against "the onrush of a naturalism bent on stripping us of our essentially human, our metaphysical reality."[88] His fiction is a devastating exposure of the Faustian pride of modern secular man, "the belief that science and intelligence are enough for the development of human life."[89] In history, the very forces that Dostoevski most dreaded have triumphed in Russia, and as Vivas notes, "the process by which man will destroy himself is already under way."[90] In such characters as Zossima, Dostoevski created a human norm by which to judge the whole course of modern history and civilization. From the vantage point of the present, Vivas observes in this regard: "We are not going back to Zossima's Russia, but to the world of Marx and Dewey."[91] Through a symbolic elaboration of life, in his fiction

---

[86] *Ibid.,* p. 76.   [89] *Ibid.,* p. 96.
[87] *Ibid.,* p. 89.   [90] *Ibid.,* p. 103.
[88] *Ibid.,* p. 89.   [91] *Ibid.,* p. 103.

Dostoevski achieved "a definition of the destiny of Western man."[92] Thus, the personal integrity of Dostoevski to his fiction was also instrumental to his achievement in the social function of his art.

The enormous value and social function of art is summarized boldly and succinctly by Vivas: "Art creates culture: it creates the values and meanings by which a society fulfills its destiny."[93] How does the literary artist achieve this great social end? Vivas describes the means by which the social function of the poet is achieved:[94]

> . . . The poet [is] a man who first gives to a nation a certain focal center in the consciousness of its own character. To do this is to exhibit to a people in dramatic terms the structure of its life and the order of rank of its values. This is what the literary artist does in the degree to which he is creative. He presents us with a symbolic fiction of a world charged with value; he defines that value in dramatic terms within the grasp of men; he shows the hierarchy that structures it; and he thus gives us the means to give vivid individual content to the generalizations on which we fall back when we take stock of our experience.

By stripping life to its essential form, the literary artist creates the symbolic normative paradigms of social culture, and thus he redeems the world from chaos and brutality. Vivas agrees with Shelley that the poet is a

---

92 *Ibid.*, p. 103.
93 *Ibid.*, Preface, xviii.
94 *Ibid.*, p. 190.

silent legislator for mankind. The poet asserts the metaphysical dimensions of man in empirical terms. He does
this by changing through his art the raw materials of
transient nature and society into an enduring aesthetic
reality. When readers perceive a new poem properly, in
its full aesthetic significance as an enduring art object,
it simultaneously reveals to them its purely aesthetic
qualities as a poem, and in its derivative cultural function it reveals the new meanings and values of emerging historical society.

As cultural artifacts, literary art embodies and reflects what is most significant in the values of every historical epoch. Nothing simply is: it is what it is only as
perceived by the individual artist in the concrete objective form in which he casts his art. Through the intuitive power of the creative artist to see through objects,
we go beyond sensory impressions and rational reflections about life. By creating a unique fusion of sensory,
intellectual, emotional, moral, social and aesthetic phenomena in the structure of his art, the artist grasps a
higher level of reality than the historian, the philosopher, or the scientist: "With morality, knowledge and
religion, art is one of the four main activities which the
animal employs to transpose himself from the animal
level to the human. Through art, man makes himself
into a human being."[95] Indeed, the other three main in-
struments of human redemption depend upon art for

---

[95] *Ibid.*, p 221.

their full realization: "Knowledge, morality and religion presuppose and build on the world we come to know by means of art."[96] Vivas quotes Henry James to the same effect: "It is art that makes life, makes interest, makes importance . . . and I know of no substitute whatever for the force and beauty of its process. . . ."[97] In its social function of raising man above his animal level, Vivas insists there is nothing that can replace art: "Art has a function to perform for which there can be no substitute."[98]

Vivas is well aware that his claim that art creates culture and provides values and human significance in life "must seem utter nonsense" to materialists, scientific rationalists, positivists, behaviorists, hedonists, and all who deny the metaphysical dimensions of reality. Such persons cannot comprehend how "mind both creates and discovers reality"[99] through art, because for them the only "reality" is the everyday material world of sensory common sense experience. All value free philosophies are anchored in materialism, and therefore deny Vivas' principle that art creates new values and meanings in society. On this point Vivas notes: "Our modern mind is instinct with hatred of value. This is part of the suicidal compulsion of our culture."[100] But the modern secular mind cannot eliminate value entirely, so it "does the next best thing: it tries to reduce

---

[96] *Ibid.*, p. 112. [99] *Ibid.*, p. 364.
[97] *Ibid.*, p. 24. [100] *Ibid.*, p. 219.
[98] *Ibid.*, p. 168.

value to desire or interest, and beyond this, to biological needs."[101] It is small wonder, then, that people who think in these materialistic terms should have such inadequate conceptions of the nature and social function of literary art, and from their viewpoint should believe that Vivas has far too exalted a conception of art.

In summary, Vivas' aesthetic theory is an original and important achievement in twentieth century philosophy. His originality is partly eclectic and partly his own unique contribution. He has mastered all that has been written about literary art in Western civilization, from Plato to the present. He has retained the valid principles of art in the theories of ancient, medieval, and modern aestheticians, but he has modified them and combined them with his own principles regarding creativity and discovery, to form a new, complex, and unsystematic whole. Although he is profoundly consistent and even single-minded in his theory of literary art, like Dostoevski he is to skeptical about human reason and logic to have a closed system of aesthetics. Such a system implies having a final explanation of literary art through human reason, and Vivas denies that reason can adequately explain the mystery at the core of the creative process, or even the symbolic effects of art in social culture. Ultimately, art is a metaphysical mystery. In a profound sense, Vivas' aesthetic

---

[101] *Ibid.*, p. 220.

theory is like his conception of literary art: it is a unique, value-laden, organically-related thesis; it is a genuinely creative conception of literary art, and those who read it with care will discover the true nature and social function of art, for themselves and for the cultural values and institutions of our age.

In addition to Vivas' positive argument for the nature and function of literary art, part of his achievement lies in his great courage and skill in attacking what he calls "the reigning philosophical orthodoxy" of our time. His principle that "creation" is literally true, and that it leads to "discovery," and his "value realism" based upon a metaphysical view of total reality, are profound challenges to all nominalists in philosophy, and to all who hold aesthetic principles based upon materialism and faith in the scientific method applied to human affairs. Vivas is a profoundly anti-ideological man in an age that is insanely ideological. He understands the many and serious intellectual delusions that lie in abstract speculative reason and theory, particularly when such rational theories are anchored in materialism and in faith in a pseudo-scientific methodology. His own aesthetic theory is anything but abstract: he constantly clarifies important points in his aesthetics through concrete details, through specific references and analyses of the fiction of Dostoevski, James, Kafka, Dreiser, and other writers. Few writers possess Vivas' knowledge, skill, and courage in exposing the inadequate conceptions of literary art held by many well known modern theorists, critics, and teachers. But perhaps the supreme tribute to Vivas' achievement is that even those who agree with his aesthetic theory can learn much from reading him, because in his original insights in aesthetics he is like the true artist who creates and discovers new meanings and values through his art.

Animadversions on the Autonomy of Art

Lee B. Brown

Lee B. Brown is Associate Professor of Philosophy at Ohio State University, and previously taught at Roosevelt University and Northwestern University. He studied at the University of Utah, the University of California, and Northwestern University. "As a student of Professor Vivas," he writes, "I learned whatever I know about the study of literature." His articles on aesthetics and metaphysics have been published in various journals.

ONE

The aim of this paper is to isolate and stress one of
the Kantian aspects of Professor Vivas' aesthetic
theory at the expense of the other. I will attempt to
make inroads into his theory of the autonomy of the
aesthetic experience, and hope thereby to strengthen
his constitutive idealist theory of art. Any attempt to
separate Vivas' theory into more and less acceptable
parts is a dangerous undertaking, for one of the prime
features of his writing is its systematic character. Although he has never written a treatise covering all the
arts thoroughly, his work has a conceptual unity quite
uncharacteristic of most mid-century aesthetics in the
Anglo-American scene. He may be charged with in-
completeness in important particulars—as in the vex-

ing topic of creativity—but all the questions he takes up
he deals with while keeping an eye on the whole fabric.
The result is thoroughly systematic. And his writings
have a weightiness almost totally lacking in modern
Anglo-American literature. There is a sense of urgency,
a sense that one cannot say one thing one place, however compelling, without danger of sacrificing profoundly important territory in other areas. The hermetic
activity of analyzing the logic of "good reasons" may
get short shrift at his hands, but substantive values in
virtue of which art gets aesthetic and moral praise are
asserted with great force.

The history of aesthetics exhibits a tension between
two extremes. One finds on the one hand attempts
(which go back to antiquity) to bind the Beautiful to
the True, and the True, in turn, to the Good. At the
other end of the spectrum, there is a tradition, fostered
more by Kant than by anyone else, which attempts to
liberate the aesthetic from all foreign entanglements.
We may date the beginning of modern aesthetics with
Kant's rigorous formulation of the nature of beauty as
contrasted with whatever may be mistaken for it. But
modern aesthetics also appeals to his epistemology.
Diverse as they be, the theories of Croce, Collingwood,
Frye, Cassierer, Langer, Gombrich, Goodman, and of
course Vivas, are anchored firmly in the Kantian tradition. Kant taught the moderns the purification rites in
honor of the aesthetic; at the same time his epistemology provided directions for amplifying his position
in boldly different directions.

Let us frame a statement of the claim of aesthetic autonomy in such terms as Vivas would accept. Aesthetic experience, it is said, is experience which although not essentially tied to emotion, may nevertheless be described in terms of an intensity of involvement— raptness, Vivas calls it—which is a response to the unity of the object. It involves an organized self-sufficiency such that the mind is inhibited from being led outside into broader chains of connection. Transitive inquiries such as preoccupy ethical or scientific modes of apprehension are inhibited. Before we proceed to come to terms with such a theory, we might pause for a brief apology to Kant, since we should recall that his defense of the autonomy of beauty was not, after all, a defense of the autonomy of poetry, indeed not even of art in general, although his qualifying considerations seem most pertinent to poetry. Whoever connects Kant with "art for art's sake" forgets the important *caveats* which belong to his theory. For he maintained that in spite of the "purposeless purpose" of the beautiful, beauty and the faculty of taste may have ends other than their own perfection in giving discipline to the production of *ideas*. This is primarily true of poetry, which in the tradition is therefore usually said to be the "highest" of the arts. The abstractions which are fitting objects of the pure faculty of taste include, as perfect instances, wallpaper design, leaves, or crystalline structures. These may be perfect examples of the purely beautiful, but even Kant understood that restricted to such stuff, the science of aesthetics would be refined down to a rather precious residue. In poetry we have what Kant called adherent beauty.

TWO

Now for Vivas, the autonomy thesis is qualified by the constitutive idealist thesis, which says that what art does, by its symbolic resources, is to put the world "at our disposal." I would like to try to disengage and impugn the autonomy thesis. I will experimentally attempt to violate the supposed purity of the aesthetic by considering some features of art in general, and specifically of poetry and fiction, the usual focus of Vivas' work. There is an *appearance* of conflict between the two theses, of course, for the one steers us away from viewing art *qua* art as instructive, referential, or true, while the second seems to take the opposite line. The Vivas answer is that there are apprehensions of, and uses of, art which, however important, are just not aesthetic. I will play the devil's advocate and see if I can find some implausibility in this claim, while reinforcing the idealist thesis. Later I will try to remove Vivas' main objection to the idea that the real world is the essential reference of art.

Clearly Vivas does not deny that we apprehend and relate the elements of the intransitively perceived object. He does deny, though, that the object's function is to refer us to things beyond it. But what about fictional beings? We may claim that there is such reference right from the start in literature, and we can see this by asking about the denotation of the proper names and descriptions of the text. Hence there come crowding into being Hamlet, Emma, Falstaff, and Minnie Mouse, the great presumably crowding together with the small. Several classical answers were proposed to dodge commitment to these Platonic beings. The sentences are all false, or devoid of truth value, or involve a language use called "story telling" (but what is story telling?). I will not consider those theories here. (None of them explains the reference of fiction to the actual world, by the way.) A brief look at this realm of fictional subsistents will be instructive as to the commitments of the Vivas theory, however.

When Vivas says that a poem is, *qua* poem, nonreferential, it is not obvious that he means this to rule out Meinongian subsistents as the referents of terms. Indeed, in his own fashion he introduces a domain of subsistents, as we shall see. But the question this raises is: What do we denote by the term "poem"? When Vivas says that a poem is nonreferential, *qua* aesthetic, he need not imply the denial of the domain of subsistents. For, in saying that a poem is nonreferential, he might not mean the word "poem" to denote a text, i.e.; inscriptions. What is claimed to be nonreferential might be the self-enclosed "world" which is "of" the text, or realized from it through a "proper" reading, and into which we imaginatively enter, even to the point of having a vivid sense of what Vivas calls a "superior knowledge."[1] Such imaginary worlds include as *inhabitants* those worthies just mentioned. So, Vivas might be saying that such a *world,* apprehended aesthetically, does not as such have some essentially aesthetic reference outside itself. In that case, he may indeed embrace Meinongian subsistents. To call attention to them, however, is not in itself to point to some reference lying beyond the poem which contradicts the intransitivity thesis. He must agree, of course, that this still leaves unexplained the semantic connection which is subsequently established between the work and the world. But it must be admitted that no one has ever said anything perfectly clear about this point, beyond some rough-and-ready psychology.

The last remark exposes *my* central consideration: Fiction is essentially *of* or *about* the world, whether mediated by subsistents or not. This fact usually strikes us more forcibly in poems of an admitted philosophical nature, but it seems to be quite generally the case. For works of literature *all* show human beings in a certain light, or *under a certain description,* just as pictures show, for example, peasants as noble, suffering, patient, strong, lazy, or stupid. We are not forced to give up the dimension of novelty, and hence of creativity, in such denotings. Nor is it given up if the fiction *idealizes* the subject matter, for it is still actuality which is ideal-

---

[1] Eliseo Vivas, *Creation and Discovery* (Chicago: Henry Regnery Co., 1955), p. 204. (Henceforth cited as *CD.*)

ized. This point is quite basic, and I am not sure how to prove it.

But what about entertainments, or fantasies? Dorothy Sayers gives us somewhat recognizable beings, e.g., gentlemen located in London. But is any such connection necessary? Well, yes, some such analogy with the world *is* necessary, and in a sense there is no *pure* literary fantasy. This idea may seem to reduce to the old idea about imitative plausibility, and I would admit it if my caveats were not so extensive. After all, our demands for connections with reality are quite humble. We require no all-embracing realism, but only a modicum of consistent connection. Given this, we will quite easily bypass strangeness, and even absurdity, in order to "live in" a story. Kafka bears witness to this.[2] And there are *kinds* of connection. Kafka's is not Fielding's, and none is *preferred*. But we do require some such basis, and even in "Jabberwocky," for example, we know that something is, physically, doing something. Whether everything strange is supposed to be transcribed into allegorical matching, or whether, on the other hand, we sometimes have some quite original reconstruction of experience, is a question which no simple rule could decide for us. Either way, we have contact with the world. We would also remember that the world so invoked is a world *as* standardly conceived.

---

[2] Kafka prompts a dream-like vision in which horrors are treated as relative commonplaces, as one might in a dream rather calmly watch injuries to one's body in a strangely denatured apprehension.

We need not necessarily be referring to brute fact. The error is in thinking that *either* there is a clean break with reality, *or* mere dull imitationism. We are not committed to slavish literalness, and the point seems to be compatible with novelty and creativity. We are not committed to some crude empiricist idea of creation as a mere reshuffling of experiences we have had.

Now these presuppositions may all be granted, and yet, Vivas could reply that they don't really count, since, although granted, they "drop out" of the aesthetic experience. (Certainly such references are usually only "facilitating," and not part of the *point* of the fiction. They are mere means to an imaginative enactment.) Well, even here I am not so sure, since it seems to me that various literary reactions to "realism"—Robbe-Grillet, for example—play with these presuppositions in intrinsically interesting ways. But I will not stake everything on the point.

The kind of reference to the world which is most often brought up has to do with specific themes: ideational material; theses; or the entertaining of options about the meaning of life, the relationship of man to God, the nature of freedom and justice, and so on. Now such material surely does pertain to the world. The tragic antinomy posed by Dostoyevesky and brilliantly analyzed in one of Vivas' pieces is not simply a statement about some rarefied possible world which Leibniz' deity didn't fulgurate. Dostoyevsky may have been presenting potentialities, but they are put forth as *real* potentialities pertaining to existence, and a prime purpose of such fiction is to direct our minds to the world in important ways. In works of great significance, of course, the world is denoted by means of highly original structurings, some of which may finally become part of our mental outlook.

The activity of fitting a poem or fiction to actuality involves making delicate discriminations and connections, but with no set tolerances of error. Such activities, being curious, inquisitive, and searching, clearly smack of the cognitive. To invoke them seems part of the clear *intention* of many works of literature, and it seems hardly reasonable to view responses to those demands as mere *breaks* in some *correct* reaction to art as art. If we do, the existence of the idea which exercised such intellectual demands ought to be thought of as an aesthetic flaw! Of course Vivas holds that if such material, in or between the lines, is not transfigured into pure dramatically organized structures, then it *is* an intrusion. But surely the story of the Grand Inquisitor exercises a pull the other way, and such examples make one loath to draw the line as Vivas does.

To this one might add the fact that whatever precious stuff we isolate as *the* aesthetic elixir, it seems rather evanescent. As one's involvement with important work deepens, it grows in other dimensions. Sometimes that original fire is rekindled. Other times the old magic is gone forever, when we see, finally, how shallow the substance really is. If the substance seems perversely selected (Celine), garbled (Hesse), cranky (Lawrence), we feel the tension between whatever we originally denominated "aesthetic" and these other factors. Gradually, we do not see these flaws as mere impediments to the apprehension of a beauty *taken for granted,* but as new evidence counting against the original judgment in favor.

We know very well how modern critics and theorists have attempted to banish ideas from poetic art. But it could be shown that the well-known views of Richards (pseudo-statements) and of Eliot (objective correlatives) are each attempts to have the cake and eat it too. These theories either say that poetry is concerned with a purely nonideational expression of emotion (or a kind of music of ideas, where the sound and some conceptually accidental connotations have some effect on emotion or feeling); or, they must admit the function of ideas as *such,* whether attended by expressive dimensions or not. Sometimes a large part of the burden of this issue is put on the question of whether publishing a book containing *apparent* assertions is really tantamount to making an assertion—hence of demanding a response to the question of truth. But if there are clearly "pseudo assertions" in literature, quite apart from whether they were seriously *meant* or not (actually I see no reason to doubt that they are), then the question of whether they are *really* asserted seems of little importance. They are provided intentionally, and are meant to elicit *some* cognitive response, even if not seeking definite assent. Vivas could argue that such assertions are unpoetic intrusions into art, and the distinctive character of much of his critical work would testify to this.[3] In practice, though, it seems to me that he does make room for some weak sense in which claims are made by works of fiction. He writes, for instance, of material in Dreiser which "contradicts" the amateur philosophizing about "chemisms."[4] And, although Dostoyevsky is praised for not rigging the data, and presenting *options,* still his novels are said to give a way of viewing human destiny, a specific form of anti-rationalism.[5] And there does seem to be a difference between gross didacticism and the presentation of philosophically pointed visions; and whether they be called assertions or not, they have been intentionally included in the fiction. They are calculated to merit at least our consideration, although not necessarily requiring a decision on our part.

But we know, alas, that none of this evidence based on intentional reference to the world, ideational content, or "showing as" will prove the point to Vivas, who can always say in reply that although what we have mentioned may be, intellectually, morally, culturally, of the greatest significance, still it is not aesthetically sig-

---

[3] They are in the spirit of Croce's masterful essay on Stendhal's unconscious irony.

[4] *CD,* pp. 11 ff.   [5] *CD,* p. 106.

nificant, save as part of the fabric of an organized world
of the fiction. In order to add any weight to these considerations, we must find more decisive evidence.

A book may be referential simply by instancing a recognized pattern—mythical types are usually cited—and
this does not imply a slavish copying. For the pattern
is not supposed to show the *only* way the world is. And
in interesting cases, the reference involves a *variation
on* themes known from other works, as in cases such as
Ulysses, or a satire by Dr. Johnson. In some cases the
cross reference is a kind of Hegelian reference by negation. The novels of Robbe-Grillet, read in pristine aesthetic intransitivity, would lose much of their point,
which is their *refusal* to live up to the structural demands traditional forms have taught us to make. They
are denials *of* stereotypical patterns, and this self-
conscious connection is virtually part of the substance
of the fiction. As with many efforts of modernism, they
are comments both on themselves, and on their anti-
theses.[6]

We can, in addition, explicitly state and capitalize
upon Vivas' claims about the cultural function of
poetry. If the substance of it becomes, subsequently,
part of our very mental equipment, and thereby refers
to the world, why should we exclude these factors as

---

[6] Robbe-Grillet's break with "realistic psychology" probably fails just
because of his refusal to supply motivations in the standard way. The
result is that *we* supply them by appealing to the very naturalistic
patterns his fiction is meant to supplant.

pertinent? But again, we probably come to an impasse. Professor Vivas will say that these cross references, however critically, philosophically, or art-historically relevant they are, are not aesthetic matters. Our devil's advocacy has still not made a dent in the armor.

Of course a nice question at this point might be how anyone *could* disprove the point. Vivas and I disagree as to whether a single quality or essence should characterize the aesthetic. I seem to be very catholic about what I am willing to take as aesthetically relevant. (Note: To the vexing meta-aesthetic question underlying this, I will not turn. I believe that on some occasions, Vivas has himself raised doubts about natural kinds.[7]) As it is, of course, someone else might isolate his own aesthetic elixir. For instance, there is a *relatively* common response to art, of no little value, which can only be described as a rushing up of emotion, a thrill in effect. Possibly this is what poor Clive Bell, so often ridiculed, had in mind when he talked about his aesthetic emotion. One might turn to this rather warmer phenomenon as the true essence of the matter.

THREE

But I do not want to gain the point by simply asking "who's to say?" There is an argument against the Vivas

[7] Eliseo Vivas, *The Artistic Transaction* (Columbus: Ohio State University Press, 1963), p. 256. (Henceforth cited as *AT*.)

position, based upon psychological or epistemological considerations which I think *will* be decisive. It is instructive, since, as I view the history of these matters, it stems from a neo-Kantian quarter. The point of the argument is that aesthetic perception has intrinsic conceptual components. Our perceiving is always a perceiving *as,* and so we cannot *separately* apprehend and mediate. (To attempt such a shift would give us just *another* seeing as.) Let me give a rather specialized, but instructive, example. One looks at a picture by Matisse, and the results may seem to approximate Vivas' purist account. But now compare that with viewing a great retrospective show of his works. One can hardly help but compare this with the *relatively* thin experience of a single work in isolation. (Forget the expert, whose mind may be in constant control of the master's works, whether they be in front of him or not.) In this context, one is aware of connections between a picture and earlier and later stages in the evolution of the man's imagination. But surely this interaction is aesthetically significant, and through it we learn more, and discern more in the individual works. We see particular examples as stages in the development of a style or technique.[8] Now even here, the purist may balk. Perhaps it will be said that all of this is external and propaedeutic, or that the Matisse

---

[8] A slightly different example is what one learns about Vermeer *after* culling out the famous forgeries and comparing them as groups.

collection constitutes a rather extended art object. But these are somewhat specialized examples of a state of affairs which pervades all aesthetic perception, and which cannot in general be explained away.

The simple fact is that we hear fugues *as* fugues, sonatas *as* sonatas. We read a sonnet as a sonnet, and look at a church as Gothic or Romanesque. To listen to a Chopin ballad as a classical piece is a kind of error. The examples may be multiplied, and one will see that no aesthetic perception is free from these conceptual factors, which often amount to concepts nested in concepts. Now if this evidence is pertinent, we are of course referred to the question of genres, and finally to intentions.[9] We cannot press the issue into all its ramifications. On genres and intentions, Vivas has decided views.[10]

Saying that all aesthetic seeing involves seeing *as* allows that, in principle, one may shift one's stance, as it were, so that an impressionist picture might be seen as a horrible example of neo-classicism. Or, a

---

[9] See Kendall Walton, "The Categories of Art," *Philosophical Review,* Vol. 79 (1970), pp. 334–367.

[10] I am uncertain as to his exact position about literary classes. See "Literary Classes: Some Problems," *Genre,* 1968. He states, somewhat sympathetically, the old Crocean and nominalist complaints against genres, but then suggests that whatever their philosophical status, we just do use them anyway, although sometimes to ludicrous extremes. And he seems to admit that in some way the appeal to genres is aesthetically useful, but he does not seem to recognize that they function as components implicitly appealed to when we perceive some x *as* a ψ.

neo-classicist picture may be seen as an utterly abstract organization, a cubist picture as an exercise in academic realism. Anyway, one might attempt such viewings. Clearly the lack of appropriate concepts at first blocks the reception of one such as Cezanne. Fry and others taught us the concepts. The point is that some ways of seeing are utterly inappropriate, and responses and judgments based on them are without validity. And we cannot talk about a response being appropriate without lateral reference to classes of things lying beyond the object perceived. Otherwise we will stare hopelessly at the object and, failing that, grasp desperately at concepts which we pray might help. We need to know some traditions, rules, assumptions, categories, before we can make sense of the art of an alien culture. Indian ragas, primitive carvings, and Japanese graphics may provide experience—indeed, intransitive experience!—when popularly translated into our terms. They are not therefore grasped in their own terms, however.[11]

---

[11] But what about the sight of an exquisite, fragile, plastic form, the origin of which may be utterly unknown? There may be responses to certain fundamental lines and shapes, or proportions of them, which is always positive and virtually universal. Birkhoff and others tried to isolate them. Well, if such is closely connected with the beautiful, then, alas, there seems to be plenty of aesthetic contexts in which beauty is not relevant. This is not new. In the Eighteenth Century, a search started for other concepts, as witness the career of the concept of the subline. Certainly expressiveness may spill beyond the bounds of the proportionate. There are surely contexts in which exquisite and graceful lines are out of place.

FOUR

When we turn to the technicalities of Vivas' own theory, and the reasons why it moves away from what we have been urging, we must, unfortunately, compress matters a bit. His statements on the topic are many, complex, and demanding. These remarks do not by any means constitute an exhaustive commentary on the numberless insights and controversial points in his theory. We must focus on a single conceptual connection the breaking of which might at least partly convince Vivas to yield. The issue has to do with ontology.

Professor Vivas spoke, as we saw, of a "superior sense of reality" as part of the intransitive experience of artistic literature. And he is quite right that one does experience a kind of "living in" the world of a great novel. It is fundamentally this which brings Vivas to matters of ontology. He asks how this "sense of superior reality" is to be explained, and denies what he formerly held, namely, that the intransitivity could itself psychologically explain the other dimension of the aesthetic experience, namely its conviction of reality. Instead, we must have recourse to ontology, as explaining it, at least in certain cases.[12] Looking at a leaf does not presumably qualify as giving the particular sort of sense of reality Vivas intends. The explanation has to do with the vision of the object in or "of" the poem—a value-

---

[12] *CD,* pp. 212–213.

freighted, self-sufficient world having some status in being.[13]

Now I believe that two phenomena need to be considered here. They ought to be distinguished, and they do not constitute equally solid basis for any ontology. On the one hand, from Plotinus to Goethe to Vivas, it has been said that the artist has "seen" something to which others are blind. There is a vision of some dimension beyond the everyday world, and perhaps even beyond the poem (which in some way is nevertheless a symbol of it). Now this I should interpret, not as a reaching into any transcendental metaphysical realm, although the shock of great art may tempt us to put it in these terms. Art may so radically reorganize the stuff of experience, that its message may seem to take us out of the world altogether. I believe that this is the root of much of Vivas' thinking. But when we look at the explicit grounds he cites as rationalia for the *entrée* of ontology, we are less certain as to his meaning.

In some cases, it appears that he is speaking of the slipping "into" the world of the novel, as if it were a reality of some sort. In that case, the conviction of which Vivas speaks sounds a good deal like make-believe, especially considering the appeal to the eloquent descriptions of William James.[14] We should

---

[13] *CD*, pp. 204–205.
[14] *CD*, p. 203.

recognize that, except in pathological cases, we only have make-believe, and not belief, although the make-believe is of course facilitated by the story structure, and may seem quite effortless. Now Vivas seems to think that a sense of conviction has something to do with the issue, but it is hard to know what this sense of conviction amounts to so that it deserves an ontological grounding in subsistent entities. Even if make-believe involved a kind of conviction, such conviction surely does not provide grounds for the truth of the conviction! And it is not easy to see what conviction has to do with the positing of subsistent beings. We do not after all make-believe that something *sub*sists. What, indeed, could that even mean? The Meinongian view can begin with imaginings of any sort, whether they have conviction or not. Conviction doesn't give them ontological weight.

But Vivas also cites L. A. Reid, who, I think, doesn't have quite the Jamesian point in mind about "living in" a story.[15] In part Reid has in mind the apprehension of something as transcendental, as *perfect,* and Vivas himself undoubtedly holds that great art becomes a sort of model of what existence "ought to be." This of course has little to do with "living in" a story, or a related sense of conviction. Thus, a vision of value might be of basic importance to understanding Vivas' theory, although the cue from Reid seems to refer to the value *of*

[15] *CD,* p. 203–204.

the art object, whereas the ontological account presented by Vivas has more to do with a vision of value which is *part of* the fabric of organized experience presented by poetry, and would be illustrated, for instance, by the love and faith conveyed in the *Brothers* by Dostoyevsky. That is different from the value *of* the novel, of course. But let us see how the theory is sketched.

It is presented as the resolution of an apparent contradiction between the fact that art gives us knowledge (which seems to involve reference and transitivity) and the fact that art is aesthetically perceived intransitively or self-sufficiently.[16] And however we solve this, we must avoid the pitfalls of imitation theory that cannot account for our inability to translate and to paraphrase poetry.[17] So, saying what it is we know, and hence avoiding utter formalism, while not yielding to imitation theory, poses the problem. And the answer is that the knowledge which poetry gives us is only a vision of subsistent values or meanings.[18] The intransitivity thesis is saved, for the vision does *not* involve a semantic relationship to existence.[19] We have a vision, not of something actual, but of something which could never-

---

[16] *CD*, p. 172.

[17] *CD*, pp. 164, 387–388.

[18] *CD*, p. 191.

[19] There will emerge, in the subsequent incorporations of the meanings into culture, such a reference.

theless be actualized, that may be incorporated into our
mental and cultural framework.[20]

The theory is challenging. From one point of view,
it means the sense of poetry is not external to the poetry,
but is, rather, immanent.[21] On the other hand, the object as embodied in the poetry is said to be *different*
from the subsistents lying beyond it, since we may say
that the immanent meaning is particularized by being
clothed in the unique garb of the poem. As embodied,
these meanings are termed "insistents."[22] Presumably,
we only grasp the meaning *in* the poem. That is, *we*
have no independent access to it. As for the poet, I do
not know whether, or how, he, unlike us, sees beyond
into the transcendental realm. In one place, Vivas appears to cast doubt on the very possibility of a grasp of
unsubstanced, purely intelligible objects.[23] At the same
time, the *subsistent* is the referent of the poem. But the
problem is that either this semantic connection is functional or it is not. If it is not, then why not simply hold
that the reference of the art is to the *world,* but to a

---

[20] I pass over what appears to be a hesitation in the texts on the question as to whether poetic resources ever can denote independently
existing things, e.g., by means of resemblances between those attributes and the things denoted. The alternative is that such denotation is
possible, but of low worth.

[21] *CD*, p. 122.

[22] *CD*, pp. 134, 213.

[23] "Reality in Literature," *Iowa Review,* Vol. 1, No. 4. Fall 1970, pp.
123–124.

world conceived in new terms? One of Vivas' specifications of this general theory is termed a constitutive symbol, and in his account of it as employed by Lawrence, we are told that such symbols are charged with a power to plumb the depths of personality and to communicate this to us.[24] We can grant that, by a dramatic organization of experience, human beings are shown in a fresh light which, however untranslatable into the sentential forms of behaviorist psychology books, still conveys information to us along a complex network of semantic avenues (including expressive ones[25]). We maintain, however, that the reference is *still* existence.

If we take the semantic relationship seriously, then we do have a *kind* of imitation theory[26] except that ordinary imitation theory has an edge. By invoking such concepts as similarity, it can explain the semantic connection. As far as I can tell, the semantic connection on Vivas' theory is inexplicable. True, the domain of subsistence (of which poets discover members) explains the fact that poetry gives us cognitions of something,

[24] Eliseo Vivas, *D. H. Lawrence: The Failure and the Triumph of Art* (Evanston, Ill.: Northwestern University Press, 1960), pp. 290–291.
[25] For a theory of expression, with the obscurities removed, see Nelson Goodman, *Language of Art* (Indianapolis: The Bobbs-Merrill Company, 1968), pp. 85–95.
[26] I won't worry about why this isn't at least a slight contradiction of the intransitivity thesis.

rather than merely *re*cognitions.[27] Again, *I* would like to say that it gives us new ways of viewing the old entities, rather than information about new ones. One senses that the "meaning in" and "meaning beyond" duality is meant precisely to cope in some way with the inexplicability of the reference to subsistence. Yes, there is a referent, but no, we can't grasp it independently (why assert that there *is* a subsistent, in that case?). So we speak of the meaning as being *immanent,* but Vivas himself has admitted that such a concept is very strange.[28] And the duality would also (in some admittedly unclear way) be responsive to the fact that there is at least a *prima facie* violation of intransitivity, for we can say that the meaning is apprehended only *in* the poem, so that the theory is consistent. One thinks of light through stained glass. Do we see it *through* or *in* the glass? Intimations of the *Jenseits* or simple internal attribute? While we see, we don't ask.

Vivas sometimes speaks of aspects revealed *through* poetry as contrasted with those revealed *in* it.[29] But we need to know what the connection is between these two sides. Let's suppose that the paraphrase gives an adequate elucidation of the subsistent. In what way is the poem itself out of gear with its referent? Perhaps

---

[27] But Vivas sometimes speaks of art not as creating, but *conserving,* value. See *AT,* p. 18.
[28] *CD,* p. 164.
[29] *CD,* p. 208.

it is too specific. But surely the paraphrase can only rely on the poem to justify its adequacy. (We do not take three things—poem, subsistent, and paraphrase—and then compare them.) In that case, the poem bears the whole responsibility, and it must *correspond* in some way to the subsistent. But in what way? Presumably it isn't a natural connection, e.g., resemblance. (A picture of a man you've never seen is, by contrast, informative.) There seems to be a mystical leap. If neither the poem nor paraphrase are adequate to the subsistent, then we seem to arrive at the same conclusion but more directly. At this point we might ask ourselves if talk about a relationship to this value-in-itself is really helpful. Drawing back and claiming that the meaning is really entirely *in* the poem simply leaves us *unclear* as to what "meaning" can mean.

Now it must be admitted that there *is* a kind of puzzle about artistic reference which doesn't stem merely from the ontology of subsistents. The symbol systems of art are referential in such a way that the reference is colored by the intrinsic features of the systems. In poetry these features of the medium are not at all easy to isolate. (Actually they are not so obvious in painting, either.) They do not (usually) have to do with the shapes of word inscriptions, although everyone knows that the sounds count. Presumably, they are properties of what is *already* a complex, namely language, and therefore include customary denotations, grammar, and the like. And within limits we can make up novel combinations of language, just as we produce novel combinations of plastic forms.

The function of artistic reference is such that the characteristics of artistic systems contribute in different ways to the conception under which objects are denoted. If a man be denoted in a picture, then certain contexts may require us to know only that it is a man. (Consider the image used at a street cross-walk.) But a painting of a man with certain flesh tones shows him exactly as *such*. In art, depiction, exemplification, and expression all do their semantic work in terms of the intrinsic attributes of the art, taken not merely bit by bit, but also as an orchestrated whole. The mystery arises when we think we ought to be able to render these "descriptions" into the stock of terms from our ordinary vocabulary, which we unreasonably assume to be some privileged or "correct" mode of transmitting information. This assumption is mistaken, as the language of gesture reminds us. Calling something "red," and pictorially denoting it with paint from a palette are not informationally equivalent. So, when we say that a Renoir denotes a healthy sexuality, we must realize that the picture itself would be utterly enervated as "translated" into some other terms, such as the terms of this sentence. For the healthy sexuality so attributed is the attribute *as* controlled by the qualities and plastic relationships of a particular picture. What we learn, we learn in the terms of the art. This, I think, does bear on the puzzlement we feel when asked to paraphrase or render it in other terms. We unwittingly assume that discursive prose is the model of communication, and yet feel the strain of trying to render other symbol systems in its terms.

My discussion is restricted. I have not dealt with the wealth of material which Vivas presents to help dispel the contradiction stated earlier in support of the ontological explanation. He appeals to historical, psychological (consciousness versus unconsciousness), and cultural material to help solve the semantic puzzle. For the most part these points seem to belong to a class of genetic accounts which, while helpful in different ways, do not on their own solve the problem, for the problem *is* an ontological-epistemological problem.

Undoubtedly issues of value theory are involved in all this. Through art, values are recognized. Are we therefore under *prima facie* obligation to espouse them? If so, then a moral or ethical role comes to the fore which would force the examination of the autonomy thesis along other lines. But if not—and Vivas does, after all, distinguish between recognized and espoused values—then it would seem more adequate to the facts to say that art provides a unique organization of experience which, to be sure, includes value espousals. I can almost completely accept Vivas' account of the Renoir whose pictures contain, he says, a *joie de vivre,* an effulgence, a healthy sexuality, a brilliance, a colorfulness which "we find in the world."[30] I would like to

---

[30] *AT,* p. 67.

add, and I'm sure he really agrees, that the picture
includes a manifold of denotative, pictorial, exemplary,
and expressive connections which allow us to see things
in fresh interconnections. (He says that Renoir allows
us "to grasp them with vividness and freshness."[31]) We
are not simply asked to recognize what we already
know and *in the same terms,* for reasons I have tried
to present. But unless we reasonably insist upon a moral
optimism in our aesthetics, we must admit that the artist
could provide us with organizations which characterize
the world in starkly life-denying terms. As to whether
these contradict Renoir and others, there is no straight-
forward answer. None of these examples gives us
merely sentential structures which either *simply* correspond or *fail* to correspond in some idealized cat-is-
on-the-mat fashion. We are influenced by degrees or
appropriateness involving mutual adjustments of facts
and symbolic representations to each other. And whatever we assume to be a sheer *given* can always be
reclassified, redescribed, reportrayed in some other
terms. Anyway, the symbol-systems of art are not translatable into those of a supposedly privileged discursive
fact-stating discourse.

The set of philosophical motivations stemming from
value theory in Vivas' account would require investi-
gations far beyond the scope of this one. I remain
content with suggesting that he would have some
ground to abandon the theory of subsistents, and the

---

[31] *AT,* p. 67.

associated theory of an autonomous aesthetic experience, if there were a way of explaining the sense in which art gives knowledge without therefore giving in to imitation theory. I think there are means for doing this, and this will take me shortly to the ultimate issue in the Vivas theory.

FIVE

Vivas considers that imitation theory presupposes some relationship of similarity or copying which is not only inconsistent with novelty but unavailable to poetry.[32] Now of course if "imitate" means "copy," there is certainly some plausibility in the complaint about imitation theory on the question of originality. Such an imitation theory would be appropriate only to realistic art. But this poses two questions: 1. Could "copying" even explain realism? 2. Would a similarity *or* a copy theory even be plausible for graphic art? Gombrich, Goodman, and others have given accounts of art which say or imply that not even "realism" can be analyzed by means of "copying," for this explanation not only ignores the role of habits and customs in pictorial perception, but presupposes mistakenly that a relevant sense of "copy" can be elucidated. It has been suggested that realism *can* be explained in terms of information "pick up," so that those pictures we know

[32] *CD,* p. 397.

how to "read" in the Gombrich sense are those taken
to be most realistic. The fact that we know how to read
them easily is not explained by any natural relationship
with reality—copying—but by their being painted in
the styles with which we are accustomed, of which we
know the idiom. The issue is, I believe, inconclusive,
but if such a theory *were* vindicated, then not even
realism in graphic art could be explained by copying.
Let us agree, for now, that it is incorrect to take either
"realism" (in the customary use of the term) *or* copying as the essence of imitationism. Indeed, we could
undoubtedly find many grounds for objection to "it, so
defined."

Pointing out that poetry apparently has no basis of
resemblance to its objects suggests that an imitation
theory framed in terms of resemblance *is,* after all,
acceptable in plastic art. Here again, recent discussions
are to the point. In the spirit of the Kantian outlook, it
has been argued that not even "picturing" can be
analyzed in terms of resemblance (resemblance, taken
with a denoting relationship, that is, since mere resemblance does not constitute picturing). Goodman, in
an interesting argument, appears to conclude from the
fact that *realism* cannot be explained in terms either of
copying or degrees of resemblance, resemblance is
therefore *no* part of the concept of "picture of."[33] Perhaps such a conclusion would be welcome to Vivas. It

---

[33] Goodman, op. cit., pp. 2–19, 34–39.

would undercut the negative point about poetry and resemblance. If we cannot even explain pictures by similarity, then it *would* seem pretty fruitless to consider literary art as imitative because of resemblance. Unfortunately, I think Goodman's argument is a *non sequitur*. It remains open, I believe, that being a picture *of* something might involve resemblance, even in relatively unrealistic cases. And it would remain *open* whether there would be some sense in which we could explain the relationship of poetry to the world by similarity. This returns us to the point about poetry. Vivas seems to be arguing hastily here. There are difficulties, of course, for poetry is a two-stage art form which obviously could not resemble its denotata in a direct way. Presumably, some imaginative realization of poetry might be said to have a structure or form which is *like* the structures or forms of life. The complexities of a full explanation of this might be discouraging, but I do not see that it should be ruled out so quickly.

On some occasions Vivas puts his point about imitation even more severely:[34]

> The object of the poem does not *exist* either as a set of particulars or as a set of universals, nor can it be for that reason grasped or apprehended independently of it.

The challenge is to shed light on how art can refer to the world without our giving way to imitation theory

---

[34] *CD,* p. 405.

and hence giving up on uniqueness and creativity. We have no right to construct a straw man in which the referentialist is a "copyist." Indeed, in these passages, Vivas seems to say that *any* reference to reality is sheerest imitationism. This is what must be challenged. Indeed, some of Vivas' own characterizations, e.g., of Renoir, do seem contrary to this thesis. And yet we do not think that Vivas has really contradicted his denial of unacceptable forms of imitation theory. What forms *are* unacceptable is precisely the question. Some elements in his theory seem to pull in the wrong direction. Perhaps they do so because it is wrongly assumed that any reference to existence *would* entail an objectionable kind of imitation theory. I can only agree with Vivas when he says that art gives us the reality "of our practical common-sense world,"[35] or that the artist gives us a "refurbished picture of our world in concrete terms."[36] I take the Kantian theme to *allow* reference, not to a pristine realm above or beyond the phenomena, but to the world. Indeed art "defines for us its sense."[37]

Our problem is that the passage cited earlier seems to challenge *any* referential dimension of art. Indeed, it would seem to impugn Vivas' own theory. In a moment we will see why he thinks it does not. The troublesome passage poses a number of questions: 1. Is *any* theory

---

[35] *CD*, p. 191.
[36] *CD*, p. 190.
[37] *CD*, p. 189

which gives art existent denotata an imitation theory
in the sense of denying creativity? Surely not, for the
art may denote or portray its object in distinctive and
novel terms. If *mere* denotation is definitive of imitation, then imitationism is not *ipso facto* incompatible
with uniqueness and novelty. 2. Is any theory which
says that the denotatum of art is available *independently* an imitation theory in the unacceptable sense?
Again the answer is no, for although the referents may
be independently available, they may not have been
available in the terms of the artistic symbolism of a
given work. Peasants are "available" independently of
Breughel, but were not therefore apprehended as *he*
apprehends them pictorially. His pictures are not therefore imitative in the sense of telling us only what we
already knew. As we saw before, art shows whatever
it shows in the terms of its intrinsic plastic means. And
something of the sort surely applies to poetry. 3. Is any
reference theory unacceptable because such reference
would have to be spelled out in terms of a resemblance
which does not invariably exist? Now this challenge
would seem to apply to the Vivas theory itself, for he
pretty clearly thinks of the semantics of poetry as *not*
involving similarity. It is almost as if he plays up this
lack of similarity in order to exhibit the difference between his view and imitation, but imposes upon the
imitationist the very resemblance which alone would
explain the semantic connection! If the point has to
do with the lack of resembling factors in poetry, we

have commented on that already. Actually, though, I think the question about similarity is located in our final question. 4. Is no reference theory acceptable because, involving resemblances as it must, creativity and uniqueness would be nullified? Here, we confront Vivas' basic assumption.

It may seem that if art denotes via resembling relationships, then art can never give us anything genuinely fresh and new, for all we are doing is reading off shuffled-up relationships of resemblance. Such a theory might as well be classified with the unacceptable copy theory of art. But it would be a mistake to do so. A work of art involves a network of denotative relationships which have to do with resemblances, to be sure, but for one thing, in the orchestrated whole it is implausible to think we have a pulverizable set of similarity-facts each of which we are acquainted with *as such* and quite independently. And even if there *be* similarity, how do we gauge as an overall phenomenon? Is the academic realist picture of Rouen more or less similar to its subject than the impressionist one? And when we consider the role of "reading" habits in our interpretation of art, which Gombrich more than anyone has brought into focus, we might well wonder if saying that some art resembles reality doesn't really conceal the fact that it is more like some relatively standardized *representation* of reality. The question is how far to go with this relativism. Goodman, who seems to want to break the resemblance connection altogether as *founding* any semantic link, may go too far. Nevertheless, it does seem hopeless to try to explain the informative role of art in terms of a gauging of objective degrees of similarity. Where, precisely, do supposedly *given* relationships leave off, and created ones take up? Or, if we want to say that *all* these relationships are "real," still no *coherent* vision of the world could but be selective, putting some connections in relief, and treating others as impertinent.

I have before me an ancient herbal with illustrations of ferns, which I am quite content to assign to art. Ostensibly, these pictures are meant to be graphically accurate, and to denote their referents as they are in themselves. But I have second thoughts about that. The colors are quite attractive, but I'm not sure I *do* want to call them accurate. A less pedantic treatment might seem more "real," more in line with stereotypical representations. Indeed, these pictures are quite specialized, and have the effect of putting certain botanical, identifying marks in relief, as it were—netted veins, wavy margins, toothed edges, fruit dots, perpendicularity, and the other referents of an identifying *vocabulary*. I no longer know if I am confronting some exact correspondence with the world. In *my* case, my image of ferns is probably somewhat controlled by these rather specialized illustrations.

Resemblances there are, but they do not constitute a stock of givens which are merely reshuffled. They are endlessly modified by subject matter, context, associative, and expressive aspects.[38] And there is what one might call feedback, which complicates the situation. The movements of a dance exemplify dynamic forms, and by their means, various denoted actions may be related. Thus, being shy and being sly may be shown *as* having connecting links, which we didn't see before. But furthermore, the very actions exemplified (head turned, bent at an angle) are, as a *result,* seen as exemplifying *expressive* properties not necessarily picked out in a purely abstract movement.[39] And it is well known that in metaphor, the frame does not merely affect our perception of the focus, but there is an influence in the other direction as well. The tired example of denoting men as wolves still illustrates this: The metaphor somewhat humanizes the wolf, making him a bit more polite, less ferocious, a *little* like a gentleman.[40] There is no doubt that a metaphor involves similarities between the focus and the frame. But a metaphor cannot be said to copy reality in any sense which rules out creativity. Nor does it give us merely what we already know. It reorganizes our perception of

---

[38] This is consistent with the "given" having a status relativized to some *customary* framework.

[39] There is a mystique, or alternatively, a suspicion, about expression. Clearly, I assume it can be dispelled by a proper analysis of its semantics. Suffice it to say here that I mean *objective* semantic connections, not psychological processes. I am aware of Professor Vivas' doubts about the topic.

[40] Max Black, *Metaphor, Proceedings of the Aristotelian Society,* Vol. 55 (1954–1955),

the world in fresh terms, and in such a way that the boundaries among types of entities are redrawn. Our picture of the world is indeed refurbished.

I fear that I must quarrel with Vivas' attempt to bring the metaphor into line with the theory of intransitivity by saying that metaphors are apprehended as "immanent component(s) of the object."[41] (Aesthetically, all the metaphorical relations are "internal.") This seems to be a way of taking the famous Richards formulation—itself a metaphor!—quite literally: Vehicle and tenor "fuse" into one another.[42] Thus, into our Kantian world enter *meanings,* which somehow *fuse* (presumably the denotata do not fuse), and this fusion is an object of aesthesis. Certainly this is creativity with a vengeance. But what is it to say that meanings fuse? I can attach sense to this in terms of assuming a relaxation of the restrictions on the applicability of terms, so that entities are grouped in novel ways, thus bringing out features hitherto unknown. So it is that one says that the metaphor *creates* similarity. Indeed, we put things together which we may even have assigned to different categories, as in "furnished souls." Such reorganization of the boundaries may "take" and finally become stale. While still alive, they pull together supposedly disconnected things, thus concentrating in an identification or predication a host of unstated, and

---

[41] *CD,* p. 227.
[42] *AT,* p. 180.

probably unstatable, similarities. In the sense of re-mapping the world, I can understand the explanation of metaphor as a fusion.

The issue of metaphor interestingly brings to the fore the connection between poetry and physics. Vivas analogizes the two at one point in order to remind us that the poet no more invents his sculpture than does "the physicist when the latter discovers the laws of the physical world."[43] Clearly this is one of those passages in which creativity, in the Kantian sense, is being pushed far in the background—indeed, out the back door—for it is doubtful that Vivas thinks of Galileo as creative in a constitutive sense. The analogy tries to make us see both artist and physicist as confronting some objectivity. It is not helpful, of course in explain-ing subsistents, or the methodology for the discovery of them. What is more important, though, is that Vivas' theory of truth in science seems to be an utterly un-Kantian correspondence view. For instance, he adverts to the positivist notion that metaphor in science is really translatable into hard empirical cash.[44] At the root of such a theory is a kind of un-Kantian assumption of some objective given to which science, when properly translated, conforms itself. But surely scientific theory is itself rooted in fundamental and distinctive concep-tual models of the world which have elements we could

---

[43] *CD*, p. 192.
[44] *AT*, p. 183.

only call metaphorical. We tend to objectify, and somewhat patronize, the root metaphors of the past (e.g., billiard-ball materialism), while discounting our own and assuming that we have been liberated into the clear air of utterly naked data supporting our (almost) finally true theories. So, we come finally to the question of truth. For Vivas there is no artistic knowledge, except in the rather specialized sense of revealing values. The subsequent assimilation of art into culture is, strictly speaking, not an aesthetic matter. If there *were* artistic knowledge, Vivas wonders what would verify it.[45] Again, we seem to be stuck on demands posed from the quarter of correspondence theory realism. We are asking for objective, uncolored facts or data which confirm sentential forms, as in the spirit of positivism. A thorough-going Kantianism would hold, I think, that truth in science is always a matter of a two-way accommodation of facts and theories. Facts which seem to disconfirm theories are always reclassifiable *in the terms of the theory.* Some would go so far as to say it isn't exactly truth which physics is after, since no theory is, as Goodman puts it, *quite* true. Granted, this leaves us with the question of how physics, poetry, and painting really differ, and the whole story has, to be sure, never been told. The clue may be in the dominance in different systems of different syntactic and semantic characteristics. Different systems give us different pic-

---

[45] *CD,* p. 172.

tures of the ways in which the elements of the world are connected. How are the elements connected *in themselves?* Perhaps an "in itself" independent of *any* symbolic mapping of it would be, in Kant's words, nothing to us.

The Kantian motifs are alive, I believe, in much of Vivas' aesthetics, but not in all of it. I want to stress what I think is the best side of his theory, but of course I cannot be sure that I speak for him when I say what I think is best.

Vivas, Lawrence, Eliot, and the Demon

Russell Kirk

Russell Kirk has been professor of history, politics, or literature at several universities and colleges. A native of Michigan, he is the only American to hold the highest arts degree of St. Andrews, the senior Scottish university. He is the author of numerous books, among them The Conservative Mind, John Randolph of Roanoke, Eliot and His Age, Beyond the Dreams of Avarice, Edmund Burke, *and, most recently,* The Roots of American Order.

History is not the work of men but of Man, the creature whom we write with a capital "M"—the animal that stumbles through time from one stupidity into another, the angelic beast or the bestial angel, the inhabitant of the city of Man and not of the City of God, who in the pursuit of virtue embraces sin, in the lust for happiness is led to misery, and in the search for God often runs into the Devil's arms. If there is one thing even more false than the belief in progress, it is the belief in progress in reverse.

—Eliseo Vivas, "Allen Tate as Man of Letters," in *Creation and Discovery*

Throughout Eliseo Vivas' writings there runs the name of D. H. Lawrence. Vivas admires Lawrence, and he detests Lawrence. That novelist was a "dribbling liar" (Lawrence's own phrase), Vivas tells us repeatedly; Vivas suggests several times that Lawrence was a coward; and Lawrence's Dark God is not adored by Eliseo Vivas. Nevertheless, Lawrence means a great deal to the moral philosopher who is his severe critic.

One is reminded now and again of T. S. Eliot on Lawrence. His antipathy to Lawrence remained, Eliot said late in life, "on the ground of what seems to me egotism, a strain of cruelty, and a failing in common with Thomas Hardy—the lack of a sense of humour." Yet Eliot published five of Lawrence's stories or sketches in *The Criterion,* defended Lawrence's paintings against the censors in 1929, and in 1960 stood ready to appear as a witness for the defense in the *Lady Chatterly* case.

This similarity of opinion notwithstanding, Vivas reproves Eliot's "severe animadversions on Lawrence's views," in Vivas' *D. H. Lawrence: the Failure and Triumph of Art* (1960). Vivas concludes his critical examination of the novelist with the argument that Lawrence has positive values as well as negative ones, declaring that for Lawrence we need "a study that corrects the exaggerations of such critics as Mr. Eliot" and the aspersions on Lawrence by Bertrand Russell.

Now I venture to suggest that both these critics, Vivas and Eliot, found in Lawrence penetrating insights; and found there, too, spiritual corruption. For both of them, the Demon lurked behind Lawrence.

Vivas quotes a passage in Eliot's *After Strange Gods* (1934), in which Eliot discerns in Lawrence "the fruitful operations of the Evil Spirit today." Eliot's criticism of Lawrence, an exercise in the moral imagination (as

contrasted with the idyllic imagination and the diabolic
imagination), is worth considering at greater length.
"What I have been leading up to," Eliot said of Lawrence then, "is the following assertion: that when
morals cease to be a matter of tradition and orthodoxy
—that is, of the community formulated, corrected, and
elevated by the continuous thought and direction of
the Church—and when each man is to elaborate his
own, then personality becomes a thing of alarming importance." Eliot finds the personality of Thomas Hardy
repellent, and turns to "a very much greater genius, if
not a greater artist, than Hardy: D. H. Lawrence." He
calls Lawrence ridiculous, what with his lack of a sense
of humour, his snobbery, his want "of the critical faculties which education should give," and his incapacity
for coherent thought. (Vivas' strictures upon Lawrence,
over the years, have been almost identical with these.)
And, Eliot adds, Lawrence suffered from sexual mor-
bidity—a failing that Vivas examines in much greater
detail.

Then Eliot proceeds to say that Lawrence was dependent upon an "Inner Light," in disregard of tradition and authority: "The point is that Lawrence
started life wholly free from any restriction of tradition
and institution, that he had no guidance except the
Inner Light, the most untrustworthy and deceitful guide
that ever offered itself to wandering humanity. It was
particularly so for Lawrence, who does not appear to
have been gifted with the faculty of self-criticism, ex-

cept in flashes, even to the extent of ordinary worldly shrewdness. Of divine illumination, it may be said that probably every man knows when he has it, but that any man is likely to think that he has it when he has it not; and even when he has had it, the daily man that he is may draw wrong conclusions from the enlightenment which the momentary man has received: no one, in short, can be the sole judge of whence his inspiration comes."

It is here that Vivas takes up the defense of Lawrence. "Lawrence, of course, never concealed that he relied on his Inner Light," Vivas replied to Eliot twenty-five years later. "But reliance on the Inner Light is not necessarily wrong. What other source of truth does a prophet have when he rises against a moribund orthodoxy, against one that he takes to be dying? Where do new truths come from? Lawrence's error lies, not in its source, but in its partiality and inadequacy to the human situation as it presents itself to Western man in our century. . . . All of this is to say that the problems that Eliot dismisses in his inimitable and magisterial 'I-know-and-you-don't' manner, are too complex for that kind of treatment. It is possible that Authority is preferable to the Inner Light, although it seems somewhat naïve to appeal to one Authority in order to discover which of the Authorities ready at hand is *the true* Authority, and although it is quite possible—possible, I do not mean it *is* the case—that the

Authority to which we appeal may find that it has the right Authority by appealing to its own Inner Light. However that may be, Lawrence's heresy cannot be disposed of by appeal to Authority, not even Mr. Eliot's Authority."

Here is a difference—but not a difference of ignorance, for Eliseo Vivas is well acquainted with the writings of Paul Elmer More, upon whom Eliot drew considerably for his concepts of the "Inner Light" and the "Inner Check." These concepts have been the most important contribution to twentieth-century criticism and ethical discussion made by the "American Humanists" or "New Humanists." The Inner Check is that mysterious power to refrain from evil which chastens human appetites. The Inner Light is a private revelation—"a pipeline to God," in the self-congratulatory phase of a governor of Michigan—most perilous.

In these concerns, the most eminent disciple of Paul Elmer More and of Irving Babbitt was T. S. Eliot, whose poetry and criticism steadfastly affirm the need for moral checks and reject private inspiration. But Eliot perceived in the arguments of More and Babbitt certain deficiencies. Unless joined to religious belief, Eliot reasoned, the doctrine of the Inner Check might slide into the infallible Inner Light or "Inner Voice" praised by John Middleton Murry. This Inner Voice, Eliot wrote in 1923, "sounds remarkably like an old principle which has been formulated by an elder critic in the now familiar phrase of 'doing as one likes.' The possessors of an inner voice ride ten to a compartment to a football match at Swansea, listening to the inner voice, which breathes the eternal message of vanity, fear, and lust."

That sort of Inner Voice or Inner Light was anathema to More and Babbitt; they meant by the Inner Check a will to refrain—quite the contrary of Rousseau's championship of "natural" impulse. But Eliot's point was that without some strong standard of judgment, some true Authority, Inner Check and Inner Voice may be difficult to distinguish. Acknowledging this difficulty, in his later books Paul Elmer More turned to Christian doctrine for authority.

Now Vivas, though he does not profess himself a Christian, is an ethical philosopher; and he understands the Humanist case. In his essay "The Objective Basis of Criticism" (1948), Professor Vivas accused Babbitt and his disciples among the literary humanists of inflexible attachment to an infallible Tradition: they "bring the present to the rigid norm of the past and instead of judging it, in Eliot's distinction, they amputate it. For them the differences between the practice of the modern artist and that of the ancients was traced to contemporary aberrations and the devils of modern history, Bacon and Rousseau. The complementary error, that of the individualist, because more virulent at present, is much more dangerous today than that of the humanists. The individualist denies the jurisdiction of the past over the present and assumes the right of the artist to unrestricted originality." So Vivas writes, doubtless with Lawrence in mind among others, in *Creation and Discovery.*

Knowing the American Humanists, presumably Vivas recalls the debate, conducted half a century ago in periodicals on either side of the Atlantic, about the "ethical imagination." In that discussion, the concept of the ethical imagination was subjected to mordant criticism by some of Eliot's associates, and Eliot himself saw perils in the phrase. In criticizing the writings of Norman Foerster, one of the American Humanists, Allen Tate wrote in *The Criterion,* during 1929, that the "ethical imagination" goes beyond the Reason which Foerster praised, but cannot stand without the support of religious convictions which Foerster rejected. Tate was no less severe upon Paul Elmer More, at that time more a Platonist than a Christian. "Moral judgments are never more irresponsible," Tate wrote then, "than when the judge deludes himself into thinking that the high and mighty of the past are behind him. Mr. More is a man whose moral habits are not subject to the purification and correction of a specific external authority, and the delusion that they are only increases their irresponsibility. In the name of restraint he is able to evoke the limit of his personal distastes."

What Eliot's friend Tate assailed in More, Vivas assails in Eliot: the invocation of Authority—but misty and doubtful Authority—to sustain personal preferences. Eliot is right about Lawrence, Vivas tells us, but right for the wrong reasons, or at least for questionable reasons. Vivas and Eliot agree, nevertheless, that—in Eliot's words at the University of Virginia—"Lawrence's work may appeal, not to those who are well and able to discriminate, but to the sick and debile and confused; and will appeal not to what remains of health in them, but to their sickness." Eliot and Vivas agree, in short, that the diabolic imagination worked through Lawrence. But on what authority do both critics arrive at this judgment? Vivas declared, in effect, that Eliot's verdict rested upon a mere provincial Anglicanism. Whether Vivas' conclusion was drawn from sources more universal, I will inquire later in this little essay. At present I do no more than suggest that Vivas' and Eliot's norms for judgment, like their verdicts, have not been so different as Vivas argues.

About 1955, when *Creation and Discovery* was published, conceivably Vivas may not have been acquainted with Eliot's review of John Middleton Murry's *Son of Woman: the Story of D. H. Lawrence*—a review published in *The Criterion* for July 1931, but not reprinted. Even if Vivas did not know it, that Eliot review contains the germ of Vivas' book on Lawrence—and of Vivas' criticism of books about Lawrence by F. R.

Leavis and others. Eliot the reviewer discerns in Lawrence precisely the failings which Vivas analyzes more
fully. Take these Eliot passages:

> Mr. Murry quotes a sentence of Gourmont which I have
> quoted myself: *ériger en lois ses impressions personelles,
> c'est le grand effort d'un homme s'il est sincére.* Well,
> Lawrence tried to do that, certainly, but to my mind he
> failed completely, and this book is the history of his fail-
> ure. Lawrence simply did not know how. He had plenty
> of sensations, undoubtedly; no man of his time was more
> sensitive; but he could neither leave his sensations alone
> and accept them simply as they came, nor could he gen-
> eralize them correctly. The false prophet kills the true
> artist. . . .

Lawrence, in short, could not or would not employ
the objective correlative—or the dissociation of sensibility, for that matter. Vivas, as well as Eliot, points
out that when Lawrence fell into the clutch of ideology,
he became a false prophet. Sensations are no adequate
substitute, if one aspires to redeem society, for moral
philosophy. Few men know philosophy, but in times
past their morals have been "a matter of tradition and
orthodoxy—that is, of the community formulated, corrected, and elevated by the continuous thought and
direction of the Church." Lacking both philosophy and
membership in community, Lawrence was compelled
to turn to the Inner Light, to a torch held by the Dark
God, whose light is as darkness. That, despite his en-

deavor to defend the Inner Light, is Vivas' analysis of Lawrence, as it is Eliot's. Then Eliot continues:

> Had Lawrence been sent to a public school and taken honours at a university he would not have been a jot the less ignorant; had he become a don at Cambridge his ignorance might have had frightful consequences for himself and for the world, "rotten and rotting others." What true education should do—and true education would include the suitable education of every class of society—is to develop a wise and large capacity for orthodoxy, to preserve the individual from the solely centrifugal impulse of heresy, to make him capable of judging for himself and at the same time capable of judging and understanding the judgments of the experience of the race. I do not think that the unfortunate initial experience of Lawrence's life led *necessarily* to the consequences that came. He would probably have been always an unhappy man in this world; there is nothing unusual about that; many people have to be unhappy in this world, to do things which seem essential and a matter of course to the majority; and some learn not to make a fuss about it, and to gain, or at least to strive towards, a kind of peace which Lawrence never knew. He is to be grieved over and his faults are to be extenuated; but we can hardly praise a man for his failure. It is by the adoption of a crazy theory to deal with the facts, that Lawrence seems modern, and what I mean by "ignorant."

Eliot, a melancholy man himself, accepted the universe and made no fuss about it; he came to know a kind of peace which Lawrence did not know, and that peace was made possible by Eliot's acceptance of orthodoxy and authority. Eliot had risen early against a moribund orthodoxy—the latter-day orthodoxy of a complacent liberalism—but he had not turned to Inner Light or Inner Voice for inspiration. His understanding of the poet's debt to tradition and the poet's duty of self-effacement saved Eliot, as a poet, from Lawrence's partial failure.

This might almost be Vivas writing. Aye, the animadversions on Lawrence are severe; so are Vivas' animadversions on Lawrence. Perhaps Vivas, an acute critic of Eliot on some points, has been unaware of the closeness of his view to Eliot's in certain major matters. Vivas' only full essay on Eliot has to do with the notion of the objective correlative, "The Objective Correlative of T. S. Eliot" (1944)—a neat, penetrating, and convincing demolition of that concept. (Vivas may have convinced even Eliot himself: this term, Eliot would say in 1961, in some degree had been developed as a temporary tactic of 'trailing my coat'; it had been useful in its time, but he would not defend the phrase with forensic plausibility years later, and suspected that literary historians of future times would find this "objective correlative" of historical interest only.)

In *Creation and Discovery,* Vivas concludes that the "objective correlative" undoes itself. "It is of the utmost importance," Vivas writes, "for criticism to realize that the emotion expressed through the objective correlative is not that which the poet felt before the poem was written. The emotion, as well as the correlative, are *found* through the process of *creation.* But if the term 'creation' is taken seriously, the consequences for

Eliot's critical approach are devastating. For it means that once finished no one can go behind the poem, not even the artist himself. Otherwise put, the emotion itself, naked and unexpressed, cannot be had for comparison with its expression through the objective correlative. And the assumption therefore that we can criticize *Hamlet* by comparing the emotion expressed in the play with Shakespeare's emotions, or that through the play we can discover the emotions that went into it, is a confusing illusion. The vocabulary of the emotions is thus confusing, if not indeed irrelevant, to literary criticism; and if it were dropped, and the critic confined himself only to the objects and situations and values communicated in the poem, there would ensue an enormous clarification in the practice of criticism."

In practice, Eliot did drop "the vocabulary of the emotions"; Lawrence should have dropped it, had it been in him to do so. (Vivas points out that Eliot seems inconsistent in his critical principles; Eliot himself points out, in *On Poetry and Poets* [1957], that his critical essays are not systematically developed—as many had fancied—upon some fore-conceived immutable principles, but rather were produced almost haphazard as responses to occasional editorial requests for reviews of particular books of the hour—often books not chosen by Eliot; either that, or were products of his "private poetry-workshop," prolongations of thinking about his own verse.) Had Lawrence been able to drop the vocabulary of the emotions from his pseudo-prophetic writings, he might have been able to exorcise the Demon.

In the course of his assault upon the objective correlative, Vivas examines the third paragraph of Part II of Eliot's "Tradition and the Individual Talent." Among Vivas' shrewd comments is this: "You just do not work up emotion into poetry the way a cabinet maker works up boards into a table." It must be said that Lawrence, in his novels and stories, was no mere carpenter; but also it should be said that Lawrence's inchoate strong emotions mistook their objects and so lacked the objective correlative. Lawrence substituted personality for ethical understanding.

It is difficult indeed to interpret Lawrence's writings without knowing much of Lawrence's life. That itself is partial poetic failure: novels and stories, if they are to endure, should stand of themselves. Eliot, who made it hard for people to learn much concerning his private life, does not require the prop of an adulatory biographer. There are in "Tradition and the Individual Talent" strong passages from which Lawrence did not profit:

"The more perfect the artist, the more completely separate in him will be the man who suffers and the mind which creates; the more perfectly will the mind digest and transmute the passions which are its material," Eliot wrote early in life. The poet is the catalyst. ". . . For my meaning is, that the poet has, not a 'personality' to express, but a particular medium, in which impressions and experiences combine in peculiar and unexpected ways. . . . One error, in fact, of eccentricity in poetry is to seek for new human emotions to express; and in this search for novelty in the wrong place it discovers the perverse. . . . Poetry is not a turning loose of emotion, but an escape from emotion; it is not the expression of personality, but an escape from personality. But, of course, only those who have personality and emotions know what it means to want to escape from those things."

All of this is too true of Lawrence. As Vivas mentions, Lawrence was a genuine poet in the larger sense of that word; but Lawrence could not separate his strong resentful emotions from his accomplishment as a poet. And his private feelings, unrestrained, damaged his novels and his stories. These private emotions led him, in Eliot's phrases, to use "the terminology of Christian faith to set forth some philosophy or religion which is fundamentally non-Christian or anti-Christian," and so it was, too, with his disciples, John Middleton Murry and Aldous Huxley. These emotions led Lawrence to denounce the over-intellectualized life —so Eliot wrote in his review of *Son of Woman*—because Lawrence himself over-intellectualized. They led him to a ruinous misunderstanding of the nature of love: "As if human love could possibly be an end in itself!" Eliot exclaims. "And all these sad young men try to believe in a spectral abstraction called Life: yet the occasional whiffs of sepulchral high spirits wafted from their Limbo are chillier than the gloom."

Vivas sees all this. He emphasizes that Lawrence hated Jesus of Nazareth, went too far in his contempt for Reason, knew *eros* too familiarly and detested *agape*. If Vivas hearkens to any Inner Voice, it is not Lawrence's Inner Voice. How does Vivas see all this, if indeed he is so suspicious of Eliot's orthodoxy and authority?

"Unwillingly in part, I admit that this is a great tragic figure," Eliot concludes his review of Murry's book about Lawrence, "a waste of great powers of understanding and tenderness. We may feel poisoned by the atmosphere of his world, and quit it with relief; but we cannot deny our homage as we retire. A fateful influence he must have been upon those who experienced his power; I cannot help wondering whether Mr. Murry was not compelled to write his book to expel the demon from himself; and if so, I wonder whether Mr. Murry has succeeded."

With those lines, compare Vivas' summary in Vivas' Lawrence book, which bears the subtitle *The Failure and the Triumph of Art,* and in which Vivas is as hard upon F. R. Leavis' *D. H. Lawrence: Novelist* as Eliot is upon J. W. Murry's *Son of Woman.* "That Lawrence's own life through its whole span was the expression of profound emotional disorder, of obdurate major disharmony, his biography, I believe, amply establishes"—so Vivas tells us. "But might not Mr. Leavis' high praise apply not to Lawrence the man but to Lawrence the poet, the maker of two great novels and a number of fine short stories? I believe I have shown that if we read *The Rainbow, Women in Love,* and *Lady Chatterly* with care we find in them, too, a profound emotional disorder, informed with genius, as the substance of their drama. To go to these books for the wisdom that our civilization needs, without rigorous discrimination, is folly."

To expel the Demon: that is what Vivas does with Lawrence, more successfully than did Murry or Leavis. Unlike Lawrence, Vivas knows that happiness is unattainable, but that salvation is quite possible: "The true destiny of man is not reached by the path of happiness but by the path of salvation, and it includes (although it is not fully defined by) the ethical life." (Could not Eliot have written that line, in *The Idea of a Christian Society* or in *Notes towards the Definition of Culture*?) "But what, someone may ask, is salvation?" Vivas continues. "At the moral level salvation is surcease from the anguish that the burden of our guilt creates in us, which is too heavy for anyone to carry. The burden cannot be thrown off, but it can be lightened by love."

Not knowing the deeper love, or actually repelling it, Lawrence was lost: his Demon was unexpelled. Eliot was saved in poetry and in life, as Vivas has been. Twentieth-century man, says Vivas, schooled man, rejects eighteenth- and nineteenth-century scientism and meliorism; I quote below from Vivas' essay on "The Substance of Tragedy," in *The Artistic Transaction and Essays on Theory of Literature:*

"We, the dupes of betrayed hopes, the men of lost

faith, the victims of relentless terror, we left meliorism
and scientism behind long ago," Vivas puts it. "Our
problem is not that of satisfying our cravings or nego-
tiating our rights. Men have always known how to take
frustration in their stride. And in this respect we are no
lesser men than our ancestors. To see tragedy as the
frustration of desire or the conflict of interest is the
privilege—a privilege I do not envy him—of the wor-
shipper of Sovereign Reason. Ours is a different age.
What we may call the Baconian lie has been exposed."

D. H. Lawrence did reveal that this Sovereign Reason, this Baconian lie, is a feeble monarch. For that
service, as for his artistic talents, Vivas and Eliot respect Lawrence. But for Sovereign Reason, Lawrence
substituted his Inner Light or Inner Voice, thus un-
chaining the Demon. What Eliot and Vivas dread in
Lawrence is that Demon of ego and appetite. During
the fourteen years since Vivas wrote his "Substance
of Tragedy," the Demon has made progress, heedless
of inner check and objective correlative. One perceives
him working through Herbert Marcuse and writers of
Marcuse's kidney, who have something of Lawrence in
them whether they know it or not, and something of
Rousseau. Vivas makes clear this diabolical power in
his *Contra Marcuse:*

> Marcuse's hatred of gadgetry and of our highly devel-
> oped technology deserves further attention because it is
> part of what I, in my ideolect, call "the Lawrentian syn-
> drome." Marcuse does not go as far as D. H. Lawrence

did, who in all seriousness told us that the problems of our
world would be solved by going back to the Elizabethans
and dressing the men in gay colors (in any sense of the
word "gay" you like to use) and showing their plump
buttocks. But can anyone deny that there is some relationship between the hatred expressed by Marcuse and the
hatred expressed by Ursula in *The Rainbow,* against ma-
chines and the men who tend them?

Lawrence did not originate this syndrome, Vivas
observes. But Lawrence reinforced it through his literary power. Since Lawrence's day, the Demon goes
further in negations. Lawrence's pseudo-philosophy
leads on to general ruin. The "revolution of nihilism,"
the totalist tendency in Lawrence remarked by both
Vivas and Eliot, has been described in its culmination
by Lawrence's own disciple Huxley (often appreciated,
like Lawrence, by Eliseo Vivas, and often coupled in
print with Eliot—to Eliot's own chagrin). Vivas is
plain about this, in his recent book on Marcuse:

> I do not believe that Marcuse mentions Aldous Hux-
> ley's dystopia, but what revolts us about the pseudo-
> humans of 632 AF, animals that look like us but do not
> seem to have much in common with us, is what revolts
> Marcuse about ourselves. According to Marcuse, the only
> way to be human, is to be negative and to yearn after
> resexualization. Hence for destruction. And after that, in
> the midst of the charred rubble and the half-burnt corpses,
> we shall play and display.

Vivas, although ashamed of having been born into
the twentieth century, is not ashamed of calling himself
a conservative. Most "defenders of tradition," Eliot

writes, "are mere conservatives, unable to distinguish between the permanent and the temporary, the essential and the accidental." But Vivas does so distinguish, and Vivas has engaged in that health-giving criticism of tradition which Eliot commends. If Vivas is not orthodox—why, one hardly would notice; surely his criticism of Lawrence is orthodox, after Samuel Johnson's fashion. I find it difficult to perceive much difference between his view of Lawrence and Eliot's view of Lawrence, as expressed in the concluding pages of *After Strange Gods:*

> There is, I believe, a very great deal to be learned from Lawrence; though those who are most capable of exercising the judgment necessary to extract the lesson, may not be those who are most in need of it. That we can and ought to reconcile ourselves to Liberalism, Progress, and Modern Civilisation is a proposition which we need not have waited for Lawrence to condemn; and it matters a good deal in what name we condemn it. . . . The first requisite usually held up by the promoters of personality is that a man should "be himself"; and this "sincerity" is considered more important than that the self in question should, socially and spiritually, be a good or a bad one. This view of personality is merely an assumption on the part of the modern world, and is no more tenable than several other views which have been held at various times and in several places. The personality thus expressed, the personality which fascinates us in the work of philosophy or of art, tends naturally to be the *unregenerate* personality, partly self-deceived and partly irresponsible, and because of its freedom, terribly *limited* by prejudice and self-conceit, capable of much good or great mischief according to the natural goodness or impurity of the man; and we are all, naturally, impure.

D. H. Lawrence was himself, but it was a self badly flawed; he was sincere, but his sincerity often was the Demon's sincerity, the sincerity of a being with too much ego in his cosmos. The Demon does not know that in the end he shall be vanquished.

Allen Tate's collection of essays *The Forlorn Demon,* reviewed by Vivas in 1954, has ambiguity in its title, drawn from Poe. Is this forlorn demon the modern man of letters, Vivas asks, "doomed to inhabit Baudelaire's *fourmillante cité?*" Or is it the daimon of Socrates, "forlorn because we citizens of the swarming secularized city of today disregarded his prohibition and attempted to do something we have no business attempting?"

However that may be, Lawrence's Demon of the perverse, his Demon that smashes all creations of culture, stalks grand among us nowadays. Some men disciplined in metaphysics and in ethics, like Vivas and Eliot, glimpse the hellish face behind the mask of the Dark God. Lawrence offers us Nature, but his Nature must be red in tooth and claw, when the mask is off.

About the time he wrote his review of Tate's collection, Eliseo Vivas wrote to me concerning a symposium on religion conducted by militant secularists. "Is this what Mustafa Mond's boys are up to now?" he inquired. He was referring to the master of mankind about 632 After Ford, according to Huxley's dystopia. Doubtless Lawrence would detest Mustafa Mond and all his works; yet the Demon wears many masks, and the Inner Voice calls strange prophets, once tradition and authority have been rejected. Vivas and Eliot, in their different fashions, are healthily orthodox in rejecting Lawrence's Demon.

For indeed Lawrence *was* a heretic, Vivas declares in his book on Lawrence, immediately after differing with Eliot. There exists a "Western" orthodoxy, Vivas instructs us. "And one of the basic notions in this body of beliefs is the idea that God is a person and that he is triune," Vivas says. "What the theist means by saying God is a person may or may not be sufficiently clear to him; but it is certainly clear enough to enable him to reject Lawrence's conception of God as a vast, shimmering impulse waving on towards an indeterminate end. And God is Providence, and the end He provides for, as the Judeo-Christian tradition asserts, is that of the individual, not that of the species. He is Providence not in the sense that He provides for our whims but, as I understand it, that He provides the end we ought to realize and that He gives us the means and the freedom to achieve that end. Eliot is right. Lawrence was a heretic because he thought he could define his end, and the individual has that end given to him to realize."

Similarly, Vivas goes on, the notion of the Trinity is a Western orthodoxy. "And only men who pick their theology from Gibbon will see in the argument which led to the idea of the Trinity a gratuitous invention of minds darkened by superstition and afflicted with metaphysical logorrhea. . . . For the tradition, God is Father —the vast shimmering impulse, the principle of creativity in history and in the universe. But He is more than a vast shimmering impulse waving towards some indeterminate end."

"Western" orthodoxy gives us also Son and Holy Ghost, Vivas argues. And here lies the heart of Lawrence's heresy. "Not only does he interpret in his own idiosyncratic manner the Father and the Holy Ghost; he denies the Son. After a fashion he acknowledged the first and third Persons." Had he acknowledged the Son, Lawrence would have been compelled to acknowledge true love, *agape,* in our world. And that would have forced Lawrence to abandon what he most cherished— his radical alienation and his radical misanthropy.

D. H. Lawrence, like his character Somers, must have an Absolute, and the Absolute must be God. But Lawrence will not receive the Son; therefore he receives his own Dark God, sensual passion ritually venerated. Lawrence thought himself a religious man. In that aspiration, Eliot and Vivas sympathize with him, for Lawrence was wiser in that than are the contemporary liberal philosophers. But, as Vivas says in his book about Lawrence, "Once more one is led to ask, How foolish, how wrong, can a brilliant man get? . . . Would it not be wise to ask us to take our sensuous Dark God, the lingam, back to the cave, or better, if we can carry it, while we swing from branch to branch, back to the trees?"

With Lucifer, Lawrence's Dark God declares, "I am, and none else beside me." Perhaps our Dark God, behind his literary mask, *is* Lucifer. Perhaps the lurking greatness in Lawrence, recognized by Vivas and Eliot, is satanic. Perhaps it is no very "severe animadversion" to descry in Lawrence's writings "the fruitful operations of the Evil Spirit today." Perhaps the Inner Voice of Lawrence, like most Inner Voices, is quite as untrustworthy as Eliot called it. Perhaps Eliot's "exaggerations" are no wilder than Vivas's declaration that in the search for God, Man "often runs into the Devil's arms."

And perhaps Vivas' "Western" orthodoxy, or even the "Judeo-Christian tradition," is an Authority less satisfying and less demonstrable than Eliot's orthodoxy, so severely criticized by Vivas. It is Christianity, not something "Western" or something "Judeo-Christian," which affirms the divinity of the Son, denied by Lawrence; nor are all Christians Westerners—witness the many in Vietnam who chose exile or death rather than submission to false gods.

Be that as it may, those of us who endeavor to resist the Dark God are grateful that an ethical philosopher stands beside a philosophical poet in appreciation and rejection of D. H. Lawrence. Few have read Vivas; not many, after all, have read Eliot. Those who worship the Dark God need read little, if anything—need not even read Lawrence. Yet in the long run the voices of Vivas and Eliot will be heard, as the voice of Augustine was heard after everything was ruin. In the end, the Demon undoes himself.

Essay Eight

Eliseo Vivas:
Philosopher in Spite
of Himself

Stephen J. Tonsor

Stephen J. Tonsor is Professor of History at the University of Michigan, Ann Arbor, Michigan. He was born in Jerseyville, Illinois, in 1923, and was educated at Blackburn College, Carlinville, Illinois, the University of Zurich, and the University of Illinois. Dr. Tonsor was awarded the Ph.D. in history in 1955, and was awarded an honorary D. Litt. by Blackburn College in 1972. He served in the Army Signal Corps as a cryptographer from 1943 to 1946. He has published widely in both professional and popular journals; his most recent book is Tradition and Reform in Education. *He has received numerous awards and prizes. Currently Dr. Tonsor is adjunct scholar at the American Enterprise Institute in Washington, D.C., and associate editor of the journal,* Modern Age. *He lectures in European intellectual history and historiography.*

I t is easier for philosophers to be poets than it is for philosophers to be literary critics. Nietzsche wrote poetry of the first order and set a style which came to characterize existentialist philosophizing which made philosophy indistinguishable from literature. Anyone who has read even a little of William James is aware of the literary artistry which is, even in dealing with the most ordinary topics, at James' command. Indeed, before philosophy was ravaged by the analytic school the philosophers were apt to shame the poets. Unamuno and Ortega, Santyana and Bergson set a high standard as poets reminding us that Plato, in spite of what he said concerning poetry, was a poet.

But philosophers are less often capable critics. It is no wonder that Eliot gave up philosophy for poetry and criticism. These two diverse talents rarely mesh. The categories of philosophy and the analytic and exacting use of language seldom make for great criticism. Even the temperament of philosophers seems in these later days inimical to literary criticism. One can't imagine the analytic dry-as-dusts as capable of construing a poem. There are, of course, exceptions and Santyana was one such. However, the exceptions have not been numerous.

And yet the combination of a poet's sensibility and a philosopher's rigorous categories are essential to the successful practice of the critic's art. Nothing illlustrates this better than the percepts without concepts which are the stock in trade of F. R. Leavis. Neither sensibility nor history alone can be substituted for the close reasoning that is the critic's special task, and where the critic fails and artistic self-awareness weakens, art itself must sink away into triviality and primitivism. Consequently the combination of an acute awareness of aesthetic norm and the poet's experience, infrequent though it is, is the *sine qua non* of great art.

To be sure the critic does not make art great. He does not even make it understandable, for the quality of all art is that it enables us to apprehend immediately and directly the world the artist wishes to reveal to us. Ethical theory does not make an action good; indeed, what the philosopher says about love is such a far cry from our immediate experience of it that we sometimes wonder why philosophers make such a great fuss. What the ethical philosopher and the aesthetician share is comprehensiveness of vision. The world of act and the world of art, no matter the perfection of their particularity, are partial and incomplete worlds. Their ultimate validity depends upon the larger framework in which they must be set. They are pointillist dots. Even their formal perfection is external to themselves and a function of both style and existential adequacy. The critic does not ratify the act but he reaches beyond it to comprehend its necessity, its appropriateness and its adequacy. Without the critic ultimate measure is lost and ultimate meaning is obscured.

Eliseo Vivas is one of the few philosophers whose possession of a poet's sensibility equips him for the critic's role. One suspects that Vivas has tried his hand at writing novels and that somewhere he has revealed a world in poetry which his critic's judgment has told him is not of publishable quality. Certainly he has the poet's eye and the poet's ability to make a world of a few vowels and consonants. Santayana wrote good though not great poetry and he too had the poet's eye. But unlike Vivas, Santayana did not have that loving regard for those mundane instances which give us a world of meaning in a vivid and unselfconscious picture. In Vivas we are often made to see a thing rather than to reason it through abstractly or, having been shown something, Vivas invites us, indeed insists, that we reason about it. William James had something of

that power, but there was always a slightly trivial edge
to it as though he had clipped his pictures from *Mc-
Clure's Monthly.*

The philosopher-poet's critical vision is sharpened
by the tension which exists between the intuitive insight
into reality or a special reality which characterizes the
poet and the capacity for abstract analytical thought
which is the special mark of a philosopher. The philosophical cat is always at odds with the poetic mouse,
and even when the encounter turns playful, the game
has a deadly kind of playfulness to it in which the mouse
may well gain the upper hand. This tension is very apparent in Vivas and is never completely resolved. He is,
indeed, a philosopher "in spite of himself," and the poet
threatens constantly to sweep the entire argument away
and dissolve the certainties of philosophy in the magic
of language.

In some ways, however, this tension between poet
and philosopher is the least interesting and the least
dramatic tension in Vivas' criticism. The second and
more important tension is that which exists between
a modernist sensibility and a classical aesthetic. This
same tension, to be sure, exists in T. S. Eliot and in
Wyndham Lewis, but one must go on to add that Eliot
never felt completely at home with modernist literature.
This accounts for his hostility to D. H. Lawrence. Eliot
was reluctantly modern. This is not true of Vivas. He
is a veritable typhoid Mary of modernist ideas. There
is not a wanton extreme of modernist fanaticism in

which Vivas has not wallowed or an obscure corner which he has not explored. Even Céline comes in for a few good words. The great dark souls of the late nineteenth and the twentieth centuries are his familiars. And it must be said that his familiarity with them goes beyond the routine and loveless knowledge of the *Censor Librorum*. Vivas' world is the world of modernity. He seems to say that it above all others gives us the most accurate assessment of the human condition. In spite of a few references to Shakespeare and Swift, his literary horizons do not seem to reach back beyond Henry James. His sensibility, then, is modernist: he is deeply read in the moderns and he discerns in them a profound artistry. When Vivas is critical of Lawrence, or of Dostoyevsky, or Céline, he is not critical from the outside. The epigraph to his essay, "Dostoyevsky, 'Poet' in Spite of Himself," is a quotation from Dostoyevsky: "I am an old 'Nechaivetz' myself." Those words are not only the words of Dostoyevsky, they are the words of Eliseo Vivas.

I do not wish to be misunderstood in my use of the term "modernity." I do not, of course, mean a dedication to "science," positivistic rationalism, technology and bureaucratic organization. Vivas stands at the end of the intellectual tradition variously described as the "antipositivist revolt" and "neoromanticism." He shares the concerns and values of the "modernists," those moral and aesthetic radicals who were so savagely attacked by C. P. Snow in "The Two Cultures." While, for example, it is clear on virtually every page he wrote on the subject of D. H. Lawrence that he opposes many of Lawrence's notions as "silly" and believes that when they intrude themselves into Lawrence's art they are aesthetically destructive, nevertheless, he does share many of Lawrence's basic assumptions, suppositions, and perceptual categories. His attachment to the modernists is an attachment to general ideas rather than to particular postures. Moreover, he is at home with the artistic technique of modernism and understands its validity. He understands what the modernist artist is seeking to achieve, he knows the formal rules which govern artistic creation in that style, and he is in sympathy with the purposes of the art. Consequently, his criticism of the great modernists never lapses into an archaizing primitivism or an iconoclastic attack upon the most recent simply because it has escaped the dead hand of the past. Vivas, consequently, is not an outsider attacking "modernism" as an aberrant manifestation of the Western spirit. His critical posture is internal to the movement and his debate with modernism is so intense because it is a family argument.

Vivas feels as intensely as anyone the tidal pull of absurdity and the void. He understands the anxiety which is the distinctive note in the modern consciousness. The deflated hopes and diminished expectations, the experience of evil as a willful expression of the ego rather than a defect of knowledge or intention, the quest for personal authenticity in the face of blind and unre-

garding cosmic forces, the knowledge of man's ineluc-
table freedom and the necessity at every moment to
choose on the basis of inadequate knowledge and evidence; all of these basic postures of modernism are
shared by Vivas.

Moreover, Vivas shares more than these attitudes
with the modernists. Like them he sees the artist and
the poet as energized and potentiated from the deepest
levels of the psyche. It is from the unconscious and
preconscious mind rather than from the analytical abstractions of ratiocination that art and poetry derive.
Freud has had an enormous influence on his thought,
though his inclinations are Jungian rather than orthodox Freudian (whatever that may be). As a consequence, the archetypal and the primitive forms of life
and thought as they existed previous to manner and
rational artifice exert a compelling attraction for him,
as they do for the modernists in general.

Lawrence expresses and I believe Vivas shares,
though it is not at all explicit in his criticism, a preoccupation with vitality, not simply on the organic level
and especially in terms of sexual expression, but vitality
as it manifests itself in artistic creativity. For Lawrence
at his best, sexuality is only an aspect of a creativity and
vitality which derives from a deep unconscious well and
at its highest level produces art, religion and society.
For the great modernists the concern has not been with
sexuality *per se*, but rather with creative potentiality,
especially as it manifests itself in the great work of cul-

ture. This is not explicit theme in Vivas but it is, I believe, an undisclosed assumption.

Connected with the primitive and the archetypal in modernist thought has been a new attitude toward, and a new understanding of, religion. Positivism and rationalism sought in vain to banish religion as an exploded form of superstitious obscurantism. The modernist preoccupation with myth, ritual and mystery has had important consequences for a new evaluation of religion in relation to the personal, communal and creative dimensions of being human. As a deeply religious man who is too sophisticated for a simplistic and reductionist orthodoxy and too radical for unbelief, Vivas is especially keenly attuned to the religious component of modernism. Eliade and Jung have been very influential in his thinking, but one senses that he discovered these theorists after the fact, and that it was his own mature religious experience and the formative character of conventional childhood religiosity that developed in him this profoundly religious attitude. For this reason, among others, he understands Lawrence very well. He sees that religion rather than sex is at the heart of Lawrence's art. Most of those who have written about Lawrence have confused religion and sex and have given to sex an undue weight. Mark Spilka is characteristic of this school. Only Vivas has seen that religion is the controlling, consuming interest in Lawrence, and has appreciated and reverenced Lawrence for that fact. Of course, Spilka and company ought to be excused, for

Lawrence himself was not very clear on the distinction between religion and sex.

Most important for Vivas' aesthetic theory and for Lawrence's poetic creativity was the impact of the Symbolist movement. This is not the place for an exposition of symbolism. That history is a complex one. A good introduction from the American side is Charles Feidelson, Jr., *Symbolism and American Literature,* and the best succinct explanation of what a symbol is from the literary standpoint is Vivas' appendix in *D. H. Lawrence, The Failure and the Triumph of Art,* on the "constitutive symbol." The new poetry which had been in the making for the whole of the nineteenth century had moved beyond metaphor and sign to symbolic utterance and these symbolic forms, forms which are rooted in "controlling myths" that give them their power and their validity. The symbol is directly apprehended and appropriated and constitutes the essential aesthetic moment. Because the symbol and the controlling myth to which it is attached are integral aspects of *nomization,* or the process by which the world is ordered, they are directly related to the apprehension of form and the construction of reality. The movement of the mind is not from the empirical perception to the symbol, but rather the symbol lifts the empirical perception to the symbol, but rather the symbol lifts the empirical perception out of the general chaos of experience. Because the process of nomization is central to any meaning, science, ethics and community are all ultimately related to symbolic utterance whether that utterance is artistic or religious.

Having identified the importance of symbolism for the aesthetic theory of Eliseo Vivas, one need hardly add that a considerable part of Vivas' admiration for D. H. Lawrence was due to the fact that he found so much of his own theory borne out in the work of Lawrence. As Vivas demonstrates with a quotation from Lawrence's "The Dragon of the Apocalypse," Lawrence knew in a rudimentary way the meaning and significance of symbolism. The function of Vivas the critic is that of showing the connectedness of Lawrence's use of symbolism with the deeper meanings of his art and with the everyday realities of our world.

These components of modernism are, however, in tension with the classical realist foundations of Vivas' aesthetic theory, and the assumptions of modernism present difficulties to anyone who insists as Vivas does that the artist both "creates" and "discovers" meaning. It is well to quote Vivas where he writes in *Creation and Discovery:*

> But how shall we resolve the contradiction involved in the claim that the artist *creates* novel objects and that he *discovers* the hidden reality of our practical, common-sense world? The contradiction is only apparent, not real, since two assertions were made from different points of view. From the standpoint of the world of experience, the spacio-temporal world of culture and history, of which the poet and his reader are part, the artist *creates* meanings, values and fitting form. But these values, meanings and their form

subsist prior to the making of the poem. The act of making is thus a *discovery* that takes place as the poet in his making goes beyond the matter of his experience; the discovery takes place when he makes the effort to extricate the import and order of his experience and body it forth in language. From the external point of view, there is novelty in his product, and spontaneity is involved in the process of making. From the standpoint of the artist, however, we grasp a different aspect of the process, since what the artist does is not to invent something new, but to extricate out of the subject matter at hand its own proper structure or order.

What Vivas seems to be saying is that the historical and cultural relativity of style and aesthetic and ethical content is only a seeming relativity, and that beneath the confusion of values and the clash of manners there is an unchanging essence, an essence only imperfectly and inadequately bodied forth by any artist. This assumption is an interesting and important attempt to resolve the most important problem in contemporary aesthetic and ethical theory. The attempt produces great tensions in criticism, however, and poses nearly insuperable difficulties for the critic.

Contemporary ethical and aesthetic theory which sees all ordering as an act of personal aggression by which the chaos of experience is given an arbitrary form is rejected by Vivas. The form, Vivas insists, lies beyond the idiosyncratic vision of the artist in the nature of reality itself. There it is discovered and imperfectly embodied by the artist in his art, by the ethical man in his actions. The artist makes possible the direct apprehension of an ordered reality through his art. This exposition of the creative act and of the ethical act has much to recommend it. I believe it is true, and yet it is only candid to admit that it poses enormous difficulties, difficulties which I do not believe Vivas has completely resolved. On the face of it, Vivas seems to give us a measuring stick, but it is immediately dissolved in the relativism and historicism characteristic of the contemporary cultural mood.

The theory Vivas offers us is far more satisfactory than the Classical Theory, as it finally banishes the theory of imitation and takes into account the truly creative activity of the artist. So long as art is the creation of a parochial and self-contained cultural realm no serious problems are posed, but once historicism and relativism have produced a plurality of orders, styles and visions, the stability of the whole system is threatened.

Let us turn directly to Vivas for a description of what the poet does. In his preface to *D. H. Lawrence, The Failure and the Triumph of Art,* he tells us:

> . . . Expatiating, what Lawrence is telling us is what we know from other sources, that the function of the poet is to sweep away the "ideas" that darken and falsify our vision. He tears the horney cataract of conceptual abstractions from the Soul's eyes, the worn out categories, the stereotyped modes of response to the living world, the brittle formulas. In their place he gives us fresh, quick, tender, unmediated revelations of the world of nature and of man. Having freed us from our "ideas," he substitutes his own freshly organized experience, through which we are able to understand

aesthetically, to grasp by immediate apprehension, those
aspects of contemporary experience that without his aid
would remain for us threatening and oppressive because
they would remain chaotic. . . .

And in his essay "The Object of the Poem" in *Creation
and Discovery,* Vivas writes:

> . . . Insofar as the object is already realized the poet merely
> imitates—he is a reporter and not a poet. He is a poet only
> when his creative activity discloses values and meanings
> which the culture is ready to espouse and adopt, which are
> knocking, so to speak, at the gate of history, seeking admis-
> sion, or have surreptitiously entered history and become
> operative in the culture but have not yet been identified,
> revealed, given a name and a dramatic mask.

As if to underline this idea, Vivas argues in his preface
to the Gateway edition:

> . . . The artist has an indispensable role to play in culture
> for which there is no substitute. He discovers creatively the
> values of a culture, he embodies them in his objects and
> thus is able to pass them on to his people. The creative mind
> has the capacity to step up to the threshold of experience
> and to discern, beyond the threshold, the shadowy forms of
> the nascent values that are about to enter the historical
> scene. . . .

One is immediately reminded of Hegel's "The very
Truth for their age, for their world; the species next in
order, so to speak, and which was already formed in the
womb of time"; and the echo is not accidental, for in
the terms which we are given only a Hegelian structure

can merge the contingent and circumstantial values of the cultural continuum with the eternally enduring forms of reality. It is possible, of course, that Vivas intends to assert that the structure of reality itself, the realm of value and form from which the poet works outward, is itself in the process of becoming; is partial, incomplete and evolutionary. This seems unlikely, for then, aside from some form of dialectical rationality, there could never be a test of artistic validity.

Perhaps Vivas means to say that the ability on the part of the poet "to make a world" to produce the suspension of disbelief is the criterion by which the poet must be judged. Perhaps the formal aesthetic truth of interior consistency and order is an adequate test of beauty and the truth which it embodies. What then of this ability to make a world as a test of artistic validity?

In discussing Lawrence's *Kangaroo,* Vivas writes:

> . . . The world of Kangaroo is a torn world, cracked by hatred, embittered by the absence of charity, a world torn by illicit passions, by blind rejections, a world without pity, an inhuman demonic world, made what it is by unwarranted claims and by a false sense of superiority. It is no wonder that it is a world that does not come off as viably human. It is a world created by a man with a devil in his belly.
>
> But in a sort of sense it is a world. And it is this power Lawrence had of never altogether failing in his failures that make him such a formidable challenge to the critic. . .

This fact, that the men who have "made the worlds" of contemporary literature have usually been men with "devils in their bellies," makes the task of the critic impossibly difficult. What, one asks, is the truth which they hold out to our times? What are the normative categories with which they present us and which enable us to comprehend and order our experience? In the inverted systems and symbols, the gnostic world orders which are the stuff of contemporary literature, where are the truths for which we must be grateful to the poet? And is this truth a truth in itself, inherent in the nature of reality, or is it the arbitrary and personal construction of the artist?

Vivas returns again and again to this problem, for it constitutes the focus of his criticism. Céline's novels are an unusually interesting case. Vivas read Céline when he was still relatively unknown in the United States, indeed when to read him and write about him was still a politically dangerous act of defiance. In discussing *Journey to the End of the Night* in his essay, "Literature and Knowledge" (in *Creation and Discovery*), Vivas says:

> . . . The novel consists of a number of characters and a succession of dramatic episodes which constitute a fictional world of deserters, cowards, stupid officers, murderers, lechers, heartless exploiters, the whole unsavory mess drenched in hatred, distrust, ill-will—in a word the novel presents us with a thoroughly evil fictional world.

Céline has made a world, and from the standpoint of the modernist aesthetic categories, it is a thoroughly satisfactory and artistic creation. Its aesthetic truth seems to be in sharp contradiction to what Vivas perceives as moral truth, just as the aesthetic truth which Lawrence presents to us is in sharp contradiction to what Vivas believes to be moral truth. Is it possible that Vivas wishes simply to separate the two truths, holding to one set of perceptions in ethics and another in aesthetics?

Far from it, Vivas writes of *Journey to the End of the Night:*

> To claim that what *Journey* does is not done to our intellect but to our attitudes exclusively—to distinguish between our cognitive and our emotive response and to claim that our reading of *Journey* elicits a purely emotive response—is to take an analytic distinction which is perfectly valid at the conceptual level as if it referred to phenomena that actually existed in us in separate compartments, and to command us to keep it separate; and this is a patently arbitrary imperative. All we need consider here is that the imperative is not an aesthetic one but a moral one and that its effect, if obeyed, would be to compartmentalize life even more than it already is, and to foster schizophrenia. . .

The first task of the critic is that which I would describe as internal and intensive. Vivas describes this activity in the following words:

> . . . Having read the novel intransitively, we can ask what the presuppositions are which must be posited in order to bring about and to sustain in the aesthetic transaction the work we have read. . .

Vivas is at his best in this effort. One reads his criticism of Lawrence with startled admiration. He insists that the interior integrity and aesthetic dynamic of the work be given its way and that we not be told but be confronted with the meaning of the work, Vivas' great achievement in his criticism of Lawrence is his refusal to be beguiled by ideology. The meaning, Vivas says over and over again, cannot in a Tolstoyian fashion be tacked on to the symbol. Preaching and propaganda, the pages of dreary rant which fill so many of Lawrence's works, all these are excluded from the category of art and justly condemned. Leavis is beguiled, as was Lawrence, by ideological content, and because he approved of it he confused it with art. The critical failure in the case of Leavis is due to the fact that he had no aesthetic scheme beyond a shallow and often vulgar sensibility. Alas, "phallic consciousness" is not an aesthetic category. The triumph of art is the defeat of ideology, and as with Dostoyevsky the really great poet is a "poet in spite of himself surrendering to his creativity and to the needs of his artistry."

Vivas reminds us again and again how compelling ideology was for Lawrence and what havoc it wreaked on his art. Later analyses of Lawrence's life and thought, particularly that by Martin Green in *The von Richthofen Sisters* and an illuminating essay by Frank Kermode, throw a good deal of light on the Germanic and gnostic sources of Lawrence's ideas. They were intruded on every possible occasion and their influence waxed as the role of Freda grew larger in Lawrence's life. That Evangelical impulse to preach a message of salvation was anti-art, and when it clouded Lawrence's vision it turned him into a shrill Dr. Goebbels of sex and pastoralism.

However, one does not need an aesthetic theory which goes beyond the structure of the work of art itself in order to exercise this sort of critical judgment. It requires objectification, neutrality and a respect for the integrity of things as they are and the dynamics which move them. Vivas does, however, go beyond an aesthetic which is intrinsic to the work of art. He insists that the values inherent in the work of art have an independent and prior validity. It is this truth which the artist brings us, a truth which is often at odds with the poet's intention. This world of the poet is a normative world, and as Vivas says in *D. H. Lawrence,* "we do not see the world reflected in it, we see the world by means of it."

But how can we know that the poet's symbol is, in fact, a penetration into the realm of values, or that these values are more than arbitrary configuration? The question is, quite simply, is the artist's conception of existence a "valid" conception? Vivas demands that the artist give us a "valid" conception of existence. He writes:

> . . . *Journey* [*to the End of the Night*] undoubtedly affects us emotively. But this is not its exclusive effect on us. For a picture of man has been presented to us which does not jibe with what we know precisely, because at least one of the factors constituting its novelty consists in excluding almost absolutely from the work itself those aspects which in actual life modify and disguise the malice of which men are ca-

pable. And the failure of the picture to jibe with what we previously knew about men instigates the need to digest the picture.

Again and again in his discussion of Lawrence, Vivas criticizes not only the aesthetic inadequacies of Lawrence's art but also its moral confusions and errors. Lawrence is wrong, Vivas says, because you and I know better. The world is simply not the way Lawrence says it is. The artist, in this case Lawrence, has either falsified experience or he has left out such consequential aspects of it that we are forced to reject his view.

The critic's appeal here, as in the case of aesthetic adequacy, is to a sort of critical universal consensus. "The total process" of criticism, Vivas tells us in his essay, "The Objective Basis of Criticism," "carried on against all comers, results in the gradual crystallization of opinions from which the errors of subjectivity have to some degree been expurgated." Which is to say that both the moral and the aesthetic critic appeal to judgments other than their own and finally to a common tradition.

This, of course, is classicism with a vengeance. It is, alas, true also that there is neither progress nor novelty in either aesthetics or morals. One may speak of styles as developing and one may suppose that the particular moral problems of any generation are unlikely to be those of another, but the notion that artists or moralists "step up to the threshold of experience," peer beyond it and provide new values and modes of perception which enable men to comprehend their experiences, carries in it such a freight of historicist and relativist content as to negate the appeal to objectified consensus. The validity of a symbol is established by its immediate recognition by the viewer or the reader. It is true because once it has been apprehended it is enduringly convincing. But how much novelty, one asks, can there be in either the ethical or the aesthetic realm? And if critical consensus is the ultimate test, are we not left with very nearly as much uncertainty as before?

It does seem to me that there are unresolved problems and difficulties with both the ethical and aesthetic theory Eliseo Vivas offers us. These difficulties are not, however, due to any inadequacy in the theory, but are rather the practical implications of a creaturely existence lived in time but an existence which is capable in its most creative and moral moments of piercing into the realm of the absolute. Vivas quotes Lawrence with approval when Lawrence writes, "It is an Absolute we are all after." Consequently both the vigor and the character of Vivas' criticism are a consequence of the tension which animates his view. He is a modernist and a classicist. He is a poet and a philosopher in spite of himself.

Arthur Schopenhauer

Erich Heller

Erich Heller was born in 1911 in Komotau, Bohemia, the son of a doctor. He graduated in 1935 from Charles University in Prague, where he studied law, philosophy, and German literature. In 1939 he emigrated to England. There he received a Ph.D. in German literature from Cambridge University, became a British subject, and, in 1948, after several years as Director of Studies in Modern Languages at Peterhouse, Cambridge, was appointed Professor of German at the University of Wales. He has held teaching appointments at numerous universities in both the United States and Europe, including Cambridge, the London School of Economics, Heidelberg, Tübingen, Harvard, Brandeis, and M.I.T. Professor Heller is currently Avalon Professor in the Humanities at Northwestern University. His essays and articles have appeared in The Cambridge Journal, The Times Literary Supplement, Encounter, Commentary, The New York Review of Books, *and other literary and scholarly journals. His books include* The Disinherited Mind; The Ironic German: Thomas Mann; The Artist's Journey into the Interior; Essays über Goethe; *and* Franz Kafka. *The Lord Northcliffe Lectures he was invited to give in the spring of 1975 at University College, London, are about to appear as a book under the title* The Poet's Self and the Poem. *This series of lectures was repeated in the summer of 1975 at the Van Leer Foundation in Jerusalem.*

There was very little to remind him of human beings in the bachelor's living-room at the *Schöne Aussicht* in Frankfurt a.M., where Arthur Schopenhauer lived for more than twenty years and died in 1860—a man of seventy-two and yet only just about to become really famous, some forty years after the publication of his great work *The World as Will and Idea* (1819).

True, there was a picture of his mother, Johanna Schopenhauer, whom during her lifetime he disliked as intensely as her many bad novels. There were also portraits of Goethe, Shakespeare, and Descartes, and, together in one frame, Immanuel Kant and Matthias Claudius. But there was no visible souvenir of his Berlin mistress who for some years had done her best to make life a little easier for the utterly unsuccessful lecturer of Berlin University, pained not merely by

the resounding successes of his colleagues Fichte and
Hegel, but also, and most sincerely, by their resounding
philosophies. The few human likenesses were, however,
considerably outnumbered by sixteen engravings of
dogs. And two objects, above all, caught the eye of the
rare visitor: the plastercast of the philosopher's de-
ceased poodle and the beautiful bronze statue of a
Tibetan Buddha.

It was a quiet room. Apart from not infrequent rows
between the irritable sage and Frau Schnepp, his devoted housekeeper, no major disturbances are on
record. Except one. It happened in 1848, in the wake of
that abortive revolutionary movement which was carried along by proletarian, liberal, and nationalistic impulses, confusedly mixed and doomed to failure. On
September 18, some shooting went on in the immediate
vicinity of Schopenhauer's house. Suddenly a great
commotion was heard at his door. "I feared," he wrote
afterwards to a friend, "it was the sovereign *canaille*."
Luckily, it was not the *canaille*, but a detachment of
soldiers who wanted to shoot from his windows. Yet
finding the position strategically unsuitable, they soon
moved on. "From the first floor of the house next door,"
Schopenhauer wrote, "the officer watched the rabble
behind the barricade. At once I sent him my opera-
glasses." "What a diversion for a philosopher, to have
the political battlefield in his study!" he remarked, and
"Heaven liberate us from all liberators!" A few years
afterwards, Schopenhauer made his last will. His con-

siderable fortune went to the relief fund for the families of soldiers crippled or killed in fighting for law and order in Germany during the years 1848 and 1849.

There can be no doubt: Schopenhauer was a reactionary. He was the tory among the whig philosophers of his age, a royalist of the mind, in stubborn opposition to those who believed that the World-Spirit was untiringly on the move, arranging from time to time large-scale plebiscites to vote in the next—dialectically necessary, even if very shaky, but ultimately rewarding—step toward the millennium. Not for him were Hegel's dialectical convulsions of history, pregnant with saviours of mankind, or Fichte's inflammatory appeals to the German nation, or Schleiermacher's religion for enlightened and educated people. Schopenhauer was the most radical anti-rationalist philosopher of the German nineteenth century.

This statement, however, may land us in difficulties. For what precisely is a rationalist? If you consult a sufficiently large number of philosophical textbooks, you are sure to find the title of rationalist given by one to Aristotle and by the second to Hegel, now to Leibnitz and now again to Karl Marx, in one place to Thomas Aquinas and in another, to John Stuart Mill. Small wonder, then, that common usage has taken the word into its own unphilosophical hands, praising with it, or stigmatizing, as the case may be, a man who tends to believe that human beings are, on the whole, quite clever enough to manage their affairs without much help from God; that evil is mainly a sort of social thoughtlessness, and sin the wrong end of a stick, the right end of which points at psychological maladjustment; and that there is always some hope for a changing world if indeed it does not actually change in the direction of hopelessness.

But whatever view we take of rationalism, and whether we try to understand it in a philosophical sense or in the sense of the pamphleteers, every possible variety of it would have provoked the brilliant rage and philosophical contempt of Arthur Schopenhauer. For he believed that the innermost principle holding the world together and driving it on in senseless rotations, was the very opposite of reason; and that therefore man was forever deceived in his ever-renewed attempts to act in accordance with "natural reason," or fundamentally to better his estate by rational arrangements. Schopenhauer once said that in his seventeenth year he was as overwhelmed by the misery of life as Buddha was in his youth. Schopenhauer's whole philosophy sprang from this impulse. Sustained by his splendid intelligence and enormous knowledge, the moral protest against the evils of existence grew into a philosophical structure both beautifully coherent and blatantly inconsistent. It shares, in fact, all the passionate coherence and logical inconsistency of that ethical radicalism which is its source. For moral indignation, protesting that this is the worst of all possible worlds, will sweep aside the intelligence which insists that it can think of a world far worse; namely a world *without* this moral indignation.

Schopenhauer was one of the profoundest and one of the most mistaken minds of the nineteenth century. This peculiar combination will seem absurd only to those who believe that philosophy is necessarily like solving mathematical problems or like examining logical propositions. But there would hardly be much left of the tradition of philosophy if we restricted the term to, say, logic. In metaphysics, ethics or aesthetics, on the other hand, there are no "solutions" of problems, but merely absolutions from them. Philosophy is largely a way of seeking and communicating deliverance from the stresses and distresses of the mind. And Schopenhauer was a metaphysician. He found his intellectual absolution from the problem of evil by postulating that the world is not the creation of a divinely benevolent intelligence, but the self-expression—the objectification, as he called it—of a blind life-force, the Will, which is a perpetual offence to man's moral sensibility. There is, in truth, no "problem of evil." The world is as it is, and the way it is strikes the humane sensibility as evil. There is only one problem of existence: the problem of the—often impeded or frustrated—will to exist; and only one solution to it: to give up willing. The *summum bonum* is not to exist; or as the ancient tragedian proclaimed, not to be born.

The Viennese writer Alfred Polgar once quoted this Sophoclean dictum and added: "Indeed, not to be born! Yet, who of us has had such luck? Among a hundred thousand hardly one." For Schopenhauer this is not a question of luck. It is a question of virtue; and to be born means participation in guilt. For every day anew we condone the original guilt by not merely accepting but actually willing our existence and, in the act of procreation, becoming consciously involved in the conspiracy of the Will. The highest virtue, on the other hand, will undo the damage of being born. No, not by suicide. Suicide is nothing but the hysterical self-consummation of the Will, the mad Will's final self-assertion. The true answer is saintliness, the will-less life of pure contemplation.

One may think that German is a clumsy language and may know Hegel's self-defeating remark about Schelling's philosophy: "It is the night in which all cats are grey." There is nothing clumsy or dark in Schopenhauer's style. It has the lucidity of Latin, the witty brilliance and rhetorical flow of French, the crispness of English and a precision which is the more precise for having been wrested from the native imprecision of the medium. Schopenhauer is a great prose writer and— one is almost tempted to say, therefore—a faulty metaphysician. But his faults are immensely significant. They are the inescapable faults of a theology without God, a doctrine of original sin without a supreme lawgiver, an acknowledgement of a divine faculty in man without divine creation, a message of redemption without a redeemer.

Read the glorification of the freedom from the Will,
the conclusion of the final volume of *The World as Will
and Idea*. Even in translation the vigor of Schopenhauer's language will reach you, something of the
profound relief this will-tortured mind found in the contemplation of "nothingness," which for him, strangely
enough, is the same as the peace that passes understanding or as the heaven of Christian saints; that
nothingness which stretches before us once the Will is
defeated: "Yet our nature, which shrinks from being
dissolved into this nothingness is but another way of
realizing that it is life we so strongly will, indeed that
we are nothing if not this very will to live, and know
nothing but it. Yet if we avert our eyes from our own
want and bondage, and turn to those who have risen
above the world, and in whom the Will, having wholly
recognized itself and having found itself present in
everything that exists, achieves the freedom of self-
negation, and who then only wait for the Will's last
vestige, which still keeps alive their bodies, to vanish
with them, we shall behold—no, not the turmoil of
strife, ambition and greed, not the endless changes from
desire to anxiety and from pleasure to misery, not the
unending and insatiable expectation of happiness which
makes up the dream of life dreamt by the will of man
—but the peace which passes all understanding, the
soul as calm as an untroubled sea, and that deep still-
ness, inviolable confidence and security, the mere
reflection of which, on faces such as Raphael and

Correggio have painted, is a complete and certain gospel: what is left is knowledge, what has gone is the Will. It is through the contemplation of such saintliness which . . . is brought before our eyes by art and vouchsafed with the stamp of inner truth, that we must shake off what darkly oppresses us in the face of that nothingness." "Only knowledge remains, the Will has vanished." It is indeed unbecoming to break such peace with philosophical questions, and one would not dare to do it, had it not been a peace with consequences.

"That inviolable confidence." The question is: confidence in what? "Only knowledge remains." The question is: knowledge of what? Schopenhauer's answer is and must be: confidence in Nothing, knowledge of Nothing. For if the abandoned Will is truly the sole sustainer of the world, if there is no world beside the Will, then there can only be Nothing where the Will is not. And yet Schopenhauer furnishes this Nothing with the holiest possessions of man: a true and selfless vision and the ultimate goodness of the contemplative life. But what truth is there to see, what goodness to contemplate? On one side the setting of the dark and will-inspired world, and on the other the rising of a luminous Nothing. Ever since, this Nothing has haunted philosophy and literature alike. Its learned name is nihilism.

Schopenhauer, of course, was no nihilist. The exploration and exposition of nihilism was left to his great disciple and renegade Nietzsche, who, significantly enough, believed that he himself had overcome nihilism

—by overcoming Schopenhauer. For Schopenhauer only just escaped nihilism by cheating his own metaphysical system of its rightful conclusion, which in itself is nihilistic in the extreme: the ultimate reality of the world is the blind, senseless, amoral Will. Its denial, so highly commendable, must needs leave us with Nothing. But at this point Schopenhauer, as we have seen, drops philosophy and picks up the philosophers' stone, making gold from nothing.

The whole of his metaphysics is shot through with this kind of alchemy. It is the alchemy of the artist, and indeed the most satisfying section of his work is his philosophy of art. It thrives, as it were, on the flawless inconsistency of his metaphysics. Art, Schopenhauer says, is only art insofar as it reflects the vision of a mind who, in the act of artistic creation, rises above his own willing self and becomes the temporary brother of the saint in the state of pure contemplation. Contemplating what? The Platonic ideas, says Schopenhauer, the eternal forms of all transient things. And what are these eternal forms, these logically so troublesome inhabitants of a domain "other-than-the-Will," a domain the metaphysical rank of which is so hard to determine? Still, whatever else they are, they are for Schopenhauer the primary and lasting models of the Will objectifying itself. And what is the Will? The answer we know in all its unpleasantness. And yet the eternal forms of that vast unpleasantness, contemplated by the artist, yield works of art, the supreme pleasure of the human race.

Is this not sheer alchemy? It is the alchemy that Nietzsche rejected.

If the world is nothing but the objectification of a senseless principle, well then, said Nietzsche, let us not play truant and in a cowardly way absent ourselves from reality to dream the nursery dreams of redeeming nothingness. If truth is an ugly thing, then works of art are not reflections of ultimate truth, but beautiful illusions. If good and evil have no roots in the fundamental nature of existence, then let us discard these chimeras of the human mind. If we are too weak to bear as much reality, let us become stronger. Thus Schopenhauer's world as Will, *denied* in the saintly contemplation of empty heavens, becomes Nietzsche's world as Will, *affirmed* in the superhuman acceptance of a life truly beyond good and evil.

From this point onward the consequences are clear. They can often, though not always, be traced back to Schopenhauer's distinct influence. The mind of Europe was ready to receive the pessimistic philosophy of the Will, as much as, on the other extreme, it liked to entertain at its more optimistic feasts the Hegelian Messiah, dispensing "rational" salvation through the progress of history. As for Schopenhauer, his great essay on "The Will in Nature" seems like the metaphysical mould in which Darwin's theory of evolution is cast, and much of Freud's psychology of the unconscious reads like a sustained rationalization of Schopenhauer's philosophy of sex, for him "the focus of the Will." Schopenhauer's metaphysics of the Will is alive in Richard Wagner's pessimistic sensationalism as well as in Baudelaire's lyrically delicious gloom, in Bergson's *élan vital* and in Shaw's more cheerful life-force. We find it in the deep pessimism which is the common mood of the nineteenth-century realist novel, the literary contemporary of the Industrial Revolution, this single-minded dedication of the Will to the acquisition of wealth and other questionable comforts. And Schopenhauer's philosophy of the "impersonal" artist, in his moments of creation half-brother of the saint, has anticipated much in modern aesthetic speculation from Nietzsche to Rilke, Valéry, and T. S. Eliot. It is easily recognized even in the contrary uses made of it as, for instance, in the case of Thomas Mann's young Tonio Kröger, cursing as "infamous" and "outrageous" his fate of having to cultivate a "strange aloofness" from the Will, that is, from ordinary human existence; of having to see, observe, and represent life without vitally sharing in it. Yet this is a fate which Schopenhauer blessed.

But beyond all theory and art, the foolish world rushed in where Schopenhauer's angels wisely feared to tread—for there was only Nothing to tread upon. Neither Kant nor his self-willed disciple Schopenhauer could really satisfy the world. For they were great stoic philosophers, and the Stoics have never supplied popular satisfactions. Kant's is the stocism of reason, Schopenhauer's the stocism of morality. There is no knowing what the Absolute is, said Kant; yet let us trust our moral intuition intimating that there is God. There is no God; rather something like the devil, said Schopenhauer; yet let us defy the devil by choosing the bliss of nothingness. But the world, of course, remained deaf to the subtleties of philosophical "but's." Most people only heard that there was no knowing and that there was no God, and felt ill at ease in a place at once incomprehensible and radically reduced in value —the ideal playground for every ideological impostor with an offer of total comprehension, total liberation and total subjugation of this doubtful world.

History has turned the pessimistic substance of which Schopenhauer's sublime metaphysics of the Will is made, into very base matter indeed. Did Schopenhauer guess that this would happen? Of course he did. For he believed that this reduction of the sublime to base matter was the perpetual, unavoidable, and therefore the only safely predictable accomplishment of history. He hated all political movements, all historical ideologies and all Hegelians. "These fools," he said of the Hegelians, "do not know that what *really* is, is the same at all times. They believe that it will develop and one day arrive." Even his tombstone had to bear witness to his contempt for history. His testament decreed that only his name should mark his grave, "my name with nothing whatsoever added to it, no date, no year, nothing at all, not a syllable."

A poodle and a Buddha in a room with the address "Beautiful Prospect," the philosophy of an evil world, of renunciation and of saintliness without God, a street full of revolutionary noise, a timeless tombstone's distrust of history, and a future under the shadow of the Will to Power—it is an odd but formidable list of questions put before the rational-liberal examination candidate. No marks, says Dr. Schopenhauer's instruction, will be given for mere optimistic or revolutionary padding.

Essay Ten

The Study of Asian Philosophy: For History; for Comparison; for Synthesis?

Robert W. Browning

Robert W. Browning is Professor of Philosophy at Northwestern University, having previously taught at the University of North Carolina and at Syracuse University. His major concerns lie in ethics, the metaphysics of process, and theory of knowledge. He has long taken an avocational interest in certain Buddhist doctrines and in the classical thought of India and China. He was an Associate Member of the Second East-West Philosophers' Conference in 1949, and of the Fourth in 1964. In 1963–64 he was a grantee for study in Asia. His publications include articles in The Review of Metaphysics, Ethics, *and* The Educational Forum. *He contributed essays to three volumes in "The Library of Living Philosophers," namely, those on C. D. Broad, S. Radhakrishnan, and C. I. Lewis. He is a member of a number of professional societies and was on the national Board of Officers of the American Philosophical Association when serving as Secretary-Treasurer of the Western Division, 1957–59.*

The scholar to whom this volume of essays is dedicated is a man of extraordinary learning and range. With potent expressive power, he championed a viewpoint with which he later broke—the break being documented by a book in ethics recognized for its salient striking force along a very long line of presumed strong points of naturalistic apologetics. His reputation in aesthetics, particularly on the philosophical levels of literary criticism, is justly international. Although he has not written for us a metaphysic as such, or a philosophy of religion, his publications disclose to the discerning major theses of philosophical anthropology which concern issues which are pivotal in these fields. His perspicacity in depth psychology is patent to all who know him; his direct scholarship in anthropology was facilitated by cooperative studies which embraced extended conversations with Professor Robert Redfield and other luminaries in knowledge of social organization. He has long combined his knowledge of depth psychology and anthropology in service to his study of personality formation for any light which may thus be thrown upon the vexed profundities of philosophy of personality. Although the present writer would share with Professor Vivas admiration for thinkers who have manifested a sense of human community—in milieus where persons are viewed and threatened between the Scylla of atomic individualism and the Charybdis of imposed collectivization—probably we would not hold common views on matters of implementation. But full respect must be accorded for the deep seriousness and perspicacious relevance with which Vivas addresses himself to issues of moment in social philosophy; his opponents must at times have felt him not only breathing but cutting like an acetylene torch.

The author trusts that this little exhortative essay is not too inappropriate to offer in honor of Professor Vivas. Hopefully its width of concern—abstracted from its shallowness of treatment—may be taken as symbolic homage to the exemplary breadth of scholarship of Professor Vivas.

The study of Oriental philosophies is hardly in good standing in prestigious quarters among Western professionals. This attitude, I believe, is unfortunate. Accordingly, I here appoint myself to find some format

for giving a lay sermon on the values to Western thinkers in studying Eastern thought. In general I do share
so many Western valuations and Anglo-Saxon limitations that it will be plain to real devotees of some Oriental orientation that I am talking to myself under the
guise of addressing others. However, I am not consciously a wolf in sheep's clothing.

One is not unmindful of the division of intellectual
labor. That one believes there to be marked values
along a certain course does not mean that all men
should tread it. That there are values in the study of
Asian philosophy does not mean that all men or all
philosophers should study it all of the time. It does
mean, I think, that some Western thinkers should study
it some of the time, and that it is not appropriate that
they should be frowned upon as peculiar by their fellows. It may furthermore be observed that, analogous to
the values generally of the humanities in an age of scientific specialization, there are complementary nonspecialist stimuli to human integrity or integralness in
the review of Western and Eastern philosophy. This is
of especial service at a time when Western philosophers
are retreating into isolated specialties.

My procedure will be, at the start, to cite some of the
motives for the study of other cultures—to secure ac-
quaintance with their thought as well as with their art
and practice—insinuating along the way the merits of
these motives. Among the ensuing intellectual enterprises, it will be well to distinguish emphases upon
history of thought from emphases upon *comparative*

philosophy and, in turn, from efforts to effect meta-physical or other *synthesis*. I will not wholly dissociate myself from the ideal of even the last, although I will not support what I take to be early and hasty attempts to achieve synthesis.

In the end I expect to resort to a sort of minimum strategy of contending for the value of non-Western studies as stimuli to the doing of social philosophy (which at the present time suffers from comparative neglect). Three reasons may be cited in addition to the desire to call attention to the deficiency. First, even those Occidental philosophers who assume that non-Western philosophy is practically devoid of truth cannot similarly scorn it as bodies of data for social interpretation. Secondly, illustratively, the classical period of Chinese philosophy turns so much—with stark simplicity—upon the differing views of human nature and the proper roles (or non-roles) of manners, morals, education, and government that one could strategically direct attention in this direction rather than dispersing it over what may be most suggestive in Buddhism and other Indian systems.[1] Thirdly, we can thus avoid or

---

[1] My allusions will be to India, China and Japan; this is due to my even greater ignorance of other Asian traditions. For a Japanese scholar's views on some of the contrasts between ways of thinking which are more or less characteristic of India, China, Tibet and Japan, one may consult Professor Hajime Nakamura's *Ways of Thinking of Eastern Peoples* (revised English translation edited by Philip P. Wiener, Honolulu: East-West Center Press, 1964). Linguistically India alone is more diverse than Europe, and it could be argued that

evade a head-on collision over the interpretation of Yogin and mystical experience.

It would be typical of most Indian thought and non-Indian Buddhist teaching, with possibly the earlier Taoist also thrown in, to hold that a certain spiritual realization is at once the supreme knowledge and supreme experience, whether called samadhi, absorption, non-dual experience, nirvana, or satori. Although the last two decades have witnessed a growing interest in such mystical experience, still most contemporary Westerners would feel that this is distinctly abnormal, the result of a sort of psychical masturbation, and to be avoided by wholesome object-manipulating men. Sooner or later, no doubt, one may be called upon to make up his mind about mysticism and alleged supernormal perceptions. But it is a distinct distortion and therefore a disservice to the cause of Oriental studies to make them turn wholly upon accepting the validity of the cognitive claims of one or more mysticisms. If one denies these claims to validity, it is a pity if one then supposes that there is nothing else in Chinese or Indian thought. Moreover, since we have mysticisms in our own culture and *prima facie* cases of supernormal perception, we need not move to the East to encounter the stimulus of any such perception. There are admittedly impressive bodies of Eastern tradition in which

---

it is as culturally diverse. I am taking it as superfluous to remark that my loose collective use of "Western" and "Asian" does not mean that I am concurring in thinking of them as blocs.

extraordinary cognitive claims seem to be made, whereas comparable claims in the West are highly exotic and are considered peripheral by the major religious tradition. In this connection, we may later touch upon the criteria of virtue and even the criteria of sanity in different cultures.

Motives toward the cognition of foreign thought and culture may themselves be dominantly *practical,* dominantly *aesthetic* (or quasi-aesthetic) or dominantly *cognitive.* We may study other cultures and histories for the "lessons" they may give, in the way of facts to be taken into account in policy, or in the way of uncovering possible repeated patterns to be sought or avoided. A scholar is not likely to make the practical motive—at least a practical political one—to be the mainspring of, or justification for, his study. Yet in a world that lives in the danger from man's own recent technology that ours does, it is not appropriate for the scholar to bury his head in possibly radioactive sands and to care nothing for the byproducts of intelligent policy (as against ignorant policy) which might flow from intercultural researches.[2]

There may be a feeling that knowledge of details is all that is needed for political technology. However, some details are not genuinely understood unless they

---

[2] The beloved Professor Cornelius Krusé observed that Clemanceau was certainly something of a nationalist who hardly loved Germans and felt that the most basic trouble with them was that there were twenty million too many of them; but still he did not take any anti-intellectual stance; instead, he wanted German language and

are related in a larger framework. And for the long run project of achieving understanding—not necessarily synthesis—apprehension of "accepted values," "comprehensive ideas" and the "enduring hopes" of others is needed. "Appreciative mutual understanding between cultures," as Professor E. A. Burtt says, "must then be won at the philosophical level if solid foundations of trust and friendships are to be established. Otherwise the supreme values and organizing ideas to which one people is committed will remain alien, opaque, and therefore unreasonable to those who have grown up in a different cultural background."[3]

Another type of practical interest is exemplified when an individual decides that the Sankhya is probably the nearest approximation to the truth of extant systems, or that a certain branch of Buddhism is the way to serenity. He submits himself to a discipline with the seriousness appropriate to one seeking enlightenment or salvation. Because of the nature of these Indian and

culture to be studied, saying that if a man is my friend I want to know him and if a man is my enemy I want to know what he is up to. Prudential non-Communist Westerners will want to know Communist ideology and national ideals for whatever clues these may yield about behavior; prudential makers of foreign policy will want to know about other cultures and the feelings and valuations which arise in persons tutored in them so that ineptnesses and tragic offenses may be avoided. The work of scholars will here be resources. I do not think that it will be characteristic of the scholars to manifest the ethnocentrism of Clemenceau in recommending their studies for attention.

[3] *In Search of Philosophic Understanding* (New York: New American Library, 1965), pp. 253f.

Japanese teachings, this is indeed the peculiarly apt way to respond to them in their own terms. They are in this ultimate sense "practical." Adherence is much like joining the Pythagorean brotherhood, Epicurus' garden, or a religious order in the West. With such an acknowledgment before us, we shall leave the topic, saying that here we are presuming a scholarly interest and not conversion. If, after study, some thinkers do decide to become devotees, that is well and good, and their ultimate responsibility. It is no part of our present advocacy. Ethnocentrism is probably such among philosophers that "enthusiasts" will be considered to be eccentrics. Some will dismiss the occurrence as a trivial datum of abnormal psychology; others will view it as of the profoundest spiritual significance. I would rather add that it is at least a remarkable phenomenon of change of psychical structure when it occurs.

There are inquiries into, and lookings at, features of other cultures where the drawing interest may be aesthetic or quasi-aesthetic. I think this needs no justification. Even when it is characterized as the curiosity of the "dilettante," it need not be deplored. One might call the experience "aesthetic" when it is the appreciation of the object for itself. Although not unique to other observers, the structures found may be novel in the experience of a given person. It is difficult to be assured of pure cases of this sort of interest, for normally there will occur byproducts of such experience and these may become recognized for some values transcending the given occasion. As well as "perceiving," one may also be "learning." As in the discovery of values in the humanities, we are at once learning about others and learning about ourselves. Assuming a common human nature, one sees more of what one might have been and orders some of his potentialities. In whatever ways we are importantly different, perceiving the other who is different helps us to see ourselves in an uncustomary way. The previously unnoticed in actualities and assumptions stands a better chance of receiving recognition. The lenses which we have previously looked through but not seen may now be made an object. Study of this object may lead to knowledge of its distorting effects. Such knowledge may thus have grown from the aesthetic matrix but is now far beyond it.

A hypothetical pure cognitive interest may be momentarily indistinguishable from an aesthetic interest when it is absorbed in the object in isolation, but its cognitive character becomes plain as one seeks connections and theoretical significance. Let it be observed that since some of the phenomena being cognized are ostensibly statements of truths within philosophical positions, such cognition of ostensible cognitions gives rise to a dimension of questions which does not emerge in the cognition of phenomena which do not make claims. Questions arise as to the validity of the claims, their worth as testimony, and criteria of assessment. We thus have normative and methodological questions, even existential questions, about other philosophies, as well as historical questions.

Let us see if any ordering significance can be noted

when we look at the three categories of motives along-
side types of intellectual enterprise that one may set out
to do. There may be some Orientalists who are advisers
in Washington or other capitals. May there be more of
them! Here, however, their immediate role may be dismissed as one of dispensing technology to geopolitical
ends or to statecraft. The dilettante with an exotic aesthetic interest will hardly be likely to write, but he may
read and look profusely. Those whom I have thought of
as scholars and philosophers are prosecuting in study,
and possibly in writing, the history and structure of Indian *darsannas,* Chinese *chias,* etc.; some are engaged
in comparative philosophy; and a few are working on
effecting a synthesis of what seems to them important
and right in the materials studied and horizons newly
suggested. For simplicity, we shall say that there are
these three emphases:

(1) upon history of philosophy;
(2) upon comparative philosophy; and
(3) upon efforts at synthesis.

No Western scholar does one of these exclusively, not
even the first, for his efforts at exposition and historical
clarification will at least lead to incidental resort to
comparison. There seems, methodologically, to be an
ascending order of inquiries. One cannot make comparisons without knowing what one is comparing. One
cannot effect synthesis without knowing what one is
synthesizing and without doing comparisons to note

agreements and to note complementarities and—yes—
to note apparent contradictions which call for some
sort of reconciliation, correction, tailoring, and clarification. There are pseudopodia which work in the opposite direction. The historian is more than a promiscuous
chronicler; his judgments of importances will presumably be somewhat influenced by his own mental comparisons and his thoughts of a philosophical nisus. The
practitioner of comparative philosophy thinks of some
level of synthesis when he characterizes some developments as complementary.

Now I am treating these three enterprises as dominantly cognitive; of course in the case of a given
philosopher who must "publish or perish," his work
may actually be more practically motivated than cog-
nitively, but we pass by his private situation. It is to be
noted that the relationships of the three emphases are
not actually as simple as my architectonic has suggested. And I do wish to assert that all three of the
enterprises are intrinsically legitimate, but I desire to
dissociate myself from all hasty programs of doing "synthesis" and to declare that comparative philosophy—
after the initial surveys are over—is extremely difficult
and subtle.

First, in so far as the historian has what I called the
aesthetic interest he may find himself not only not left
alone but cast in the rôle of collector of data for the
doer of comparative philosophy and for the synthesizer.
If in principle he accepts this assignment in the in-

tellectual division of labor, he may nevertheless find himself disturbed by the use made of his results. Specifically, he may feel that those who are committed to comparison and to synthesis are, as living limited professional minds, actually devoted to oversimplification. How does the comparer work except by selecting some structures as more fundamental, or even by fastening upon some features for showing similarity and some features for exhibiting contrast. In any case he is vocationally prone to vast omissions and to neglect of subtleties. For example, Professor Filmer S. C. Northrop's sweeping contrast between dominance of the aesthetic continuum in the East and dominance of the conceptual in the West, with concepts in the East being derived from intuition and concepts in the West being set up by postulation, was markedly enlightening, rough as it was. He showed it to be a tool of inquiry for entering into fields of law and social relationships as well as philosophy. And yet any historian worth his salt could hardly help taking offense at Northrop's thesis for its failure to note exceptions and make qualifications. The historian with his eye upon uniqueness will have similar feelings about "synthesis." Precious variety is likely to be forgotten and lost, intellectually and even socially, if the synthesizer is allowed to push his own eclectic recipes into some position of prestige. Santayana may be allowed to speak for this point of view: "From a literary or humanistic point of view I think that it is the *variety* and *incomparability* of systems, as of kinds of beauty, that make them interesting, not any compromise or fusion that could be made of them." Again, " 'synthesis' . . . could only be reached by blurring or emptying both systems in what was clear and distinct in their results. Now in natural evolution it is not the results that are alike. They grow diverse as they grow richer and more perfect. What is similar, perhaps identical, in all things is their origin or starting point."[4]

Now I shall affirm the long-run legitimacy of efforts at synthesis, and I shall observe that neither Santayana nor I have it in our power to restrain some tendencies toward one world culture. Whether men will move toward a unified world homogeneity or whether they will not (owing either to immoral ethnocentrism or to a sensitively moral regard for the constellations of values) I surely cannot say. But I may partially disarm some critics by partially agreeing with them. I shall return to this theme after taking note of the somewhat distinctive activity of a very few Western thinkers.

No independent general rubric is being assigned to an activity which nevertheless deserves special mention. Reference is made to the searching of pieces of non-Western philosophical literature for arguments which may further our own researches or bolster our own positions. For example, one might ransack the Nyaya-Vaisesika and the early schools of Southern Buddhism for "new" arguments which bear upon the status of ideas

---

[4] George Santayana, "On Philosophical Synthesis . . .," *Philosophy East And West*, I: 5.

or upon the controversy between neo-realism and critical realism (presentative or direct realism *vs.* representative realism). One may look at Kung-sun Lung for confirmatory support of elemental notions in semantics or look at him and Chu Hsi to see if they suggest any help with our problem of universals. A logician may look at Jainist, Buddhist or Hindu logic to see if he finds anything to disturb his own taxonomy of kinds of inferences. Idealists may search Ramanuja or Shankara or Vasubandhu for further arguments in behalf of idealism or for aid with some of the problems connected with error or with the status of the finite self. Now we shall class this kind of activity as a species of comparative philosophy; it is then at most "piecemeal" work in comparative philosophy. Some might say that it is only Western philosophy doing a little mining in Eastern ores to feed the Western intellectual economy—the exploitative import side of colonialism in the realm of ideas. Although such a characterization is not without point, it is lacking in justice. That the activity is throughout accompanied by a domineering, even arrogant, attitude is a gratuitous blanket assumption.[5] Furthermore, it is just this sort of activity, if success-

---

[5] The falsity of the assumption is manifest in the judicious studies of Professor Karl Potter, who has unobtrusively been bringing Western analytic concepts to bear upon his reading of Indian philosophical literature—and finding some occidental distinctions to have been well antedated. Reciprocally, Professors D. M. Datta, K. N. Jayatilleke, and many others utilized Western tools beneficially in illuminating traditional orthodox and unorthodox systems of Indian epistemology.

ful, which would—whatever be the ethnocentrism exhibited—bring about higher respect in the West for Eastern studies. If tracts of Eastern philosophy can help solve Western problems, it is indeed worthy of respect and investigation. This prompts the question: Why has so little of this piecemeal comparative philosophy been done, and why is there so little aid being received by Western thinkers from Eastern resources?

No attempt will be made to apportion weightings to the following considerations which at once occur to one. Western philosophy may simply be ahead; or, more modestly, it may be ahead in dealing with its problems as Eastern philosophy may be further advanced with its characteristic practices and problems. Eastern philosophy is not visibly in one of its great creative periods —it may be on a rising crescendo now—and living ferment is more stimulating than ancient books in a foreign language and in a foreign idiom of life. Most all Asian philosophy is prescientific; although most of the history of Western philosophy is also prescientific, current discussions are circumspectly in the scientific age. Moreover, it may be easier to overlook mixtures of pseudo-science with philosophy in one's own tradition than in another culture, and it is certainly assumed that our science is not just Western science but simply "science," intercultural and supracultural. That little aid has been received in modern times is not surprising; aid requires some kind of contact, and few have gone where they could make any contact.

This last deserves a little expansion. I am sure that a

weighty factor is this: Eastern literature, particularly
Indian and Buddhist literature, is prodigious; it is an
unknown jungle to us. A Western philosopher knows
he must get hold of the works of Plato and Aristotle
rather than of Paracelsus or Apuleius' *Golden Ass;* he
does not similarly know what to take hold of in Eastern
publications. And some who have with good will undertaken, say, the reading of Buddhist literature, whether
in translation from Pali or Sanskrit or Chinese recen-
sion, not to mention from Tibetan, have found it so
repetitive that they cannot carry on. If they are looking
for minerals which their intellectual smelter requires,
they feel that percentagewise the Asian ore is of such
low yield that calculation shows that they must pru-
dently cease to mine it. (Many Western thinkers do not
read Hegel; it is not that he is devoid of ideas, but
that they feel the obscurity is not worth overcoming in
order to find the occasional gems. Again, many Westerners do not pursue symbolic logic; they estimate that
the time spent in learning the operation of the machine
and polishing it had better be given to a direct assault
on the problems with present tools.) Now in so far as
the piecemeal comparative philosophy does not take
place because a thinker sees that he may be fatigued or
even lost in the Asian literature if he once starts, the
situation may change after the work of more general
surveyors, field geologists and prospectors has been
done and made known.

Even when the intent of the Westerner is to further

his own inquiries growing out of his own tradition, his finding of relevant confirmatory or suggestive argument in Asian sources is a form of comparative philosophy. His attitudes may vary when he finds not what he is looking for but something that he cannot, on his present basis, assimilate. Then he may reject it as wrong, because he sees it to be wrong or because of its non-assimilability with his convictions. If, however, he is stimulated to broaden his basis, to achieve a new perspective because of what he could not previously encompass, then I should say that he is doing a bit of synthesis. His comparative work has turned into integral or synthetic work.

More general comparative philosophy and more general synthetic efforts, of course, are carried on by people who attempt frontally to take in the whole of systems being compared or available for integration. What gets encountered is not restricted to what is found to be associated with their own specialized interests within their own tradition.

The suspicion is plausible that one reason some Western professionals frown upon the minority of their colleagues who take some interest in Oriental thought is that they suppose them to be advocates of premature synthesis. They picture these more or less evangelical deviants as laboring under the assumption that there is roughly 50 percent of the truth in the East and 50 percent of it in the West, and that they, putting the two together in one generation—nay, perhaps in one decade—will be twice as wise as their fellows. Extended comment is superfluous. One can do history of philosophy with a minimum of comparative philosophy and no attempt at synthesis. We do not take all of our own medieval scholars as committed to compromising their respective "modern" points of view by effecting an eclectic mixture with the objects of their historical researches. One may pursue comparative philosophy without any intent of effecting syntheses on the first ground level of encountered explicit contentions. To be sure, there may be a kind of synthesis on some "meta-level" of the parameters he has found as planes of comparison (e.g., theory of human nature and culture) from which the activities of the respective philosophizing are supposed to issue. But this constitutes no synthesis of the contents of the contentions.[6]

---

6 Thinking of East–West philosophers' conferences and of the organ, *Philosophy East and West,* one's impression is that there was much more talk about "synthesis" in the 1940s and 1950s than more recently. Assuming this to have been a fact, it may have sprung in part from the milieu in which there still remained more dispositions toward system-building than in the last decade or two, and it may have been due in part to direct prodding from Professor Charles A. Moore, the father of the conferences and of the journal. If one may trust titles as an index of orientation of contents, the impression is confirmed. The completing issue of 25 volumes of *Philosophy East and West: A Quarterly of Asian and Comparative Thought* contains a "Twenty-five Year Index," pp. 503–514. Under the heading of "Methodology," pp. 509–510, there are some eighty articles among which 24 have "synthesis" in their titles. Three fourths of these appeared in the first five volumes, doubtless a number by invitation. Another small clustering occurs in Volumes XII and XIII. The present editor, Professor Eliot Deutsch, who assumed his duties in 1967,

However, I do not wish to leave this criticism with simply showing its possible irrelevance. Instead, I will move head on for the legitimacy of synthesis at the same time as I remark upon where practically we now are in relation to it. If in one way or another philosophy is held to contain no truths and to have no concern with truths, my argument would seem to fail. If philosophizing were solely, for example, some nonpropositional intuition of meaning or of reality, one—particularly an outsider—would have great difficulty in knowing what he was to synthesize. But only by an extreme stipulation could philosophy be so restricted. Even were some such goal its consummation, as some say, there would presumably be a path along which preparatory truths and falsities, or sound imperatives as opposed to mistaken ones, could be uttered. If there is a process of clarification, presumably there are rejections of meaning that can be made. Again, if one looks upon all phi-

---

has made clear that for his clientele he desires intensive studies and not general comparisons—nor syntheses, nor exhortations. Cp. p. 389. One may quite concur that for those already interested, *apologies* had pretty well run their course. However, for Western philosophers generally one cannot at all concur that this would be an apt judgment.

In recent years the society which is associated with the journal mentioned above has held a series of workshops upon problems indirectly evoking comparison (e.g., "existence," "causation," "law and morality") and upon explicit comparative studies (as on Whitehead and Buddhist thought). Nor have all comparisons been between Asian and Western notions; there have been intra-Asian comparisons when focus has been engaged upon Wang Yang-ming or upon *dharma* and *li*.

losophies as expressions of culture in the way in which, say, plastic arts are, then there is no meaning in a project of synthesizing them into a body of discursive truth. If, however, each philosophy involved is looked upon as claiming certain truths about the world, then there is point to the questions as to which of these claims are true and which are false and what one is to do with undecidables; and there is point to the possibility that a consolidated view which comes from another culture may contain some truths which a genuine enquirer had better incorporate. Of course in our statement here we have assumed an objective meaning of truth and (what need not be the same thing) that there is or are one or more objective procedures for approximating to some of the content of it. The point is that if one has a definition of truth which accords it objectivity and if he takes given philosophies to claim to formulate some of this truth, then he does not easily avoid questions of truth and falsity in respect to the systems he is reviewing and comparing. *Mutatis mutandis,* similar remarks could be made for the idea of moral truth when it would be held not to be descriptive of an antecedent moral order but nevertheless formulated by some objectively reasonable criteria in the face of the realities.

One factor of no little interest which is packed into the notion of "synthesis" may be raised by the query of how far "philosophy" is being conceived as in principle one supracultural enterprise. Mathematics and each natural science have (at least until recently) been so conceived by Western practitioners. Sociological reporting on our contemporaries in response to some hypothetical questionnaire concerning "objectivity" might disclose that different reactions—and not just one reaction spread on a spectrum of degrees—might be elicited with respect to different "fields" within the antique omnibus "philosophy." For example, construing any attendant imperatives to be hypothetical only, pure logic (as against applied) and philosophy of science might well be taken—like the growing sciences themselves—to be supracultural and in a basic sense "descriptive" even when done on a meta-level. Metaphysics, too, I myself would say, has historically been in intent descriptive of the universe which *is;* as such, this queen of cognitive enterprises (now deposed and living in exile from "Anglo-Saxon countries") was not classed as normative—although different "morals" may well have been drawn from the supposed nature of things when construed in different cultures, yes, and in the caves of individual thinkers with their personal idols. Meta-studies about given ranges of data—even when the data are phenomena in the domain of the social, where claims of truth, appropriateness, validity or right may be made—are likewise undertaken as both descriptive and supracultural. Doing the studies may be guided by implicit norms, but no endorsement is made of the norms which are taken simply as complicated portions of the social phenomena under review.

Accidents of location or other forms of advantageous access may favor some workers as compared with others, but the enterprises prosecuted may be deemed supracultural. After the explorations of three generations of anthropologists[7] and after the "emotive"

---

[7] Perhaps it is easy to overassess and easy to underassess the impact made upon philosophers by anthropologists. Some detailed research, particularly as relating language and world-views, may finally have had weighty effect in philosophy; real appropriation naturally awaited the semanticist's or the metaphysician's own ripening of the pertinent questions. There is little doubt that Aristotle has had predecessors and many successors in seemingly at once saying that he was doing an ethics for man and saying, tacitly, that the ethos of one's own civilization was superior to that of barbarians and accordingly should be looked to for the best sources of data. Anthropologists have been "useful" in prolifically offering illustrations of the social relativity of moral codes, but philosophers apparently have not been greatly disturbed by the *ignoratio elenchis* and the occasional sweepingly exciting but false assertions made in philosophy by their colleagues outside. If anthropologists can continue their wonderful resistance to the intimidations of behavioristic methodologists and if perhaps empirical or phenomenologically-minded philosophers can condescend to be interested in details, particularly details of concrete consciousness of what has familial resemblance to feelings of obligation, feelings of beauty, feelings of evidential force, feelings of environing powers and realities, then I for one would forecast a bright day for the ensuing cooperative endeavors. "Moral sense" philosophers were once on a par with "aesthetic sense" aestheticians, but one suspects that characteristically moralists would be much more ready to surrender any title to normative aesthetics, vacating the territory to meta-aestheticians, than they would be to abandon normative ethics. And understandably so—out of practical pressures—but they may too readily have grown weary of trying to formulate any residual meaning of "human nature" to serve as a pole of something intercultural and thus supracultural. Some contemporaries who fruitfully employ modes of game-playing are disturbed by the question of whether the game of morals,

theories of ethics of positivists and their forebears and
their descendants, one may encounter a deal of caution
and relatively little outright confidence about the once
unabashed "normative" enterprises, specifically old-
fashioned ethics, aesthetics, and social philosophy.

It is not becoming to take the initial stance: My philosophy is true and yours is false. It is hardly cricket to
begin with the assumption: My philosophy aims at
descriptive truths about the world and your philosophy
is expression of—if not "rationalization" of—your attitudes toward the world. But of course it is logically
possible that my philosophy in certain particulars is
true and yours false. And after inquiry we might find
that to a significant degree, and to a larger degree than
is characteristic in Western suppositions about philosophy, several Eastern so-called "philosophies" are more
directions for, or stimulation toward, attaining certain
experiences than declarations about the structure of
the world we inhabit or about the categories needed for
the articulation of its actual or possible structures. Indeed, I am inclined to hold that this is the case.

Now I do fancy it helpful to us to approach a given
intellectualized position not only with our new tools of
asking about the different employments of language
exhibited but also with our familiar trichotomy of

---

or the language of the game of morals, is one which, unlike chess, one
must play. Coerciveness could be grounded in man as a social or
cultural being, while the specific coercions would be functions of the
particular encompassing culture.

Logic, Fact and Value. I feel that I am taking initial steps toward understanding—at least toward the prevention of misunderstanding—when I can sort positions into those whose primary thrust is descriptive and those whose primary thrust is directive or valuational. Likewise, within the analysis of a more or less systematic persuasion it is helpful to sort out its explicit and tacit propositions into kinds of contentions and then in turn to try to account for the connections in terms of logical deduction, inductive or abductive support, and practical purpose. (Everyone, I suppose, who treats of Western thought notes an anthropocentric practical interest on the part of Socrates in contrast with some Ionians, characterizes Epicureanism and Stoicism as practical philosophies, and recognizes distinct features of Patristic and Medieval thought. Among the great merits of Sabine's *History of Political Thought* is his frequent use of his categorical trichotomy of Reason, Fact and Value, as well as his perspicacious observation of the social context of the thought under investigation.) If we recognize the dominant practical character of Confucian philosophy toward social ends, or the dominant practical character of Zen toward producing certain valued experiences or the dominantly practical character of original Buddhism toward personal salvation, we are saved from some possible misunderstandings which might arise from trying to fit everything into ordered declarative descriptive sentences. Of course, however, just as atomism may excite the major interest of some reader of Epicureanism, so one may be chiefly interested in Buddhistic skandas and theory of the self as proffered theories.

Burtt, in some earlier publications, held that the Western categorization of Reason, Fact and Value enjoys no correlate in Eastern thought. Thus, what Burtt's criticism amounts to in brief is: "You supposed you were doing intercultural or supracultural 'historical' and 'comparative philosophy.' Instead, you were doing them from your own cultural point of view." I believe that we must probably plead guilty to this, practically speaking, and certainly at least be mindful of it as a heuristic caution. But I intend this as a relative pleading guilty to having exhibited an instance of the truth of relativism. The very statement, however, of such relativism presupposes a meaning to the ideal of supracultural or intercultural objectivity, and—to adapt an old Roycean argument about error—the very recognition of the error or relativity in a given case indicates that in one way one is beyond it. One is seeing something of the reality of another view when one sees that one's proffered schema does not fit it. And I think Burtt himself in a later statement would agree. For he writes:

> But while every person *is* an individual—and his individuality needs never to be lost—through his power of unlimited sensitivity he is also universal. Vigorously or feebly, he can stretch his awareness beyond every present boundary, including the boundary set by the presuppositions of the culture to which he belongs.[8]

---

[8] *In Search of Philosophic Understanding*, p. 254.

I am not as confident as he about our unlimited sensitivity if he means to refer to something actual.

Similar critical remarks could be made about the actual cultural limitations of such efforts at synthesis as do obtain, without denying the validity of the ideal of intercultural synthesis and with positively asserting that there is no discoverable antecedently fixed line of a cultural barrier beyond which a given thinker cannot go.

Probably the regnant ideals of "synthesis" and of "system" have—quite appropriately—been determined by proponents of the coherence "theory" of truth. The two notions, indeed, lie in the metaphysician's vocabulary familiarly, not really as two but as aspects of one. The resultant "ideal" is extremely severe if the requirement that all accepted propositions be mutually supportive is insisted upon. At the opposite extreme, the lowliest form of logical "synthesis" might be that of mere consistency, where logically independent propositions are admissible as well as, of course, those which have one or other form of "positive" logical relationship —perhaps including loose and informal ones which do not appear in texts on deduction but which are brought over from induction, abduction and accepted forms of practical reasoning. A thinker need not, it seems to me, be convicted sweepingly of adherence to an ontology of logical atomism if basically he wishes now to abstain from system-building in the grand manner. One might even grant Spinoza and a number of right wing Hege-

lians their point—and Whitehead his presumably different "necessary system of general ideas"—and still insist
that, soberly considering where we are epistemically,
we had better operate partially as empiricists, gathering
what are to our limited minds logically independent
mundane truths. Leibniz, as he may be read, seems to
be asserting that the Supreme Monad can be a perfectly
successful rationalist, but those of us with lesser scope
and intellectual power had better in practice discover
what we can as if it were contingent, long before we
can see its necessity under the principle of sufficient
reason.

Suppose that in the present context one normally
does think of "synthesis" as entailing integration into
one well unified whole. Then it is not impertinent to
suggest that there may be "weaker" forms of "synthesis." Thus one might preempt an enclave for pro-
tecting some mongrel forms of integral apprehension,
and one might deem these to be less objectionable than
the more reprehensible forms of "eclecticism" and than
sheer aggregational encyclopedism. One might proffer
the label "conjoined synthesis" for what obtains where
mutually supporting evidence of the integrated has been
far from achieved but where none the less the holder
supposes himself to have some sense of the encompassing matrix from which he apprehends the conjoined
positions; he holds them in suspension—more or less
separate or unrelated except through their connection
with the matrix, though doubtless not without a num-

ber of comparative philosophical relationships. If the plurality or duality of views thus held suspended seem more plausibly to portend themselves as rivals, he may wish to name his encompassing state of consciousness a case of "disjunctive synthesis." The separation is then stronger than when he feels them to be supplementary despite his having been unable to delineate the ways in which they actually do complement each other.

The same or somewhat similar range of efforts at integral thinking could be spoken of in terms of perspectivism. Less radical forms of pespectivism occur when the holder feels that he has a way of relating the perspectives such that they may in main be validly referring to aspects of his one encompassing world. The thinker is driven to radical perspectivism, however, when he perceives the rival perspectives as ones from which different worlds are asserted; the rival theories are incompatible with each other; the rival theorists are called upon to be intellectually intolerant toward the—to them—misleading or false competitors. Although from a commonsense standpoint the "theories" seem to have arisen from different matrices among the stretches of our common life, still, as they develop, one or more has so reworked the vague world of the plain man as to deny accepted features of the common world. The protagonist is not satisfied—unless this world be allowed to be identified with the one he champions. Others perchance may grant the uniqueness of the fractious view, but they cannot concede its claim uniquely to have the truth.

Recently Western philosophy of science has been in a big stir over the possible variance of meaning in what looked like the "same" term appearing in two theories —specifically two "rival" theories, usually with one as a candidate for succeeding the other or, indeed, with one which did historically supplant the other. With much acuity and learning Professor Thomas Kuhn has argued that even in physics—assuredly in the cases of "revolutions" in physics—the retention of the same label for a concept is misleadingly read if it is taken as having the same meaning in its new post-revolutionary context. For, as idealists have long said and as linguistic analysts have much documented, a meaning is constituted in context (even if part of its context is what it is supposedly referential toward among lower-level demarcated things). A whole nest of problems has arisen over the grounds of rejection and acceptance of theories if straight disconfirmation and confirmation will not do. Suspicions of extra-scientific rôles of the regnant scientific community have emerged, with consequent charges of "psychologism," "sociologism," "relativism," and "skepticism."

Philosophers have long been beset with this nexus of problems and they have wrestled with it, though their "terms" have not been of the sort which occurred in mathematical equations and which permitted the assignment to them of numerical values by experimental determination. "Meaning-variance" of terms has been patent between different metaphysical "theories." Efforts have been put forth to define with clarity, but also many have held that the meaning of the term can only be got in context. The "discipline" of philosophy has roughly followed Professor Paul Feyerabend's advice to maintain the variety of theories (including bizarre ones), and to foster the growth of rival theories some of which do not formally contradict each other nor of course stand in the relation of one including or implying the other. The rivals may be intuitively incompatible, although it is difficult to locate where one contradicts the other. It was presumed by many philosophers that some theory (or theories) would be found to be better than others—not by any one decisive experimental test but perhaps by some general fit to experience.

Those who undertake to do comparative philosophy therewith have augmented their field of rival "theories." For them, issues of invariance of meaning of a term appearing in an original and in its translation are acute, as are bounds of insignificant and significant variation. Sensitivity to context has been an immemorial rule. Those thinkers who might aspire to "synthesis" are beset with all these antecedent problems, further compounded by questions of consistency, inconsistency (or other forms of incompatibility), indirect supporting evidence, general fit, and what "general fit" is being fitted to.

One virtue of a number of contemporary phenomenological undertakings is that, at minimum, they constitute initial efforts (whether successful or not) toward delineating features of a common world of experience. Such work may help to elicit a sense of an encompassing common matrix. Similarly, Wittgenstein's ultimate appeal to "forms of life" suggests an intended grounding in experience—in this case nothing *a priori* nor rationalistic. The overtones of perusing Wittgenstein's intellectual album of observations and interrogations may convey an impression of the probable pluralism of forms of life—and therewith of a correlative relativism of justification of theories and a relativism of justification of types of conduct (though he did not live long enough to be articulate in these domains, if indeed he would ever have had an interest in so doing).

There is a sense, I would want to say, in which articulate philosophers already live in one world culture. They can, in principle, talk to one another and enter into dialogue with one another whenever they can speak the same natural language. (We may ask bilingual colleagues here what it is like to "do" philosophy in a second non-native language. Is it really a grappling with two worlds?) There are, in the end, conditions (and in this sense limits) to literal communication in any case anywhere. There is not some single large gulf between Eastern and Western communicators. Perhaps there are quite as large canyons to be bridged between, say, a Western logical positivist (if any exist) and a Western Heideggerian than there are between an Eastern Advaitin and a Western Bradleian. Probably, however, the commonsense worlds of two persons in a given culture are more alike than commonsense worlds in different cultures.

If we did not have some understanding across cultures as also between private individuals, we could not put the question of the impossibility of understanding. Our cultural privacy is not so great but what we can carry on dim intercultural dialogues about cultural relativity.

That I take the getting of truth seriously and that I think my fellow man may have some of it which I do not possess will make me interested in synthesis. But this does not mean that I will find it easy to locate just where that truth lies which I do not possess, nor that I know just what it means if my fellow man has put it in propositional form or some other form. When I make my best effort at stating it I may still be told that I have distorted it into my own categories.

My personal feeling is that attempts at "synthesis" are rather premature. A great deal of effort needs to go into would-be intercultural comparative philosophy before essaying systematic integration. Yet I recommend no prohibition—even by social pressure—of synthesis. Even if the cultural relativities show themselves conspicuously, there may be some valuable stretching of insight beyond the familiar. Let whoever feels himself somewhat prepared try it. But I shall not join "crash programs" for growing synthesis quickly; at best we shall thus get hot house plants, and most all of them will be frosted when set out in the real world.

We may have an ideal of philosophy *simpliciter,* not Eastern or Western, just as we assume an objectivity of science across cultures. But, as I take "philosophy," it is on a different footing than science—its footing is total and general. The products of the scientific activities are meant to be descriptive in the generic sense, where description includes causal explanation and recourse can be had to hypothetical entities if these are sufficiently tied conceptually to the experienced. Perhaps it is still plausible that definitions within a given subject matter can be made operationally. What extantly passes as a philosophy may contain ethics and other valuational prescriptions besides possessing a metaphysics which is allegedly descriptive. Criteria for sorts of reality and for the pertinent kinds of evidence are involved. And, as for the metaphysics, its most general concepts are, I think, incapable of operational definition. As in communication elsewhere, a leap is required; here the leap is greater and apparently on the basis of alleged systemic relations to what may be familiar.

In doing science one accepts a discipline, and there accrues a public character to the results in accord with the discipline. In *a* philosophy the same thing may happen—if the given philosophy imposes it. In the general *matrix* of philosophy the situation is not the same; there is a freedom of mind prior to the acceptance of a discipline, a freedom to play beyond different disciplines. The situation is that of being surrounded by vague undetermined ultimates, with perhaps the tacit task of making them somewhat determinate. If there are difficulties in grasping the formulations of a cosmologist in one's own culture, there are greater difficulties in translating and understanding the ultimates of some philosophers in other cultures. How shall we understand Tao or Brahman or Sunya or the Buddha-nature in all things? It is small wonder that some do want us to get the advantages of being tied in one way or another to ordinary language; I do hope that they do not want birth-control of ideas. It seems to me to be a meta-philosophical truth that the nature of the matrix situation of philosophy is forgotten when one decides to purchase scientific objectivity in philosophy in the way in which it is secured in a science. (Possibly it is not always forgotten but rather sometimes deliberately escaped by decisive stipulations; the price of this is then the cutting off of conversation with some others who are trying to think as ultimately as they can.)

I append now a few questions, some of which have been already suggested, my intent being to convey that comparative philosophy, beginning in the social area or elsewhere, could be a very live affair.

First is a methodological question, albeit relating to realities. If one is to do comparative philosophy, how should he demarcate "philosophy" in different cultures? Anthropologists and philosophers of religion have had some difficulties in deciding whether "religion" names some one thing and in concurring upon criteria to be used in applying the term. Is there a similar problem over "philosophy," the basic situation being that different people in different cultures are doing different things but that at best we predicate "sameness" where there are the lesser degrees of difference?

Assuming a meaning has been found or attached to "philosophy," how is it related to its respective cultures where located? It is not uncommon to say that some philosophies are "quintessential expressions" of some cultures—Plato of Athens, Confucius of millennia of Chinese life, Dewey of America. What does this mean? Is this intended to declare that the philosophy is a revealing effect but not significantly a cause (which at least is more than taking it to be an ideational piece of superstructure which is not particularly revelatory of the executive order beneath it)? Or is it compatible with also allowing it to be socially efficacious? How should one apportion influence of the culture on a philosophy and influence of a given philosophy on a culture? One must say that a culture makes possible a philosophy in the sense of furnishing its habitat, even if the philosophy is revolutionary. It is plausible that the popularity of a philosophy is considerably a function of felt needs in a culture, and that thus a culture imposes selective ecological conditions upon beliefs.

On the other hand, selected philosophies may exercise an influence beyond what they were selected for, and the very giving of form to certain feelings may somewhat strengthen them and somewhat alter them. For one example, one can plausibly point to social conditions which selected Confucianism into a position of ideological dominance; but after its selection the features selected had a weighty influence toward certain kinds of definiteness in Chinese culture.

Is "human nature" everywhere "the same"? Of actual living human nature, how much is it determined by the raw inherited equipment and how much is its character due to the cooking by conditioning? Do human beings in some cases have genuinely different sorts of experiences, so that their data for philosophy is different? Of course our natural language has a vocabulary for emotions. Our interpretations of the experiences of others are translated into our vocabulary. May we find that our vocabulary is deficient? Problems of the knowledge of other selves in detail arise—not whether they exist and experience but of what they experience. In the process of attempting to cope with these, more general questions of the adequacy of verbal expression in a language emerge, questions of the relation of form to feeling and more particularly of the conceptual to the immediate and of the sense in which certain structures may be said to be implicit in a concrete passage of experience.

One possible reason for studying other cultures is to

find phenomena which are not had or are rare within one's own culture. This is one avenue for finding psychological truths which are not known to us. Suppose one believes, for example, that Freud is not irrelevant to ethics; then will he not want to test the intercultural validity of the pertinent hypotheses?

Philosophers who refuse to alienate empirical content from philosophy want to know both what a person is and what types of personal formation emerge in certain cultural matrices. Ultimately, I suppose we shall be quite content to surrender various details to anthropology and social psychology; but I opine that not only do we want to contemplate personhood but we want to grasp general principles of ethology, of an empirical ethology. The emergence of personal structures is highly pertinent to ethics, aesthetics, philosophy of religion and philosophy of social organization. We may tend to assume that moral experience is everywhere pretty much the same as experience; what differs are its objects. We may tend to assume that aesthetic experience is everywhere the same, but again objects admired in one culture do not strike a person from another culture with similar force, at least not without a period of training. We may have assumed that worship is everywhere the same but toward different gods.[9] And

---

[9] Comparative religion went on for generations—at least done in the West without much participatory dialogue from those whose adherences were suffering comparison. But new dialogue has opened, intra-culturally and interculturally. Comparative religion has, I opine, been

that "mysticism" names one phenomenon. We may have failed to ask ourselves whether the bonds of social cohesion are inescapably different in the family than in larger social groupings, and whether clan, tribal, national, class and possibly international loyalties are or are not all built from the same affective sources. In psychology of religion, there has been distinction of some psychological types (James' work being a classic); and two generations ago so influential were some subcultures in the American scene that any respectable book in psychology or philosophy of religion had to have at least one chapter on "conversion"; now this phenomenon occurs less dramatically if also not less frequently (except in the area of socio-political com-

---

heavily oriented toward comparison of doctrine, and in this sense it has been like—and at times a segment of—comparative philosophy. As religion heavily involves feelings, practice and cultus, one might have expected practitioners of comparative religion to have undertaken much comparison of consciousness, of feelings, especially of feelings taken to be appropriate, most valuable, even revelatory. No doubt some work as been done in this extremely difficult pursuit, but one wonders if (freed from any traditional suppositions of its impossibility due to notions of "privacy") there is not vastly more to be done—and done, of course, with the greatest delicacies of perceptivity. Nondoctrinaire phenomenologists have—in concrete forms of philosophical consciousness and religious consciousness—a great field before them. And how much they find commonness in our mutual world and how much they extend our world with worlds new in feeling to us is yet to be determined. Patently an incidental product of such study will be contributions to our hackneyed but vexing problems of how to translate key terms (not excluding the solution of refusing to translate).

mitments), and is largely neglected. Besides older distinctions of the sublime and the beautiful, phenomenological analyses have led to nuanced distinctions, ranging "down" to the cute and the neat. But I do not know whether anyone has established an English equivalent of *shibui* in Japanese or explained why rusticity and chrysanthemums are so much more powerful on the Japanese mind than on ours. The intercultural status of aesthetics, save at a general ethological level, may be in question. That some phenomena related to personality structure are accepted as pertinent to ethics and that some interpretations of them will be explicitly or tacitly made in ethical theory hardly needs argument. For illustration, take apparently one phenomenon occurring in some persons in Western culture—what was comprised under the global meaning of "conscience." Sometimes one reads that the Greeks had no conscience, or at least no word marking it, although of course they had shame, sense of proportioned propriety and honor. It has been alleged that conscience is a Semitic and Christian phenomenon. More accurately, it is meant that it arises where there are certain cultural features, which happened to have been instanced in Judaism and Christianity and not in classical Greece—perhaps the feature of a monarchical Deity who is at once benevolent and highly concerned to enforce his moral rules. Exegetically it can be argued that, say, Locke, the Cambridge Platonists, not to mention Quaker theologians, Hutcheson, Hume, Kant and associationists all think that they are not ignoring the phenomena but that they have somewhat differing estimates of its significance. Price and Kant and even Sidgwick (if under "conscience" we will include distinctively moral consciousness) surely give a significance to it that the associationists do not. Does every man have "conscience," or is it a product of a certain kind of conditioning which is not socially universal? If the latter, do we want a social education which yields it? If the former, we can study its different forms as well as degrees and try to relate it to Japanese "shame," awareness of Indian dharma, etc.

The layman has learned from the anthropologist that the content of virtue is different in different cultures. It could even be the case that the personality structure relating itself to the content is also different. Again, we might extend the topic of personal competence within a culture (which includes virtue) to ask whether sanity would have the same boundaries in different cultures and whether types of neuroses and species of insanity have easy cross-cultural identifiability. Difference of incidence in different cultures of identifiable types of neuroses might be of some normative interest as well as constituting sociological data.

Lastly here but not the most easy of topics is whether reason as a theoretical faculty, not to mention reason as operative in value conflicts, is the same possession in all men.

Approaches to the Artist as a Young Language Teacher

Hugh Kenner

Hugh Kenner has been Professor of English at The Johns Hopkins University since 1973. He previously taught at the University of California at Santa Barbara, serving as Chairman of the Department of English from 1956 to 1962. He received his Ph.D. from Yale in 1950, and has been a Guggenheim Fellow. Widely published, his books include Dublin's Joyce, The Counterfeiters, The Pound Era, Bucky: A Guided Tour of Buckminster Fuller, Homemade World: The American Modernist Writers, *and* The Stoic Comedians: Flaubert, Joyce and Beckett.

The reader who has persevered to page 152 of *Fin-negans Wake* has just encountered an overbearingly garrulous professor who set out three pages previously to answer a question and by now has chiefly succeeded in making us forget what the question was (something about shaving a shoul). Conceding that his explanations so far are probably above our understandings, the professor next offers to "revert to a more expletive method" and with much pomp of throatclearing commences to tell a story:

> The Mookse and The Gripes. . . .
> Eins within a space and a wearywide space it wast ere wohned a Mookse. . . .

A Mookse? In 1950, not in *Finnegans Wake* but in the less coherent universe whose epicenter is Columbia

University, another professor made use of the word "Mookse" in the following extraordinary sentences:

> Joyce had a queer mind. He was always seeing analogies. When he saw a Mookse, twenty parallels occurred to him. They range in kind from Yardley's soap to the frog who would a-wooing go. . . .

"When he saw a Mookse"! What—talking of queer minds—are we to make of the state of mind in which that proposition was framed? For it postulates that Mookses are there to be seen, though when seen by other eyes than purblind Joyce's, eyes hitched to saner heads, they give rise to smaller arrays of analogy, or perhaps to none. To see a cow, to think cow and no more than cow, of such, we may agree, is the kingdom of normalcy. (Harding, who coined the word "normalcy," could have concurred.) And if James Joyce had but been content with seeing a Mookse, and saying no more than "Mookse, Mookse," *Finnegans Wake* might have been an easier book. The question remains, how one goes about seeing a Mookse; or rather the question, how Professor W. Y. Tindall (*James Joyce: His Way of Interpreting the Modern World,* 1950, p. 112) trapped himself into talking as though Mookses were there to be seen.

The answer of course begins with the simple fact that Professor Tindall had been reading *Finnegans Wake,* where (and only where) there do be Mookses which we may come to suppose that we can see, though

we should be powerless to explain what they look like.
What can we learn from *Finnegans Wake* about
Mookses? The word first appears on the fifth line of
page 152, which line reads in its entirety,

The Mookse and The Gripes.

From this we are sure of one thing anyhow, that a
Mookse is not a Gripes.

To be sure of this much is perhaps small comfort, but
it is the beginning of linguistic wisdom. Two words affirm perhaps not two entities, but anyhow a twoness, a
difference. "In languages," wrote Fernand de Saussure,
"there are only differences," and it soon turns out that
Joyce might have been writing these Mookse-haunted
pages expressly to afford examples for students of
Saussure's *Cours de linguistique générale,* a book published only after both Joyce and its author were dead.
De Saussure found it profitable to discuss words solely
as members of a linguistic system, without reference to
the non-linguistic "things" of which it is customary to
assert that they are signs. Thus "cat" is not a label tied
onto a cat; "cat" is a word which primarily is *not* several tens of thousands of other English words. And its
value—Saussure does not say its "meaning"—derives
from the "simultaneous presence" of many other expressions which it is not: *felis domestica* for example,
since when I say "cat" one thing I am doing is declining
to talk like a zoologist.

La langue est un système dont tous les termes sont solidaires
et ou la valeur de l'un ne resulte que de la presence simul-
tanée des autres.   (Saussure, p. 159)

As Maurice Merleau-Ponty later explained it, in Saus-
surian linguistics the choice of a sign entails evoking
"some of the other expressions which might have taken
its place and were rejected, and we must feel the way in
which they might have touched and shaken the chain
of language in another manner and the extent to which
this particular expression was really the only possible
one if that signification was to come into the world."
(Quoted in Gerald L. Bruns, *Modern Poetry and the
Idea of Language,* 1974, p. 98.)

Anyone inclined to protest that "cat," dammit, means
cat ought to consider what "Mookse" means and how,
and before he can snort that "Mookse" means nothing
at all he will have to explain the Tindall Hallucination,
which permitted the framing of that confident phrase,
"When he saw a Mookse. . . ."

Well then, "The Mookse and The Gripes"; and
among Merleau-Ponty's "other expressions that might
have taken its place and were rejected," the first that
springs to mind is "The Fox and the Grapes." It is an
odd property of *Finnegans Wake* that it brings vividly
to mind so many words it does not use. They are often
more vivid than the words on the page, and they exist
in the mind's ear to specify what the words on the page
are not.

So a Mookse isn't a Gripes, and also isn't a Fox

(nor is Gripes the same as Grapes). Yet whatever
Mookse and Gripes may prove to be, we sense that
their relationship is like that of Fox to Grapes in the
fable. Mookses, it may be, covet Gripeses but will later
claim they didn't really: "sour gripes." (Eureka! Don't
"sour" and "gripes" make a bonded pair, though there
is no "sour" in the text? In a comparable example one
might concoct, "the fattening tower of pizza" plays on
two senses of "lean" without using the word.)

To continue:

> Eins within a space and a wearywide space it wast ere
> wohned a Mookse.

Here another whole sentence comes to mind, the first
sentence of *A Portrait of the Artist as a Young Man:*

> Once upon a time and a very good time it was there was a
> moocow coming down along the road and this moocow that
> was down along the road met a nicens little boy named Baby
> Tuckoo.

"His father told him that story," the narrative goes on;
and what did little Stephen make of it, seeing that official English contains no such words as "moocow" and
"nicens"? But little children don't know what official
English contains, and don't much worry about sets of
verbal labels glued onto nonverbal entities. They are
used to hearing about what they have never experienced. A moocow, that is something in a story; it can
come down along the road, and it can meet you. And in

these respects a Mookse is like a moocow. (We're getting on.)

I'll mention, in this connection, another pair, Lewis Carroll's Mock Turtle and Griffin. If "The Mookse and The Gripes" reminds us of Carroll's phrase, then a Mock Turtle is one more thing a Mookse both recalls and isn't. The existence of Mock Turtles need give no trouble; it is something deduced from the undoubted existence of Mock Turtle Soup. If Turtle Soup (we know) is made from Turtles, then Mock Turtle Soup from Mock Turtles. And if reason protests that "Mock Turtle" is no more than a whimsical mistake, a back-formation from a form of words found on soup-tins, then reason has glimpsed a principle it might consider more than it does, that we have all learned most of the words we know by induction from the other words they keep company with; that we were likely comfortable with the word "elephant" long before we ever saw one, and would be comfortable with it should we never chance to see one. Seeing one, as when Joyce allegedly "saw" a Mookse, though an interesting experience is linguistically unimportant.* We may even want to add that "learning" a subject is predominantly learning how

---

* Pound's comment on the difficulties of his *Cantos* was that if you've never seen an elephant, "naturally the word is obscure." This means that the verbal interconnections in the *Cantos* tend to rely on our extra-linguistic knowledge, to the nature of which the verbal clues are sparse. So Saussure is not a cure-all. And we can see why *Wake*-ese is so heavily redundant: twenty pages crammed with half-a-thousand river-names to assist a reader who may pick up twenty.

to talk about it, and so the meaning of this talk; thus
the main business of law school is lawyer-talk and of
medical school, doctor-talk ("ptussis"; "epistaxis": thus
I enter my doctor's office with a belly-ache and come
out with gastroenteritis and a bill for $20, the charge
for a laying-on of linguistic hands).

Back to Mookses. It is surprising, by this time, how
much we know about them. There is more to be known.
When "... within a space" replaces "... upon a time,"
and "space" comports with "wearywide" and "wast"
(waste?), and "ere wohned," where we should have
expected "there lived," takes advantage of the German
wohnen, dwell, to introduce Sam Butler's word "ere-
whon" (=nowhere), we derive a strong sense (to say
the least) that Mookses are space-creatures: Gripeses
therefore by contrast time-bound. And strings of La-
tinate words, especially bureaucratic-ecclesiastical Latin ("vacticanated"; "impermeable"; "impugnable";
"chalkfull of masterplasters"*) soon apprise us to think
"Mookse" in the area of thought where we also think
"Pope." (But *Mookse* does not equal *Pope,* or "Pope"
would do.)

What we are being taught by this method of both
evoking and excluding possibilities is not the "meaning" but what Saussure would have us call the *value*

---

* Cf., "borgeously letout gardens strown with cascades, pintacostecas,
horthoducts and currycombs," from which we recover numerous
papal Roman words that aren't there, e g Borgia, pentecost, orthodox, aquaduct, catacombs.

of the word "Mookse." It is not *deduced,* and does not inhabit, hard-edged but transparent, the Euclidean space deductions occupy: the mortality of Socrates, the constant sum of a triangle's vertices. It is intuited, faster than rational thought, and acquires the substantiality of unicorns and phoenixes. If we persevere, and having come this far we are likely to do so since as pages of *Finnegans Wake* go these are easy pages, we shall eventually be inclined to suppose that if we were to see a Mookse we should know it on sight. That, it must be, is how Professor Tindall was eased into the inadvertent supposition that Joyce sometimes saw them.

Still, the skeptical reader may be tempted to consign the existence of Mookses to that area of childish confusion where Mock Turtles can be stipulated, a confusion grown people put behind them. But learning speech is not confined to childhood. Grown people learn to speak too, when they are paying someone (such as James A. Joyce, B.A. in Trieste) to teach them a second language. In the process they learn to speak very fluently of things no native speaker gives a thought to: for instance, if French is being learnt, *la plume de ma tante,* the pen of my aunt.

For the better part of a decade James Joyce devoted most of his waking hours to teaching Triestinos English. We should place beside this biographical fact the remark that any language when we are learning to speak it has the property of creating worlds quite as unreal as that inhabited by Mock Turtles and Mookses. *La plume de ma tante,* far from being an obsession shared by Frenchmen, is a phenomenon generated in language classes by two elementary facts: that the earliest French nouns a pupil picks up by the "direct method" are apt to pertain to classroom objects (e.g., "plume") and family relationships (e.g., "tante"), and that the way of forming the French possessive is so primary a topic he needs to be drilled in it before he has at his disposal more words than these. Round and round, then, the ghosts of language glide, member after member of the slim company at the pupil's disposal slipping into its place on the proper side of the formula for the possessive, face to astonished face with a surreal partner:

$$
\left.\begin{array}{l} \text{Le} \\ \text{La} \\ \text{Les} \end{array}\right\} \quad\text{———}\quad \text{de} \left\{\begin{array}{l} \text{mon} \\ \text{ma} \\ \text{mes} \end{array}\right\} \quad\text{———}.
$$

—la plume de ma tante, les crayons de mon père, le papier de ses soeurs, Le Monocle (wrote the waggish Wallace Stevens) de Mon Oncle. Afterwards you could spend a lifetime in France never mentioning your aunt's pen, yet sensing as no Frenchman ever can that its being is intrinsicate with that of the French language.

We have mentioned the "direct method," that of Berlitz, which was relatively new when Joyce commenced his teaching career. Its rules are simply stated. Instruction is "one to one." It proceeds solely in what educators call the target langauge, in Joyce's case English, and the student learns how things are said in English by constant conversation, constant emulation of the spoken example, constant framing of reply and statement within a system of competence which will commence from little or nothing and gradually expand. The instructor need not even know the student's normal language; indeed from some points of view it will be better if he does not, since there will then be no danger of his lapsing into it, at moments of exasperation or impasse, to talk *about* the target language. Language is not talked *about*.

If we give this a moment's thought we perceive three peculiar consequences. (1) At the start, nearly idiot concentration will be brought to bear on saying almost nothing at all correctly, and memories of this will shape and pervade what follows. (2) For the duration of a fifty-minute hour teacher and student will be united by the need to *make conversation* without having anything important to say: hence an odd interpersonal tension. (3) Slowly, as they proceed, a universe of discourse, commencing from a very few words like glove and shoe and umbrella and rapidly accreting population, will sustain itself in the room between them, cohered by grammar and usage, and will *generate* such realities as are talked "about." That is the principle by which Mookses are born, and the world into which they are born, like the world of French aunts' pens, is wholly that of language.

After a while, it may be, the student on his own time will essay a target-language book or two, and will learn words, for instance the book-word "aloft," only to gather from his teacher when he tries it out at their next meeting that "aloft," its status as a perfectly "polite" word notwithstanding, is a word that, by and large, one doesn't *say*. (When did you last say "aloft," unless you're a sailor?) Or the verb "bear." One may by linguistic custom bear gifts as well as children, but if you say you come bearing gifts you're understood to be jocular, and the wise teacher will tell his student that in non-obstetrical contexts the word is best avoided.

(One perceives Joyce acquiring from such likely conversations an uncanny sense of "literary" vs. "speakable" words. "In languages there are only differences.")

But (mysteriously) words like "bear" and "aloft" pass unremarked in books, according to some principle on which dictionaries give little help. Here it is useful to invoke Saussure's principle, remarking that when it is encountered in a book the chief nuance of the non-speakworthy word is to call attention to some special quality—no matter what—by virtue of which it has replaced the word one would *say*. Though Joyce never read Saussure—nor did anyone else, until eight years after Joyce's death—it seems a fair guess that he discovered this principle for himself, during his countless hours on the Berlitz treadmill. We can sense it behind the opening lines of *Ulysses* (written in Trieste, some time before mid-1915):

> Stately, plump Buck Mulligan came from the stairhead, bearing a bowl of lather on which a mirror and a razor lay crossed. . . . He held the bowl aloft and intoned:
> —*Introibo ad altare Dei.*

It is customary to call this "naturalism," the plain fidelity of word to fact from which (it is ritually complained) the latter half of *Ulysses* deviates wilfully. This is meant to mean that we can work back with confidence from the words depicting to the action depicted, or (in the contrary direction) that someone observing those actions and possessed of a good command of English would as if automatically find those words to depict them.

Let us try. Here comes Mulligan. What is he doing with that bowl? He is carrying it in his hands. Ah, but is he perhaps *bearing* it? The pupil leafs through his dictionary. How to distinguish a *bearing* from a *carrying?* The dictionary is no help at all. "Carrying" is a word in good standing, and "carrying" is what gets written, and the first precept of documentary naturalism is observed*; and something is lost.

To specify what is lost we take our eyes off Mulligan and inspect the language-field, and we note, of the sentence as Joyce wrote it, two properties: that "bearing" gets part of its effect by *avoiding* the ready word

---

* ". . . so many *things,* almost in an equal number of *words.* . . . and preferring the language of Artizans, Countrymen, and Merchants, before that of Wits, or Scholars." —Thomas Sprat, 1667. "Bearing" can't claim to be an artisan's or countryman's word.

"carrying" (something special going on here) and part of it by alliterating with "bowl" (some ritual connotation here, as in carrying a cross, furling a flag, doing a deed). We should not know it was the right word by observing the action—what incautious common sense would say it "means"—but by consulting the available words, and the neighboring words. So the words have created more than was empirically "there," employing the same resources by which words can create Mookses.

So with "aloft." Since no nautical context admits it as a sailors' word, it becomes a *literary word,* i.e., a word borrowed from a speaker who isn't there. It replaces "up," and it says, "What the Buck does here resembles a quotation from the kind of book whose author is undiscriminating about words like 'aloft.' " His liturgical parody is a lapse of taste, like this putative author's. Joyce had written some years earlier of his young self that "people seemed to him strangely ignorant of the value of the words they used so glibly." Glib is the word for the writer who tosses in words like "aloft," and glib is the word too for Mulligan's irreverence. (For Joyce, irreverence was a serious business.)

Ah, but how do we know the writer of *Ulysses* isn't that kind of writer, since he tosses in the word "aloft" before he has finished the fourth line of his narrative?

There are two answers. We know this if we come to the opening page of *Ulysses* having read its predecessors, *Dubliners* and *A Portrait of the Artist as a*

Young Man. Or, if we come without this preparation, we shall know it before we have gone far with *Ulysses* itself, in observing its careful, discriminate zoning of usage. We know, in short, by attending to the systematic differences entailed by other groupings of words than these on page one.

To reemphasize: it is not in "reality" that the first page of *Ulysses* installs us but in a language-field, and the book's later extensions of that field are consistent with this principle. Out of that initial field the scene atop the Martello Tower condenses, real in the same way that a Mookse is real. It is true that whereas no one knows where, if not in a book, Mookses are findable, a Dublin bus-line will take us to the Martello Tower at Sandycove, atop which we may observe "the round gunrest" Buck Mulligan mounts. But this visit belongs to a different, though partly coincident, order of experience from the experience of reading the page. On the page the noun "gunrest," otherwise mysterious, accepts the adjective "round" and the verb "to mount," and these facts confer on it the reality a reader needs. Beyond that, the scene no more entails a non-verbal tower than it entails a non-verbal Buck Mulligan. If a tower can be produced, a Buck Mulligan cannot be produced. Research can produce a man named Oliver Gogarty, now dead but demonstrably alive and in that tower in 1904, but a Gogarty alive is not a Mulligan in a language-field. Later the book will produce a "Leopold Bloom" for whom no single counterpart is discoverable at all, and still later a "Mr. Best" found in a library. This last seems a tricky case since it was possible until 1959 to question a living Richard Best, frequenter of Dublin libraries, but when someone did that he protested that he was not a character in *Ulysses* but a living person.

Such remarks, though in principle applicable to any novel, prepare us to understand *Ulysses'* way of diverging from other novels, concentrating as it does on the habits of its verbal fields until the "naturalism" of the opening pages comes to seem no more than a coincidental illusion. Joyce's earlier writings are compatible with it, but not wholly. The methods of *Dubliners* (commenced mid-1904) would generate many* of the Martello Tower effects, and like the later *Portrait* the stories explore the allure words can have before their meaning is known. The boy in "The Sisters" fascinated by "paralysis," the boy sets out for a bazaar called "Araby," young Stephen pondering "tower of ivory" and "suck," these boys like all young people have more experience of language than of the world. Slowly the world will dispel much linguistic glamor; we are shown the magic going out of "Araby." Deglamorization, that is a familiar 19th century theme; the author of *Dublin-*

---

* Not all. Half-way down the first page a glimpse of white teeth with gold fillings is followed by a sudden "Chrysostomos," a learned pun on "golden-tongued" which unassisted by so much as a "Stephen thought" evokes the unspoken thoughts of the silent Stephen. There is nothing like this in *Dubliners.*

ers and of *A Portrait of the Artist as a Young Man* inherits concerns that Wordsworth shared with Dickens.

What is new in *Ulysses* is that linguistic phantoms entoil adults in comedy, not children in pathos; the adult most entoiled is of course the reader. That is why it seems pertinent to recall that by the time he commenced the book about 1914 Joyce had for some years been teaching English to adults. An adult contending with an unfamiliar language is like someone half-overpowered by laughing-gas, and there is no one in *Ulysses* for whom some areas of English are not unfamiliar: Molly Bloom commencing her day by asking the meaning of a word ("who's he when he's at home?" —one might ask the same of a Mookse); Gerty Mac-Dowell brooding fondly on the picture "Halcyon Days" in the outhouse ("the colours were done something lovely") after having looked up in Walker's Pronouncing Dictionary "about the halcyon days what they meant"; or the narrator of the episode called "Eumaeus" who aspires so grandly to a man-of-the-world literary idiom ("something out of the common groove") to celebrate what is after all Leopold Bloom's finest hour (*"My Experiences,* let us say, *in a Cabman's Shelter"* is Bloom's modest gloss), and has such a terrible time getting sentences finished.

"Eumaeus" comes late in the book, the sixteenth episode of eighteen, and commentators are fatigued by that time. It repays more alertness than it usually gets. Joyce contrived it, we may say, in his role as

Berlitz teacher, mindful of a principle T. S. Eliot was
to enunciate some years later, that a man who can *talk*
English beautifully "may compose a letter painfully
written in a dead language bearing some resemblance
to a newspaper leader, and decorated with words like
'maelstrom' and 'pandemonium.' " ["Byron," 1937; see
On Poetry and Poets.] In the dark no-man's-land between spoken and written idioms, it emits starshell after
starshell by the brief glare of which we glimpse figures
of hearty speech frozen in grotesque embrace with
phantoms of shapeless literariness.

> Preparatory to anything else
>
> > [how magnificiently empty!]
>
> Mr Bloom brushed off the greater bulk of the shavings and
> handed Stephen the hat and ashplant and bucked him up
> generally in orthodox Samaritan fashion, which he very
> bady needed. . . .

There, as the book's third part opens, are "brush" and
"shaving" and "Buck," words that in the opening of
the first part reached toward one another in a wholly
different field. Brushing aside (so to speak) a halluci-
natory Mulligan with shaving-brush, we query "orthodox Samaritan fashion." May one put "orthodox"
beside "Samaritan"? No, one had better not, because
"orthodox" has more powerful affinities with "Jew"
than with "fashion," and "Jew" is antithetic to "Samaritan." But the word "Jew" is not here? Ah, but (quite
apart from the fact that Mr. Bloom is a Jew) the word

"Samaritan" brings it here. So words do battle with the ghosts of absent words.

Next we learn of the hope that they "might hit upon some drinkables in the shape of a milk and soda or a mineral," and there rises within each of us a ghostly schoolmaster to protest that drinkables are not for hitting, and liquids proverbially have no shape; moreover by what appeal to absent idiom does "a mineral" become the shape of a drinkable?

Soon a cab is sighted, and we observe "Mr. Bloom, who was anything but a professional whistler" endeavoring "to hail it by emitting a kind of a whistle." Penumbrally these words conjure up some Mookse-like "professional whistler" (to be distinguished from an amateur whistler), and "a kind of a whistle" which presumably is not a mainstream whistle. Considering, moreover, the criteria that would normally distinguish "a kind of *a* whistle" from "a kind of whistle," we may glimpse a phantom instrument emerging from between Mr. Bloom's agile lips.

Wonder crowds upon wonder. The two next "put a good face on the matter and foot it" (how pliable is the anatomy of "the matter"!). Immediately thereafter Mr. Bloom, patient Laocoon, is said to be *handicapped* by a *circumstance,* which, if we are to credit etymology, stands around him hand in cap, before it is suddenly equated with the absence of a button. But he enters "thoroughly into the spirit of the thing" (as we fumble round for that inspirited "thing") and "heroically" "makes light" of the mischance (*Fiat lux*). Next they "dandered along past by where the empty vehicle was waiting without a fare or a jarvey"; we do not know whether to marvel more at the reduplicated emptiness or at the concatenated "along past by where," a freight-train of phantom grammatical constructions.

For it is in "Eumaeus," more than anywhere else in *Ulysses,* that the principles of *Finnegans Wake* are on display, congesting foreground and middle distance with verbal phantoms. (Open *Finnegans Wake* at random, and you will likely meet syntax as disordered as that of "Eumaeus.") No episode in *Ulysses* would pose more insurmountable obstacles for a translator. "Dandered along past by where. . . ."!—what might a committee of Frenchmen hope to do with that? And how might one begin one's explanation, say to an earnest pupil in Trieste, that it simply isn't quite English? English, after all, is what has permitted it.

Evidently "Eumaeus" would be no fun at all did we not believe in its author's firm control over its idiomatic disasters. All fifteen preceding episodes have been in one way or another preparing us for it, and teaching us how to read it when we shall come to it. As "brush" and "shaving" and "Buck" in the first sentence may remind us, its words are the familiar words, its materials the familiar materials, once more recycled.

It is commonplace to remark how much of its own material *Ulysses* continually recycles: how many times, for instance, the adultery of Blazes and Molly is en-

acted and reenacted in prospect, in fantasy, in retro-
spect (and never in narrative). Each episode reclaims
and reenacts material from its predecessors, clutching
from them even handfuls of verbal material, trans-
posed each time to yet a new linguistic domain. Pa-
tiently reverting again and yet again to the same
banalities of locution and conduct, making its small
talk of shaving-suds and postcards and buttons, running
them through ever one more stylistic permutation,
Ulysses from one point of view resembles nothing more
than it does a marathon course of language lessons,
conducted "by the direct method" in discrete sessions,
each vaguely recalling all the ones that have gone before, each making a brave new start, each discovering,
along with new fluencies, unprecedented now modes
of linguistic degeneracy (pupils often speak a new language most "correctly" in the first few weeks of instruction). For English is never learnt, that is one of
the book's lessons. Though nearly all the characters
are native speakers, it is hard to find one to whom English does not present difficulties. And the greatest
difficulties of all plague that personage every novel,
every piece of writing adumbrates: the very author,
arranger of these words. He began the day possessed
of a firm neat narrative manner, trim as Lemuel Gulli-
ver's. He ends it, a marathon spree of language behind
him, seemingly unable to keep persons or tenses
straight, or to put into a sentence (what, he seems to

be wondering by then, is a sentence?) even the most rudimentary punctuation.

Undaunted, for the next seventeen years he will struggle to devise a seventeen-part course that shall teach us, always and only by the direct method, a language that exists nowhere but in one book, the language of *Finnegans Wake*. It ends on the word with which most English courses begin, the definite article. Though no pupil has ever emerged with real distinction from this curriculum whose subject is itself, still none can escape salutary reflections on what it means to write, what it means to read, and what minds do when they do what they do exactly all the time, which is frame subsystems within a vast system of ordered differences, capable of realizing indifferently soap, buttons, God, Odysseus, a Mookse.

The Published Works
of Eliseo Vivas (1901–   )

Allan Shields, Editor

Allan Shields has been Professor of Philosophy at San Diego State University since 1949, except for 1968–70, when he served as Dean of the College of Humanities and Fine Arts at the University of Northern Iowa. He is a frequent contributor to professional journals and has published widely on many subjects, including music, education, and national parks. In addition to a novella, The Tragedy of Tenaya, *he is the author of* Bibliography of the Works of F. C. S. Schiller, with an Introduction to Pragmatic Humanism *(with H. L. Searles) and* A Bibliography of Bibliographies in Aesthetics. *He is currently at work on a volume of essays on American aestheticians.*

1922

"Pio Baroja y Nessi." *The Literary Review.* (December 23, 1922), 339.

1923

"A Chilean Mystic." Review of Gabriela Mistral, *Desolacion. The Literary Review.* (July 28, 1923), 865.

"Minute Studies." Review of Henry A. Holmes, Martin Fierro and Nicholas B. Adams, *The Romantic Dramas of Garcia Gutierrez. The Literary Review.* (October 13, 1923), 130.

Review of Benjamin Fernandez y Medina, *La Flor Del Pago, Cuentos. The Literary Review.* (November 17, 1923), 268–9.

"The Lower Depths." Review of Pio Baroja, *Weeds. The Literary Review.* (December 1, 1923), 300–2.

1924

"A Spanish Play." Review of Eduardo Marquina and Luis Fernandez Ardavin, *Rosa de Francia. The Literary Review.* (March 29, 1924), 633.

Review of Andreas Gonzales Blanco, *Maria Jesus, Casada y Martir. The Literary Review.* (1924?—information incomplete).

"Man's Conflicts." Review of D. H. Lawrence, *The Boy in the Bush. The New Leader.* 1, 42 (November 1, 1924), 9.

"The Unknown Critic" (by himself). *The Nation.* 119, 3101 (December 10, 1924), 638–9.

"Where Conquest Would Be Freedom." *The Independent.* 112, 3867 (April 26, 1924), 223–5 and 229.

"A Spanish Impressionist." Review of Arozin (Jose Martinez Ruiz), *Don Juan. The Nation.* 118, 3063 (March 19, 1924), 320.

"An Old Master." Review of H. Warner Allen, ed., *Celestina or The Tragicomedy of Calisto and Melibea. The Nation.* 119, 3083 (August 6, 1924), 148.

"A Spanish Woman Novelist." Review of Concha Espina, *Mariflor and the Red Beacon. The Nation.* 119, 3084 (August 13, 1924), 168.

"Baroja Among Us." Review of Pio Baroja, *Red Dawn. New York Herald Tribune Books.* (November 2, 1924).

"Outside the Tradition." Review of Romon del Valle-Inclan, *The Pleasant Memoirs of the Marquis de Bradomin. New York Herald Tribune Books.* (December 14, 1924).

1925

Review of Frank B. Deakin, *Spain Today. The Nation.* 120, 3105 (January 7, 1925), 21. (Anonymous review.)

"A Postil to D. H. Lawrence." Review of D. H. Lawrence, *The Rainbow. The Guardian.* 1, 6 (April 1925), 267–9.

"Mr. Ibanez Takes to the Stage Again." Review of Vincente Blasco Ibanez, *Alfonso XIII Unmasked. New York Herald Tribune Books.* 2, 33 (1925?—information unverifiable).

"A Negative Zarathustra." Review of Miguel de Unamuno, *Essays and Soliloquies. New York Herald Tribune Books.* 2, 33 (May 3, 1925), 2–3.

"Benavente as a Dramatist." Review of Walter Starkie, *Jacinto Benavente. New York Herald Tribune Books.* 2, 38 (June 7, 1925), 10.

"A Literary Magnate." Review of Vincente Blasco Ibanez, *The Old Woman of the Movies and Other Stories. New York Herald Tribune Books.* 2, 40 (June 21, 1925), 9.

"A Relic." Review of Don Juan Manuel, *Count Lucanor, or The Fifty Pleasant Tales of Patronio. New York Herald Tribune Books.* 2, 34 (May 10, 1925), 11.

"Heirlooms." Review of E. Allison Peers, *Spanish Mysticism. New York Herald Tribune Books.* 2, 8 (November 8, 1925), 11.

"Sicilian Tragedies." Review of Giovanni Verga, *Little Novels of Sicily. New York Herald Tribune Books.* (April 19, 1925), 14.

"The Microcosm of New York." Review of Konrad Bercovici, *Around the World in New York. The Nation.* 120, 3118 (April 8, 1925), 388.

Review of Gabriel Miro, *Figures of the Passion of Our Lord. The Nation.* 121, 3133 (July 22, 1925), 123.

"Miguel de Unamuno." Review of Miguel de Unamuno, *Essays and Soliloquies. The Nation.* 121, 3142 (September 23, 1925), 336–7.

1926

"Son of Ulysses." Review of Joseph T. Shipley, *King John. New York Herald Tribune Books.* 2, 17 (January 10, 1926), 15.

" 'From the Portugese?' " Review of Eca de Queiroz, *The Relic. New York Herald Tribune Books.* 2, 4 (October 11, 1926), 13.

"The Critic's Answer." *The Nation.* 123, 3205 (December 1, 1926), 600–1.

"Entertaining Persiflage." Review of Salvador de Maderiaga, ed., *The Sacred Giraffe. The Nation.* 123, 3186 (July 28, 1926), 89.

"A New Look At Cervantes." Review of Americo Castro, *El Pensamiento de Cervantes. The Nation.* 123, 3203 (November 24, 1926), 535–6.

1927

"The Ideal College." *The New Issue.* (March 1927—information incomplete.) (Pseudonym, Richard Cory.)

"Notes." *The New Issue.* (March 1927—information incomplete.)

"A Note on Modern Tragedy." *Wisconsin Literary Magazine.* 27, 1 (November 1927), 11–16.

"Unamuno's Quixote." Review of Miguel de Unamuno, *The Life of Don Quixote and Sancho, According to Miguel Cervantes de Saavedra. New York Herald Tribune Books.* 14, 12 (December 4, 1927), 18, 20.

"Recent Spanish Literature." *The Nation.* 124, 3227 (May 11, 1927), 530–1.

"Unamuno's Epilogue." Review of Miguel de Unamuno, *L'Agonie du Christianisme. The Nation.* 124, 3225 (April 27, 1927), 481–2.

"Toward a Revaluation." Review of Han Ryner, *The Ingenious Hidalgo Miguel Cervantes. The Nation.* 125, 3235 (July 6, 1927), 20–1.

"A Philosophy of Renunciation." Review of George Santayana, *Platonism and the Spiritual Life. The Nation.* 125, 3247 (September 28, 1927), 316.

"Transcendental Romanticism." Review of Miguel de Unamuno, *The Life of Don Quixote and Sancho, According to Miguel Cervantes de Saavedra. The Nation.* 125, 3255 (November 23, 1927), 578.

1928

"Historian of Our Stupidity." Review of H. L. Mencken, *Prejudices, Sixth Series, and Selected Prejudices. The Nation.* 126, 3270 (March 7, 1928), 272–3.

"Santayana's Roots." Review of George Santayana, *The Realm of Essence, Book First of Realms of Being. The Nation.* 126, 3275 (April 11, 1928), 410–11.

"Culture's Feet of Clay." *The New Student.* 8, 1 (October 1928), 6–8.

"Thoreau: the Paradox of Youth." *The New Student.* 7, 23 (March 7, 1928), 5–9.

"John Dewey's Humanism." Review of Joseph Ratner, ed., *The Philosophy of John Dewey. The Nation.* 127, 3304 (October 31, 1928), 457–8.

"A Modern Poet." Review of William Ellery Leonard, *A Son of Earth. The Nation.* 127, 3309 (December 5, 1928), 624.

1929

Review of Gladys Oaks, *Nursery Rhymes for Children of Darkness. The Wisconsin Literary Magazine.* 28, 2 (February 1929), 27–8.

"Intellectualism in Vacuo." Review of Richard McKeon, *The Philosophy of Spinoza,* and A. Wolf, ed., *The Correspondence of Spinoza. The Nation.* 128, 3320 (February 20, 1929), 233–4.

"Southern Prophet." Review of Jose E. Rodo, *The Motives of Proteus. The Nation.* 128, 3327 (April 10, 1929), 429–30.

"Popular Morals." Review of C. E. Ayres, *Holier Than Thou; The Way of the Righteous. The Nation.* 119, 3347 (August 29, 1929), 228–9.

"Robinson Jeffers." *The New Student.* 8, 7 (April 1929), 13–15.

1930

"Rabelais." Review of Albert J. Nock and C. R. Wilson, *François Rabelais: The Man and His Work,* and Samuel Putman, *François Rabelais: Man of the Renaissance. The Nation.* 130, 3373 (February 26, 1930), 250–2.

"Páginas de un diario." *Elite.* Caracas, Venezuela, Año VI, 266 (18 de Octubre de 1930), 15–16 (Eliseo Vivas Salas).

1931

"Wisconsin's Experimental College." *The Nation.* 132, 3429 (March 25, 1931), 322–5.

1932

Review of Joseph Wood Krutch, *Experience and Art. The Wisconsin State Journal.* 141, 64 (December 4, 1932), 3.

1933

"One More Christian." Review of John A. Mackay, *The Other Spanish Christ. The Nation.* 136, 3532 (March 15, 1933), 293.

"Guedalla Facing South." Review of Philip Guedalla, *Argentine Tango. The Nation.* 136, 3535 (April 5, 1933), 380.

1934

"About Modern Poetry." Review of John Sparrow, *Sense and Poetry. The Wisconsin State Journal.* 144, 8 (April 8, 1934), 4.

"Critic of American Culture." Review of Van Wyck Brooks, *Three Essays on America. The Wisconsin State Journal.* 144, 57 (May 27, 1934), 4.

"Ezra Pound." Review of Ezra Pound, *ABC of Reading. Wisconsin State Journal.* 145, 21 (October 21, 1934), 4.

"Max Eastman." Review of Max Eastman, *Art and the Life of Action. Wisconsin State Journal.* 145, 42 (November 11, 1934), 7.

"Francis Bacon." Review of Charles Williams, *Bacon. The Nation.* 138, 3587 (April 4, 1934), 393.

"Baruch or Benedictus." Review of Harry A. Wolfson, *The Philosophy of Spinoza,* and S. M. Melamed, *Spinoza and Buddha. The Nation.* 139, 3607 (August 22, 1934), 222–4.

"Education and the Crisis" (Rejoinder). *The New Student.* (May 1934), 9 and 13. (Information not confirmable.)

"Jean-Jacques's Doctrines." Review of Charles W. Hendel, *Jean-Jacques Rousseau, Moralist. The Nation.* 139, 3611 (September 19, 1934), 334–5.

1935

Review of Edward F. Rothschild, *The Meaning of Unintelligibility in Modern Art*. *Wisconsin State Journal*. (April 1935—information incomplete.)

Review of Joseph Wood Krutch, *Was Europe A Success? Capital Times*. 35, 86 (March 10, 1935), 22.

"Art, Morals, and Propaganda." *International Journal of Ethics*. 46, 1 (October 1935), 82–95.

"Four Notes on I. A. Richard's Aesthetic Theory." *The Philosophical Review*. 44, 4 (July 1935), 354–67.

"A Liberal Historian." Review of Carl L. Becker, *Everyman His Own Historian*. *The Nation*. 140, 3642 (April 24, 1935), 487–8.

"Analysis of Renoir's Art." Review of Albert C. Barnes and Violette de Mazia, *The Art of Renoir*. *The Nation*. 141, 3660 (August 28, 1935), 250.

1936

"Buck Looks Back." Review of Philo M. Buck, *The World's Great Age*. *Wisconsin State Journal*. 148, 40 (May 10, 1936), 4.

Review of Ralph Linton, *The Study of Man*. *The Capital Times*. 38, 99 (September 27, 1936), editorial, page 22.

"A Note on Value." *The Journal of Philosophy*. 33, 21 (October 8, 1936), 568–75.

"The Aesthetic Judgment." *The Journal of Philosophy*. 33, 3 (January 30, 1936), 57–69.

"Mr. Santayana's Wisdom." Review of George Santayana, *Obiter Scripta*. *The Nation*. 142, 3694 (April 22, 1936), 524–5.

"Mr. Prall's Aesthetic." Review of D. W. Prall, *Aesthetic Analysis*. *The Nation*. 142, 3701 (June 10, 1936), 752.

"Mr. Santayana's Philosophy." Review of Irwin Edman, ed., *The Philosophy of Santayana*. *The Nation*. 143, 17 (October 24, 1936), 495–6.

"A Proper Study." Review of Ralph Linton, *The Study of Man.*
The Nation. 143, 22 (November 28, 1936), 639.

1937

"Our Nietzsche." Review of *The Philosophy of Nietzsche* (Modern Library). *The Nation.* 144, 25 (June 19, 1937), 710–11.

"A Definition of the Aesthetic Experience." *The Journal of Philosophy.* 34, 23 (November 11, 1937), 628–34. (See "Sobre La Experiencia Estetica," 1941.)

"A Note on the Question of 'Class Science.' " *Marxist Quarterly.* 1, 3 (October-December 1937), 437–46.

"Reality in Art." *University of Kansas City Review.* 4, 1 (Autumn 1937), 36–42.

Review of Israel Knox, *The Aesthetic Theories of Kant, Hegel, and Schopenhauer. The Nation.* 144, 7 (February 13, 1937), 192.

"Bankrupt Realism." Review of James B. Pratt, *Personal Realism. The Nation.* 144, 11 (March 13, 1937), 300–1.

"Anti-Metaphysical Philosophy." Review of Rudolf Carnap, *The Logical Syntax of Language,* and Julius Weinberg, *An Examination of Logical Positivism. The Nation.* 144, 21 (May 22, 1937), 599–600.

"The Philosophy of Aldous Huxley." Review of Aldous Huxley, *Eyeless in Gaza. Marxist Quarterly.* 1, 2 (April–June 1937), 315–19.

"Professor Hartshorne's God." Review of Charles Hartshorne, *Beyond Humanism. The Nation.* 145, 1 (July 13, 1937), 24.

"Mussolini's Philosopher." Review of Roger W. Holmes, *The Idealism of Giovanni Gentile. The Nation.* 145, 16 (October 16, 1937), 410–11.

"Toward An Improved Strategy." Review of Kenneth Burke, *Attitudes Toward History. The Nation.* 145, 26 (December 25, 1937), 723.

1938

"A Note on the Emotion in Mr. Dewey's Theory of Art." *The Philosophical Review,* 47, 5 (September 1938), 527–31.

"Drieser, An Inconsistent Mechanist." *Ethics.* 48, 4 (July 1938), 498–508.

"Force in Empirical Ethics." *Ethics.* 49, 1 (October 1938), 85–92.

"Nature, Common Sense and Science." *Philosophy of Science.* 5, 3 (July 1938), 300–09.

"The Use of Art." *The Journal of Philosophy.* 35, 15 (July 21, 1938), 406–11.

"Types of Philosophy." Review of Irwin Edman, *Four Ways of Philosophy. The New Republic.* 93, 1205 (January 5, 1938), 262.

"The Problems of Morals." Review of W. T. Stace, *The Concept of Morals. The Nation.* 146, 3 (January 15, 1938), 76.

"The Error of Philosophy." Review of Etienne Gilson, *The Unity of Philosophical Experience. The Nation.* 146, 8 (February 19, 1938), 219–20.

"Beauty As Quality." Review of Stephen C. Pepper, *Aesthetic Quality. The Nation.* 146, 17 (April 23, 1938), 481–2.

"A Conservative Testifies." Review of Ruiz Vilaplana, *Burgos Justice. The New Republic.* 94, 1221 (April 27, 1938), 366.

"The Dialectic According to Levy." Review of H. Levy, *A Philosophy for Modern Man. Partisan Review.* 4, 6 (May 1938), 51–54.

"The Philosophy of Control." Review of George Herbert Mead, *The Philosophy of the Act. Partisan Review.* 6, 1 (Fall 1938), 113–17.

"Logic and the Scientific Method." Review of John Dewey, *Logic, The Theory of Inquiry. The Saturday Review.* 19, 2 (November 5, 1938), 18.

1939

"Finalidad del Arte." *Revista Nacional de Cultura.* Caracas, Venezuela, 8 (Junio 1939), 3–5.

"John Dewey's Achievement." *Partisan Review.* 6, 3 (Spring 1939), 79–91.

"The Fanatic As Type." *The Sewanee Review.* 47, 2 (April 1939), 166–74.

"The New Encyclopedists." *The Kenyon Review.* 1, 2 (Spring 1939), 159–82.

"Value and Fact." *The Philosophy of Science.* 6, 4 (October 1939), 432–45.

"Art As Expression." Review of R. G. Collingwood, *The Principles of Art. The Nation.* 148, 4 (January 21, 1939), 98–99.

"Hyperindividualism." Review of Paul Weiss, *Reality. The Nation.* 149, 2 (July 8, 1939), 50–51.

1940

Review of A. Wolf, *A History of Science, Technology, and Philosophy in the Eighteenth Century. The Nation.* 150, 12 (March 23, 1940), 401–02.

"Ethical Empiricism and Moral Heteronomy." *The Philosophical Review.* 49, 4 (July 1940), 447–53.

"From *The Life of Reason* to *The Last Puritan."* Schlipp, Paul Arthur, ed., *The Philosophy of George Santayana* (Evanston: Northwestern University Press, 1940), 315–50.

"The Legacy of Freud." *The Kenyon Review.* 2, 2 (Spring 1940), 173–85.

"Introduction to Dewey." Review of Sidney Hook, *John Dewey. The Nation.* 150, 1 (January 6, 1940), 22–23.

"Too Wild A Cow For Our Matador." Review of William York Tindall, *D. H. Lawrence and Susan His Cow. Partisan Review.* 7, 1 (January–February 1940), 67–69.

"Critique of Santayana." Review of Milton K. Munitz, *The Moral Philosophy of George Santayana. The Nation.* 151, 2 (July 13, 1940), 37.

"Positive Ethics." Review of Moritz Schlick, *Problems of Ethics. The Kenyon Review.* 2, 1 (Winter 1940), 109–12.

"The Philosophy of Peirce." Review of Justus Buchler, *Charles Peirce's Empiricism. The Nation.* 151, 20 (November 16, 1940), 483–4.

1941

"Sobre La Experiencia Estetica." *Revista del Caribe* (September 1941—information incomplete.) (See "A Definition of the Aesthetic Experience," 1937).

"Humanism: A Backward Glance." *T'ien Hsia.* 11, 4 (February 1941), 301–13.

"Lawrence's Problems." *Kenyon Review.* 3, 1 (Winter 1941), 83–94.

"The New Naturalism." *Kenyon Review.* 3, 4 (Autumn 1941), 446–59.

"Mr. Russell on Empiricism." Review of Bertrand Russell, *An Inquiry Into Meaning and Truth. The Nation.* 152, 10 (March 8, 1941), 275–6.

1942

Review of Philo M. Buck, *Directions in Contemporary Literature. Daily Cardinal.* 51, 138 (April 4, 1942), 4.

"Language In Action." *American Sociological Review.* 7, 2 (April 1942), 256–60.

"Reply to Mr. Wheelwright." *The Kenyon Review.* 4, 1 (Winter 1942), 91–98.

"From Prometheus to Maitreya." Review of Charles Morris, *Paths of Life. The Kenyon Review.* 4, 3 (Autumn 1942), 419–22.

Review of Crane Brinton, *Nietzsche,* and George Allen Morgan, *What Nietzsche Means. American Sociological Review.* 7, 6 (December 1942), 883–6.

Review of Herbert J. Muller, *Science and Criticism. Accent.* 4, 1 (Autumn 1943), 58–60.

"Art and Freedom." *The Journal of Philosophy.* 40, 19 (September 1943), 517–23.

"Art and Life." Shipley, Joseph T., ed., *Dictionary of World Literature* (New York: Philosophical Library, 1943), 49–50.

"Henry and William (Two Notes)." *The Kenyon Review.* 5, 4 (Autumn 1943), 580–94.

"Value." Shipley, Joseph T., ed., *Dictionary of World Literature* (New York: Philosophical Library, 1943), 607–9.

"On Symbolism." Review of Suzanne K. Langer, *Philosophy in A New Key. The Kenyon Review.* 5, 2 (Spring 1943), 301–4.

"Aesthetics As Libertarian Faith." Review of Horace M. Kallen, *Art and Freedom. The Nation.* 156, 23 (June 5, 1943), 814–5.

Review of Horace M. Kallen, *Art and Freedom. The Journal of Philosophy.* 40, 19 (September 1943), 517–23.

1944

"A Natural History of the Aesthetic Transaction." Kirkorian, Yervant H., ed., *Naturalism and the Human Spirit* (New York: Columbia University Press, 1944), 96–120.

"The Objective Correlative of T. S. Eliot." *American Bookman.* 1, 1 (Winter 1944), 7–18.

"M. Maritain's Aesthetics." Review of Jacques Maritain, *Art and Poetry. The Nation.* 158, 17 (April 22, 1944), 488–9.

"The Spanish Heritage." *American Sociological Review.* 10, 2 (April 1945), 184–91.

1946

"Franz Kafka's Fine Writings." Review of Angel Flores, ed., *The Kafka Problem* and *A Franz Kafka Miscellany,* transl. Sophie Prombaum and G. Humphreys-Roberts. *Chicago Sun Book Week.* (November 3, 1946), 9.

"A Forerunner of Existentialism." Review of Soren Kierkegaard, *Works of Love. Chicago Sun Book Week.* (August 11, 1946).

"Animadversions on Naturalistic Ethics." *Ethics.* 56, 3 (April 1946), 157–77.

"Henry y William [James]." (Dos Apuntes). *Asomante.* Ano II, 2, 3 (September 1946), 44–45.

1947

"Don Alonzo to the Road Again." Review of John Dewey, *Problems of Men,* and Sidney Hook, *Education for Modern Man. The Western Review.* 11, 2 (Winter 1947), 59–71.

1948

"Julian Huxley's Ethics." *Ethics.* 58, 4 (Summer 1948), 275–84.

"Kafka's Distorted Mask." *The Kenyon Review.* 10, 1 (Winter 1948), 51–69. (See "Kafka's Distorted Mask," 1962.)

"The Objective Basis of Criticism." *The Western Review.* 12, 4 (July 1948), 197–210.

"Two Notes on the New Naturalism." *The Sewanee Review.* 56 (July 1948), 477–509.

1949

"The Objective Correlative of T. S. Eliot." Stallman, R. W., ed., *Critiques and Essays in Criticism, 1920–1948, Representing the Achievements of Modern British and American Critics* (New York: Ronald Press Company, 1949), 389–400.

"Theorists Without Theory." Review of René Wellek and Austin Warren, *Theory of Literature. The Kenyon Review.* 12, 1 (Winter 1949), 161–5.

1950

The Moral Life and the Ethical Life (Chicago: University of Chicago Press, 1950), xix, 390 pp.

"The Function of Art in the Human Economy." Harris, Julian, ed., *The Humanities: An Appraisal* (Madison: University of Wisconsin, 1950), 143–51.

"The Function of Criticism Today." Harris, Julian, ed., *The Humanities: An Appraisal* (Madison: University of Wisconsin, 1950), 49–66.

"The Moral Philosophy of Corporate Man." Review of E. Jordan, *The Good Life. Ethics.* 60, 3 (April 1950), 188–97.

"The Heresy of Paraphrase." Review of C. M. Bowra, *The Creative Experiment. Poetry.* 75, 4 (January 1950), 217–24.

Review of Paul Arthur Schilpp, ed., *The Philosophy of Ernst Cassirer. The Journal of Aesthetics and Art Criticism.* 3, 4 (June 1950), 275–6.

"Philosophy for Nineteen Eighty-Four." Review of R. Sellars, et. al., *Philosophy for the Future: The Quest of Modern Materialism. The Sewanee Review.* 58, 3 (Summer 1950), 505–13.

"Lorca's Background." Review of Arturo Barea, *Lorca, The Poet and His People. Poetry.* 76, 1 (April 1950), 46–51.

1951

"Kafka's Distorted Mask." Ransom, John Crowe, ed., *The Kenyon Critics, Studies in Modern Literature from The Kenyon Review* (Cleveland: World Publishing Company, 1951), 58–74.

"Criticism and the Little Mags." *The Western Review.* 16, 1 (Autumn 1951), 9–18.

"Aesthetics from Above." Review of James K. Feibleman, *Aesthetics, A Study of the Fine Arts in Theory and Practice. The Western Review.* 15, 3 (Spring 1951), 229–34.

"Our Spiritual Heritage." Review of Gilbert Highet, *The Classical Tradition, Greek and Roman Influences on Western Literature. The Western Review.* 15, 2 (Winter 1951), 152–4.

"The Two Dimensions of Reality in *The Brothers Karamazov.*" *The Sewanee Review.* 59, 1 (January 1951), 23–49.

1952

Review of George Boas, *Wingless Pegasus: A Hand Book for Critics,* and Morris Weitz, *Philosophy of the Arts. Ethics.* 62, 3 (April 1952), 222–4.

"Literature and Knowledge." *The Sewanee Review.* 60, 4 (October 1952), 561–92.

Review of Paul Henle, ed., et al., *Structure, Method, and Meaning, Essays in Honor Henry M. Scheffer. The Journal of Aesthetics and Art Criticism.* 10, 3 (March 1952), 279–80.

1953

Vivas, Eliseo, and Murray Krieger, eds., *The Problems of
Aesthetics, A Book of Readings* (New York: Rinehart and
Company, 1953), 639 pp.
"The Nature of Aesthetics." Wild, John, ed., *The Return to
Reason* (Chicago: Henry Regnery Company, 1953), 201–
17.
"The Object of the Poem." *The Review of Metaphysics.* 7, 1
(September 1953), 19–35.
"The Neo-Aristotelians of Chicago." Review of R. S. Crane,
ed., *Critics and Criticism, Ancient and Modern. The Sewanee
Review.* 61 (January 1953), 136–49.

1954

"What is a Poem?" *The Sewanee Review.* 62, 4 (Autumn
1954), 578–97.
"Jordan's Defense of Poetry." Review of E. Jordan, *Essays in
Criticism. Review of Metaphysics.* 8, 1 (September 1954),
162–75.
"Allen Tate As A Man of Letters." Review of Allen Tate, *The
Forlorn Demon, Didactic and Critical Essays. The Sewanee
Review.* 62 (Winter 1954), 131–43.

1955

"A Semantics for Humanists." Review of Philip Wheelwright,
The Burning Fountain. The Sewanee Review. 63, 2 (April
1955), 307–17. (See also 1956.)
Creation and Discovery, Essays in Criticism and Aesthetics
(New York: Noonday Press, 1955), xxiv, 460 pp.
Creation and Discovery, Essays in Criticism and Aesthetics
(Toronto: Longmans, 1955), 460 pp.
"Dreiser, An Inconsistent Mechanist." Kazin, Alfred, and
Charles Shapiro, eds., *The Stature of Theodore Dreiser, A
Critical Survey of the Man and His Work* (Bloomington:
Indiana University Press, 1955), 237–45.

"Mr. Wimsatt on the Theory of Literature." Review of W. K. Wimsatt, Jr., *The Verbal Icon: Studies in the Meaning of Poetry. Comparative Literature.* 7, 4 (Fall 1955), 344–61.

1956

Review of Philip Wheelwright, *The Burning Fountain. Perspectives USA.* 14, 14 (January 1956), 167–75. (German and Italian editions, Winter, January 1956.) (See also 1955.)

1957

"Mr. Leavis on D. H. Lawrence." Review of F. R. Leavis, *D. H. Lawrence: Novelist. The Sewanee Review.* 65, 1 (January 1957), 123–36.

1958

"Four Meanings of 'Education.' " *Papers and Studies* (a pamphlet). The Institute for Christian Learning, February 1958. 16 pp. (Delivered during seminar in Evanston, Illinois, on the topic, "Philosophical Unity in the Educational Process.")

"The Two Lawrences." *Bucknell Review.* 7, 3 (March 1958), 113–32.

Creazione e Scoperta, Saggi di critica e di estetica (Bologna: Il Mulino, 1958), xii, 351 pp.

"The Substance of *Women in Love.*" *The Sewanee Review.* 66, 1 (Autumn 1958), 588–632.

"Evolutionary Aesthetics and Aristotle." Review of Iredell Jenkins, *Art and the Human Enterprise,* and Gerald F. Else, *Aristotle's Poetics: The Argument. The Yale Review.* 48, 1 (September 1958), 135–9.

1959

"Contextualism Reconsidered." *The Journal of Aesthetics and Art Criticism.* 18, 2 (December 1959), 222–40.

"Mi Ritrovai Per Una Selva Oscura." *The Sewanee Review.* 67, 4 (Autumn 1959), 560–66.

"The Tragic Dimension." Review of Richard B. Sewall, *The Vision of Tragedy. The Yale Review.* 48, 4 (June 1959), 587–93.

"For and Against 'The Founder.' " Review of Sidney Hook, ed., *Psychoanalysis, Scientific Method, and Philosophy. National Review.* 7, 26 (October 10, 1959), 398–400.

1960

"A Theory of Man." Review of Margorie S. Harris, *Francisco Romero on Problems of Philosophy. The Randolph-Macon Alumnae Bulletin.* 54, 1 (November 1960), 4–6.

D. H. Lawrence, The Failure and the Triumph of Art (Evanston: Northwestern University Press, 1960), xvi, 302 pp.

"In Defense of Non-Objective Art." *Modern Age.* 4, 4 (Fall 1960), 412–15.

"Science and the Studies of Man." Schoeck, Helmut, and James W. Wiggins, eds., *Scientism and Values* (Princeton: D. Van Nostrand Company, 1960), 50–82.

Review of Paul Weiss, *Our Public Life. Ethics.* 70, 2 (January 1960), 168–71.

"Creativity in Art and Education." *The Arts Symposium on the Creative Process.* Randolph-Macon Women's College (March 1960). Reprinted in *Teachers College Record.* 62, 2 (November 1960), 140–48.

1961

D. H. Lawrence: The Failure and the Triumph of Art (London: George Allen and Unwin, 1961), xvi, 302 pp.

"Animadversions on Imitation and Expression." *The Journal of Aesthetics and Art Criticism.* 19, 4 (Summer 1961), 425–32.

"Freedom: The Philosophical Problem." *Modern Age.* 6, 1 (Winter 1961–2), 7–20.

"Reiterations and Second Thoughts on Cultural Relativism." Schoeck, Helmut, and James W. Wiggins, eds., *Relativism and the Study of Man, Papers by Leonard Carmichael and others* (Princeton: D. Van Nostrand Company, 1961), 45–73.

"Metaphysics for 632 A. F." Review of Norman O. Brown, *Life Against Death. The Sewanee Review.* 69, 4 (October 1961), 677–90.

1962

"Kafka's Distorted Mask." Gray, Ronald, ed., *Kafka, A Collection of Critical Essays* (Englewood Cliffs, N.J.: Prentice-Hall, 1962), 133–46. (See also, "Kafka's Distorted Mask," 1948.)

"Art and the Artist's 'Citizenship.'" *Modern Age.* 6, 1 (Spring 1962), 155–64.

"Relativism: Its Paradoxes and Pitfalls." Intercollegiate Society of Individualists, Philadelphia, Pennsylvania (October 1962), 19.

"The Two Dimensions of Reality in *The Brothers Karamazov.*" Wellek, René, ed., *Dostoevsky, A Collection of Critical Essays* (Englewood Cliffs, N.J.: Prentice-Hall, 1962), 71–89.

1963

The Artistic Transaction, and Essays on Theory of Literature (Columbus: Ohio State University Press, 1963), 267 pp.

The Moral Life and the Ethical Life (Chicago: Henry Regnery Company, Gateway Editions, 1963), xxviii, 292 pp.

"Art and the Artist's 'Citizenship.'" Schoeck, Helmut, and James W. Wiggins, eds., *The New Argument in Economics, The Public Versus The Private Sector* (Princeton: D. Van Nostrand Company, 1963), 216–31.

"Freedom: The Philosophical Problem." Morley, Felix, ed., *The Necessary Conditions for a Free Society* (Princeton: D. Van Nostrand Company, 1963), 120–41.

"The Revolution in Personal Values." Reid, T.E.H., ed., *Values in Conflict.* 32 Couchiching Conference, C.I.P.A. Toronto: published for Canadian Institute on Public Affairs by University of Toronto Press, 1963. 92–111.

"Something for Everybody." Review of Stanley Burnshaw, ed., *Varieties of Literary Experience. The Sewanee Review.* 71, 2 (Spring 1963), 343–47.

"The Liberal Ethos." Review of Ralph de Toledano, *Seeds of Treason. Modern Age.* 7, 2 (Spring 1963), 206–10.

"Narcissists and Others." Review of Henri Peyre, *Literature and Sincerity. The Yale Review.* 57, 4 (June 1963), 617–22.

1964

D. H. Lawrence, The Failure and the Triumph of Art (Bloomington: Indiana University Press, Midland Book, 1964), xvi, 302 pp.

"Naturalism and Creativity." Tomas, Vincent, ed., *Creativity in the Arts* (Englewood Cliffs, N.J.: Prentice-Hall, 1964), 84–96.

"Notes on Truth." *The Personalist.* 45, 2 (Spring 1964), 176–92. Reprinted in *Philosophy Today.* 8, 1–4 (Spring 1964), 46–55.

"On the Conservative Demonology." *Modern Age.* 8, 2 (Spring 1964), 119–33.

"The Mind of Richard Weaver." Review of Richard Weaver, *Visions of Order: The Cultural Crisis of Our Time. Modern Age.* 8, 3 (Spring 1964), 307–10.

"Essays After a 180 Degree Turn in Thought." Review of John Dos Passos, *Occasions and Protest. Chicago Tribune Books Today.* (December 20, 1964), 3.

1965

"Apologia Pro Fide Mea." *The International Review.* 2, 2 (October 1965), 126–37.

"The Self and Its Masks." *The Southern Review.* 1, New Series, 2 (Spring 1965), 317–36.

"Things and Persons." *Modern Age.* 9, 2 (Spring 1965), 119–31.

Introduction to Friedrich Nietzsche, *Schopenhauer as Educator,* transl. James W. Hillesheim and Malcolm B. Simpson (Chicago: Henry Regnery Company, Gateway Editions, 1965), vii–xx.

Introduction to Richard Weaver, *Life Without Prejudice, and other Essays* (Chicago: Henry Regnery Company, 1965), vii–xvii.

"Dostoevsky: Philosopher or Novelist?" Review of Edward Wasiolek, *Dostoevsky: The Major Fiction. Modern Age.* 9, 3 (Summer 1965), 302–9.

"Something is Missing." Review of Charles Frankel, *The Love of Anxiety and other Essays. New York Times Book Review.* (July 18, 1965), 6–7.

1966

"Were They Radicals or Intellectuals?" Review of Christopher Lasch, *The New Radicalism in America. The Intercollegiate Review.* 2, 4 (January 1966), 251–60.

Creation and Discovery, Essays in Criticism and Aesthetics (Chicago: Henry Regnery Company, Gateway Editions, 1966), xv, 460 pp.

"Animadversions Upon the Doctrine of Natural Law." *Modern Age.* 10, 2 (Spring 1966), 149–60.

"Philosophy of Culture, Aesthetics, and Criticism." *Texas Quarterly.* 9, 1 (Spring 1966), 231–41. (See 1967 for transl. in *Op. Cit., selezione della critica d'arte contemporanea.*)

1967

"Filosofia della cultura, estetica e critica: alcuni problema." *Op. Cit., selezione della critica d'arte contemporanea.* Maggio 1967, numero 9, Napoli, Italy. (This is a translation of "Philosophy of Culture, Aesthetics, and Criticism." See 1966.)

Introduction to Sigmund Freud, *The Origin and Development of Psychoanalysis* (Chicago: Henry Regnery Company, Gateway Editions, 1967), v–xxxv.

1968

"Is A Conservative Anthropology Possible?" *Social Research.* 35, 4 (Winter 1968), 593–615.

"Literary Classes: Some Problems." *Genre.* 1, 2 (April 1968), 97–105.

"A Good Guy or a Bad One." Review of D. F. Pear, *Bertrand Russell and the British Tradition,* and Mortimer Adler, *The Defense of Man and the Difference It Makes. Modern Age.* 12, 2 (Spring 1968), 174–82.

1969

"Atrabilious Thoughts on A Theory of Tragedy." Knauf, David M., ed., *Papers in Dramatic Theory and Criticism* (Iowa City: University of Iowa, 1969), 9–23. (Presented at the University of Iowa, April 6–7, 1967.)

1970

"Literary Criticism and Aesthetics." Scholes, Robert, ed., *Philosopher Critic* (Tulsa, Oklahoma: University of Tulsa, 1970), 18–39.

"Reality in Literature." *Iowa Review.* 1, 4 (Fall 1970), 116–27.

"Incoherent Nihilist." Review of Herbert Marcuse, *Five Lectures, Psychoanalysis, Politics and Utopia. National Review.* 22, 27 (July 14, 1970), 739–42.

"Ordeal of Civilization." Review of John Luckas, *The Passing of the Modern Age. National Review.* 22, 40 (October 20, 1970), 1116–7.

1971

Contra Marcuse (New Rochelle, N.Y.: Arlington House, 1971), 236 pp.

"Marcuse as Torquemada of the Left." *New York Times.* (June 15, 1971), L-43.

"The Object of the Poem." Adams, Hazard, ed., *Critical Theory Since Plato* (New York: Harcourt, Brace, Jovanovich, 1971), 1069–77.

"The Spanish Heritage." Moreno, Francisco José, and Barbara Mitrani, eds., *Conflict and Violence in Latin American Politics: A Book of Readings* (New York: Crowell, 1971), 3 14.

Review of George P. Stein, *The Ways of Meaning in the Arts.*
The Journal of Aesthetics and Art Criticism. 30, 1 (Fall
1971), 117–20.

"Too Clever By Half." Review of George Steiner, *In Blue-*
beard's Castle: Some Notes Towards the Redefinition of
Culture. National Review. 23, 51 (December 31, 1971),
1477–78.

1972

Contra Marcuse (New York: Dell Publishing Company, A
Delta Book, 1972), 236 pp.

"Allen Tate as Man of Letters." Squires, Radcliffe, ed., *Allen*
Tate and His Work; Critical Evaluations (Minneapolis: University of Minnesota Press, 1972), 78–91.

"In the Presence of Art." *Symposium Humanities.* 1, 1 (Winter
1972), 85–106.

"In Memoriam: Frank Meyer." *Modern Age.* 16, 3 (Summer
1972), 312–3.

1973

" 'Poetry' and Philosophy." *The Iowa Review,* 4, 3 (Summer
1973), 114–26.

1974

"Dostoevsky, 'Poet' in Spite of Himself." *The Southern Review.*
10, 2 (April 1974), 307–28.

1975

"Teachers and 'Teachers.' " *Modern Age.* 19, 3 (Summer
1975), 226–35.

"Alonzo as 'Teacher.' " *Modern Age.* 20, 1 (Fall 1975), 355–
63.

"Critical Assizes." *The Blue Guitar, Revista Annuale di Lit-*
teratura inglesa e Americana. Facultà di Magistero, Univer-
sità di Messina. 1, 1 (1975), 59–87.

Review of Jack J. Spector, *The Aesthetics of Freud: A Study in*
Psychoanalysis and Art. Leonardo. 8, 1 (Winter 1975).

1976

"From Left of Center to Right." *Modern Age.* 20, 1 (Winter 1976).

"On Human Origins: Freud, Huxley, and Malinowski." *Modern Age.* 20, 2 (Spring 1976), 130–40.

A NOTE ON THE TYPE AND DESIGN

This book was linotype set in the Times Roman series of type. The face was designed to be used in the news columns of the *London Times*. The *Times* was seeking a type face that would be condensed enough to accommodate a substantial number of words per column without sacrificing readability and still have an attractive, contemporary appearance. This design was an immediate success. It is used in many periodicals throughout the world and is one of the most popular text faces presently in use for book work.

The cuneiform inscription that serves as the design motif for our endpapers is the earliest known written appearance of the word "freedom" (*ama-gi*), or liberty. It is taken from a clay document written about 2300 B.C. in the Sumerian city-state of Lagash.

Book design by Design Center, Inc., Indianapolis
Typography by Weimer Typesetting Co., Inc., Indianapolis
Printed by Hilltop Press, Inc., Indianapolis

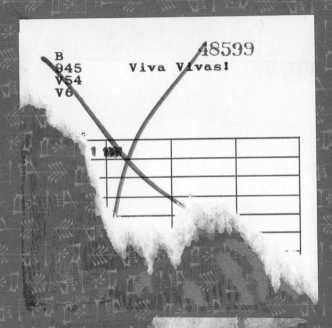